Progress in IS

Progress in IS encompasses the various areas of Information Systems in theory and practice, presenting cutting-edge advances in the field. It is aimed especially at researchers, doctoral students, and advanced practitioners. The series features both research monographs, edited volumes, and conference proceedings that make substantial contributions to our state of knowledge and handbooks and other edited volumes, in which a team of experts is organized by one or more leading authorities to write individual chapters on various aspects of the topic. Individual volumes in this series are supported by a minimum of two external reviews.

Dilli Prasad Sharma • Arash Habibi Lashkari
Mona Parizadeh

Understanding Cybersecurity Management in Healthcare

Challenges, Strategies and Trends

Dilli Prasad Sharma
University of Toronto
Toronto, Canada

Arash Habibi Lashkari
York University Toronto
Toronto, ON, Canada

Mona Parizadeh
University of Calgary
Calgary, Canada

ISSN 2196-8705   ISSN 2196-8713   (electronic)
Progress in IS
ISBN 978-3-031-68033-5   ISBN 978-3-031-68034-2   (eBook)
https://doi.org/10.1007/978-3-031-68034-2

This Springer imprint is published by the registered company Springer Nature Switzerland AG
The registered company address is: Gewerbestrasse 11, 6330 Cham, Switzerland

If disposing of this product, please recycle the paper.

Preface

The book is part of the comprehensive Understanding Cybersecurity Series (UCS) knowledge mobilization program, aiming to provide diverse cybersecurity resources for researchers and readers from various backgrounds, especially industry managers.

In 2020, the first team released the initial online article series, "Understanding Canadian Cybersecurity Laws," which received recognition and was awarded the Gold Medal for Best Blog Column in the Business Division at the 2020 Canadian Online Publishing Awards. Building on this success, the team published the first book, *Understanding Cybersecurity Law and Digital Privacy: A Common Law Perspective*, in 2021 through Springer Nature Switzerland AG.

Continuing the research efforts, the second team launched the second article series in 2021, titled "Understanding Cybersecurity Management for FinTech (UCMF)," accompanied by the publication of the related book *Understanding Cybersecurity Management in FinTech: Challenges, Strategies, and Trends*. This book highlights the significance of cybersecurity in financial institutions by showcasing recent cyber breaches, attacks, and financial losses.

Starting in 2022, the third UCS team embarked on the third online series, "Understanding Current Cybersecurity Challenges in Law," addressing emerging trends and critical legal issues concerning cybersecurity globally. This series, consisting of six parts, explores digital jurisdictional authority and user-generated digital content ownership. The series is complemented by the publication of the third book, *Understanding Cybersecurity Law in Data Sovereignty and Digital Governance: An Overview from a Legal Perspective*, which offers an in-depth understanding of current cybersecurity challenges and their legal implications. Simultaneously, another team also worked on the fourth book, *Understanding Cybersecurity Management in Decentralized Finance: Challenges, Strategies, and Trends*. This book comprehensively reviews cybersecurity in blockchain technologies, analyzing platforms like Ethereum, Binance Smart Chain, Solana, Cardano, Avalanche, and Polygon. It explores cybersecurity issues in smart contracts, and related blogs are currently being published through the IT World Canada website.

Starting in 2023, the fifth team worked on the fifth book, *Understanding Cybersecurity on Smartphones: Challenges, Strategies, and Trends*. This book focused on understanding cyber threats and adversaries on smartphones, examining cybersecurity threats, vulnerabilities, and risk management. The book offers practical solutions for securing and protecting smartphones while raising awareness of the importance of smartphone security.

In addition to these endeavors, the sixth UCS team has focused on understanding the criticality of cybersecurity in healthcare, advocating for robust measures to protect patient data, maintain system integrity, and mitigate evolving cyber threats. This book offers practical solutions for securing and protecting healthcare data and the environment for patients, doctors, and hospital IT teams while raising awareness of the importance of healthcare environment security.

Canada	Dilli Prasad Sharma
Canada	Arash Habibi Lashkari
Canada	Mona Parizadeh
June 2024	

The original version of the book has been revised. A correction to this book can be found at https://doi.org/10.1007/978-3-031-68034-2_12

Acknowledgments

For all of those fighting for Woman, Life, and Freedom.

Contents

Chapter 1
The Healthcare Environment

1.1 Introduction

Navigating the healthcare sector is a complex endeavor. This sector isn't just about patients and doctors—it includes insurers, policymakers, and many others. As it rapidly evolves, it's molded by technological innovations, changing regulations, and the ever-adapting needs of patients. At its heart lies the commitment to deliver quality care that's both accessible and affordable.

A significant trend is the shift toward patient-centered care (Van Lerberghe et al., 2008), which values personalization over generalization, ensuring treatments align with individual circumstances. Moreover, technology isn't just an add-on—it's a driving force, pushing the boundaries of treatment capabilities and operational efficiency (Turea, n.d.). And the vision isn't just about curing ailments but actively preventing them, placing community health at the forefront (Starfield et al., 2005). Alongside these advancements is a renewed push to level the playing field, ensuring everyone, no matter their background, has access to healthcare (on Population Health HDTG of TFAC, Security H, 2004).

This chapter delves into the intricacies of the healthcare landscape, covering its various components, the stakeholders involved, the services provided, and the inherent challenges. With a comprehensive understanding, we can collaborate to achieve optimal healthcare delivery.

© The Author(s), under exclusive license to Springer Nature
Switzerland AG 2024
D. P. Sharma et al., *Understanding Cybersecurity Management in Healthcare*,
Progress in IS, https://doi.org/10.1007/978-3-031-68034-2_1

1.2   Categories of Healthcare

The healthcare industry can be divided into different sectors and settings that reflect individuals' and communities' diverse and unique health needs. The categories include healthcare providers, healthcare financiers, life sciences, and care settings (hospital or non-hospital).

Beyond these sectors, the healthcare industry operates within the public and private realms, each with distinct features and funding strategies. When we talk about the kind of care, there are three main levels: primary, secondary, and tertiary, which show the range and specialization of the care given. Understanding these divisions is crucial in planning and delivering the best healthcare.

1.2.1   Healthcare Sectors

The healthcare environment comprises various sectors that play integral roles in delivering healthcare services and driving advancements in technology and research. Healthcare sectors are classified differently across countries, but overall, we can break them down into three categories: healthcare providers, healthcare financiers, and life sciences (Fig. 1.1).

1.2.1.1   Healthcare Providers

Healthcare providers are vital sectors in healthcare, which include medical practitioners and healthcare professionals, as well as companies that offer medical services and facilities.

- *Healthcare professionals* maintain health by applying evidence-based medicine and providing patient care. They study, diagnose, treat, and prevent various physical and mental impairments from meeting the needs of the communities they serve. They offer medical advice research and develop operational methods to advance evidence-based healthcare. They may also supervise other healthcare workers (Gupta et al., 2011). Some healthcare professionals include medical practitioners, chiropractors, dermatologists, dietitians and nutritionists, homeopaths, optometrists, physical therapists, psychologists, and social workers.
- *Medical services and facilities:* They are fundamental in providing quality medical care and ensuring patient satisfaction. They can create an environment that supports safe and effective care delivery. Infrastructure and facilities in the healthcare system contribute to improving the quality of care, accessibility, affordability, safety, and patient-centered care and enhancing the overall healthcare experience (Leslie et al., 2017; Das et al., 2018). The following are a few examples of different types of healthcare facilities:

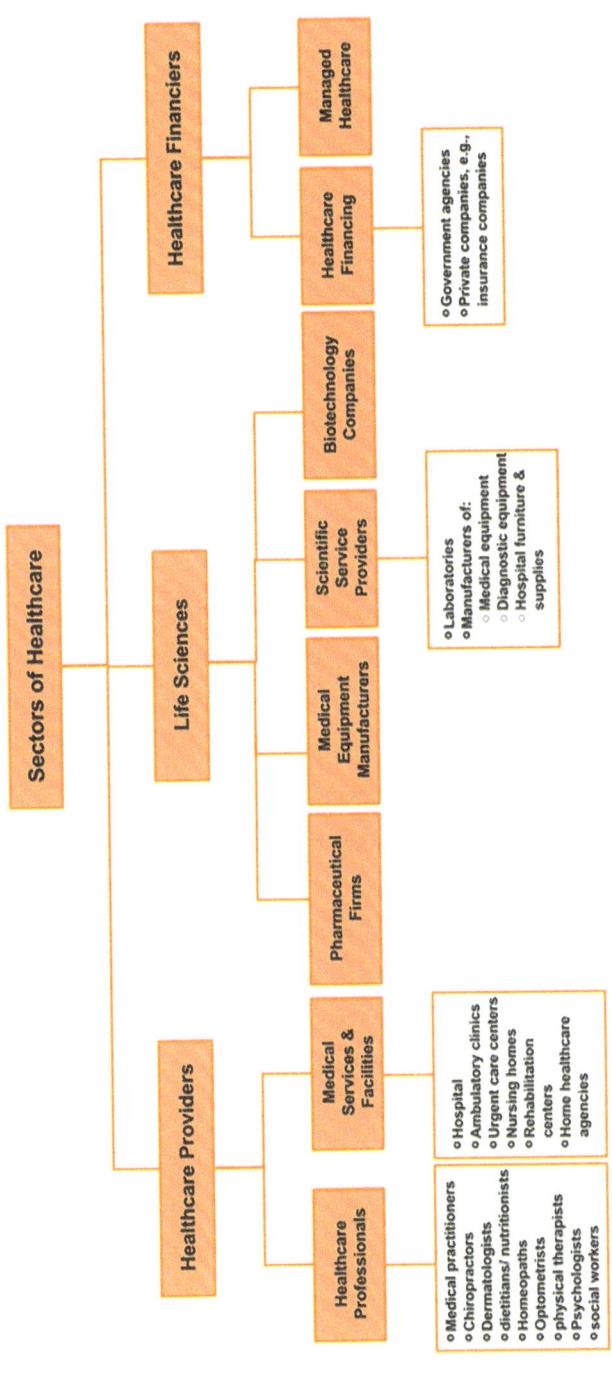

Fig. 1.1 Sectors of healthcare

- *Hospitals:* These facilities provide various medical services, including emergency care, surgeries, diagnostic tests, and specialized treatments.
- *Ambulatory clinics:* They are outpatient facilities that offer primary care services, such as routine check-ups, vaccinations, on-site screenings and diagnostic imaging, and minor treatments.
- *Urgent care centers:* These centers provide care for non-life-threatening medical issues that require immediate attention but not a trip to an emergency room. They often have extended hours and provide services like treating minor injuries and illnesses.
- *Nursing homes:* Nursing homes, also known as skilled nursing facilities, offer long-term care and assistance to individuals who require medical supervision and assistance with daily activities.
- *Rehabilitation centers* offer specialized services for patients recovering from surgeries, injuries, or illnesses. These centers focus on restoring physical function and improving independence through therapies and interventions.
- *Home healthcare agencies:* They provide medical care, therapy, and assistance to patients in their homes, especially those with chronic illnesses or recovering from surgery.

1.2.1.2   Healthcare Financiers

Health systems rely heavily on healthcare financing. Providing financial incentives to healthcare providers, mobilizing funds, distributing financial risks, and allocating healthcare services are all responsibilities of healthcare financers. These financiers can be government agencies or private companies that offer health insurance policies and fund healthcare services.

Managed healthcare is another approach used in the healthcare system. It is designed to organize, coordinate, and control healthcare services through designated entities like insurance companies or health maintenance organizations. Managed healthcare aims to control costs while maintaining high-quality care.

1.2.1.3   Life Sciences

The life sciences sector encompasses various segments contributing to the healthcare system, including pharmaceutical firms, medical equipment manufacturers, biotechnology companies, scientific service providers, and medical equipment and supplies manufacturers.

- *Pharmaceutical firms:* Pharmaceutical firms are crucial in developing medications for various diseases and conditions.
- *Biotechnology firms* are also a segment of the life sciences sector, conducting research and development to create new drugs, equipment, and treatment methods.

- *Service providers:* Service providers, including laboratories and companies involved in diagnosing, treating, and monitoring patients, contribute to accurate diagnosis and disease monitoring.
- *High-tech medical equipment companies* contribute to medical technology advancements and innovation by manufacturing advanced medical machines and diagnostic devices. Innovative companies that provide the full spectrum of medical equipment, hospital supplies, products, and services are also integral life sciences segments. This sector consists of different types of manufacturers, such as:
  - *Medical equipment manufacturers supply electromedical* and electrotherapeutic apparatus, surgical instruments and appliances, supplies and instruments, and laboratory cleaning and sterilization equipment.
  - *Diagnostic equipment manufacturers and laboratories:* They produce in vitro diagnostic substances, glucose meters, and toxicology laboratories.
  - *Hospital furniture and supplies manufacturers:* They provide hospital beds and furniture.

Overall, healthcare providers are responsible for offering a wide range of medical services and facilities to meet the diverse needs of communities; healthcare financiers play a crucial role in financing these services and distributing financial risks; and the life sciences sector contributes significantly to medical advancements and patient care and safety. Together, all segments of the life sciences contribute to developing drugs, medical equipment, and innovative healthcare solutions, enhancing patient care and safety, and advancing the healthcare system as a whole.

1.2.2 Hospital and Non-hospital Settings

Understanding the various types of hospital and non-hospital settings and their role as healthcare service providers is also essential for effective healthcare planning and delivery.

1.2.2.1 Types of Hospitals

Hospitals vary widely in their structure and purpose. They can be sorted based on ownership, profitability, location, and services (Liu & Kelz, 2018; Ahmed et al., 2015).

Ownership-wise, there are public, private, and academic medical centers. Private hospitals are individually, or group-owned, public ones are government-funded, and academic centers align with medical schools, emphasizing research, education, and specialized care.

In terms of profitability, non-profit hospitals reinvest earnings for community benefit, for-profit hospitals aim to generate profits, and government hospitals serve public needs (Liu & Kelz, 2018; Horwitz, 2005).

Location plays a role, too. Urban hospitals in busy areas boast a plethora of specialized services and tech. Due to their remote locales, rural areas often struggle with adequate resources and attracting medical talent (Liu & Kelz, 2018; Ahmed et al., 2015).

Finally, hospitals can be general, offering various services, or specialty-focused, zeroing in on areas like pediatrics or mental health. Diverse settings, like outpatient clinics and specialty care centers, are also available (Ahmed et al., 2015).

1.2.2.2   Non-hospital Sides of Healthcare

The non-hospital sides of healthcare play a crucial role in providing healthcare services and offering patients diverse models of care that extend beyond traditional hospital settings. Non-hospital settings include clinics, community health centers, home care settings, and basic operations of various healthcare settings such as physician offices, pharmacies, outpatient laboratories, chiropractic centers, dentistry, optometry, oncology centers, adult day care, and hospice care. Assuring patient safety, mitigating legal and financial liabilities, and supporting healthcare professionals are essential in these environments. Managing risk in non-hospital settings requires comprehensive programs addressing clinical and operational risks, proactive risk identification, and effective communication (Gann, 1997).

1.2.3   Public and Private Healthcare

The healthcare landscape comprises public and private entities with strengths and challenges. Private healthcare spans "for-profit" hospitals, independent practitioners, and "not-for-profit" providers—while public healthcare, rooted in promoting general health, is governed by national systems. The private sector often boasts efficiency and less waiting but faces issues of affordability and access. The public sector emphasizes fairness and has a societal focus but might grapple with bureaucracy and limited resources. Payment methods differ too: private leans on insurance or direct payments, while the public is tax-funded (Jofre-Bonet, 2000; Kaabi et al., 2022; Merviö, 2013).

Merging the best of both, a hybrid model could offer quality, affordability, and universal access, enhancing overall health. This mix could ensure healthcare accessibility, public health promotion, emergency responsiveness, and diverse choices for better well-being. Yet, the two sectors, having different aims and financing structures, could clash. Effective management then hinges on recognizing each sector's pros and cons. Proper policies and coordination can leverage the strengths of both public and private hospitals (Merviö, 2013; Culyer & Jonsson, 1986). With a deep understanding of these differences, policymakers can craft informed strategies, refining healthcare for all.

1.2.4   Healthcare Levels

In the healthcare system, different levels of healthcare practice represent increasing specialization and technical complexity related to the organizations and the delivery of healthcare services, along with higher care costs. The healthcare levels are classified into the four tiers explained below based on their complexity, scope, and level of care they offer. Healthcare providers across these levels provide various medical services, including evaluation, diagnosis, treatment, and referrals to the next level of care based on specific health needs. Understanding these levels of healthcare is imperative for comprehending the organization and delivery of healthcare services (Mäkelä et al., 1994; Glazier, 2007).

1.2.4.1   Primary Care

Primary care is the first contact point in the healthcare system. It is a patient-centered service that addresses various health needs throughout a person's life, including physical, mental, and social well-being (Van Lerberghe et al., 2008). General practitioners or family physicians typically provide primary care, focusing on promoting health, early detection of diseases, and coordinating the patient's overall healthcare. A key aspect of primary care is continuity of care, with patients preferring to consult the same practitioner for routine check-ups, preventive care, initial consultations, and illness and chronic conditions. Due to the wide range of ages, socioeconomic backgrounds, and health conditions that primary care practitioners treat, they must possess a broad knowledge of several areas. As patients are filtered out of primary care, they move into higher levels of specialized care.

1.2.4.2   Secondary Care

Secondary care addresses more complex medical conditions requiring specialized knowledge and expertise. It involves specialized medical services specialists provide upon referral from primary care providers. Many of these services are provided in hospitals or clinics, although some may also be available in community settings. A secondary care practitioner usually serves patients with more severe or complex health conditions requiring a specialist's expertise, such as psychiatrists, cardiologists, obstetricians, dermatologists, pediatricians, and gynecologists.

1.2.4.3   Tertiary Care

Tertiary care is the highest level of specialized care associated with advanced and complex medical procedures, long-term disease management, and specialized treatments for severe or rare conditions. Organ transplantation, neurosurgery, and intensive care services are examples of tertiary care. Typically, it is provided by highly trained specialists at regional or national centers using advanced medical technologies. Some examples of tertiary services include specialized cancer management, neurosurgery, cardiac surgery, organ transplants, plastic surgery, burn treatment, advanced neonatology, palliative care, and other complex medical and surgical interventions. Government-run facilities, private institutions, or a combination can provide these services.

1.2.4.4   Quaternary Care

Quaternary care extends tertiary care and refers to highly specialized and advanced medicine levels. This level of care, typically offered in a limited number of national or international centers, involves experimental medicine, uncommon diagnostic or surgical procedures, critical evaluation, and patient-centered approaches to ensure patients receive appropriate and necessary care. Due to the limitations, patients receiving these services may experience more extended hospital stays and increased mortality due to the complexity or rarity of their conditions.

1.3   Stakeholders in Healthcare

Various stakeholders contribute to shaping and influencing the functioning of the healthcare system. They are individuals, groups, organizations, or systems that influence or are affected by healthcare decisions and actions. In healthcare, it is crucial to recognize stakeholder relationships and manage them effectively. They may have different interests, needs, and expectations, and their involvement and support are essential for healthcare organizations and healthcare delivery. Understanding the dynamics and relationships among stakeholders and effectively managing their participation is critical to the success and sustainability of healthcare organizations and the delivery of quality healthcare services to patients.

1.3.1   Categories of Stakeholders in Healthcare

There are three basic categories of stakeholders in the healthcare system: external, internal, and interface stakeholders (Kaur & Victoria, 2011).

1.3.1.1 External Stakeholders

External stakeholders encompass various individuals and organizations, including patients, community healthcare professionals, non-governmental organizations, suppliers, policymakers, and the government. These stakeholders have an external relationship with the healthcare system and influence it through the resources and services, regulations, and policies provided.

1.3.1.2 Internal Stakeholders

Internal stakeholders work within healthcare organizations, such as hospitals, clinics, and nursing homes. They include healthcare professionals, administrative staff, management, and support staff. Internal stakeholders are directly involved in the day-to-day operations of the healthcare system and are responsible for providing quality care and services to patients.

1.3.1.3 Interface Stakeholders

Interface stakeholders act as a bridge between external and internal stakeholders. They are individuals or groups who closely connect with the healthcare system's external and internal aspects. This could include healthcare professionals working in hospital and community settings or suppliers interacting with healthcare organizations and external parties.

1.3.2 Healthcare Stakeholder Management

Managing stakeholders in the healthcare sector involves several steps, including identifying key stakeholders, assessing their level of influence and interest, understanding their needs and expectations, and actively engaging and communicating with them. This process helps diagnose and understand stakeholder relationships, categorized as adversarial, collaborative, dependent, or supportive. Healthcare organizations can tailor their strategies to effectively manage and engage stakeholders by identifying these relationship types. Management strategies in healthcare systems include involving stakeholders' concerns and grievances in decision-making processes, providing timely and transparent communication, and establishing stakeholder group mechanisms for feedback and collaboration. By actively managing stakeholder relationships, healthcare organizations can improve patient outcomes, resource allocation efficiency, and overall system performance.

1.3.2.1 Engaging Key Stakeholders in Healthcare

Developing relationships with key stakeholder groups and engaging them at each stage of a healthcare program's design and evaluation encourages involvement, gathers input, and ensures continuous improvement. Their engagement helps align program goals, secure resources, and manage expectations. The following strategies can be employed to engage stakeholders effectively (Petkovic et al., 2020; Bonawitz et al., 2020).

- *Identifying program champions:* This is an effective strategy to find those who can assist in program rollout, offer expertise, and promote program continuation (Shaw et al., 2012). These champions can support training, implementation, problem-solving, orientation, and material availability and provide feedback and encouragement to staff, contributing to the program's success.
- *Communicating regularly:* Another critical strategy is regularly communicating with stakeholders. Sharing program successes, failures, and new initiatives helps build support and maintain stakeholder engagement and demonstrates the program's value.
- *Managing the expectations:* Staff can manage stakeholders' expectations by acting as the critical point of contact for program information, ensuring stakeholders receive accurate and current information, and responding to their questions or concerns. Identifying and sharing early results that stakeholders consider successful can contribute to engagement and program sustainability.

1.4 Public Healthcare Programs and Services

Public healthcare programs and services provide a variety of initiatives that facilitate maintaining, restoring, and promoting health. These programs are designed to meet the healthcare needs of individuals and communities and to improve overall health outcomes (Andermann, 2016; Kumar & Preetha, 2012). These efforts aim to maximize the advantages for the most significant number of individuals and involve various strategies, policies, and actions implemented by governments, organizations, and individuals to prevent diseases, injuries, and other threats to public health (Edemekong & Tenny, n.d.). The following are a few examples of public healthcare programs and services:

1.4.1 Public Health and Safety

Public health and safety assists individuals and communities in staying safe and informed about food, drugs, medical devices, and violence prevention (Andermann, 2016).

- *Food safety:* The public health system is responsible for ensuring the safety and quality of the food supply chain. This involves monitoring food production, handling, and distribution, conducting inspections, implementing safety standards, and responding to foodborne illness outbreaks.
- *Drug safety:* The public health system is committed to providing timely information to consumers about drug safety, including recalls, market withdrawals, and safety alerts.
- *Medical device safety:* The public health system is responsible for regulating and monitoring the safety and performance of medical devices and issuing recalls, safety alerts, or product advisories when a device poses a safety risk or is deemed ineffective.
- *Safety from violence and abuse:* Public health efforts also focus on the recognition and prevention of child abuse and neglect, domestic or partner violence, elder abuse, sexual violence, youth violence, and community violence.

1.4.2 Health Education and Promotion

Public health addresses disease management and champions education and proactive wellness measures for individuals and communities. These undertakings foster disease prevention, enhance health results, and nurture equitable societies (Kumar & Preetha, 2012; Hahn & Truman, 2015).

- *Health education:* This area imparts accurate health information to deepen individuals' grasp of health hazards, prevention methods, and wholesome lifestyle decisions. Platforms like schools, community groups, health institutions, and media and online platforms facilitate this education.
- *Healthy lifestyle:* Central to public health is endorsing habits that stave off chronic illnesses, such as quitting smoking, eating nutritious meals, exercising, and practicing stress relief.
- *Mental health:* Public health magnifies mental health through awareness campaigns, destigmatization efforts, and ensuring adequate resources and support systems are in place.
- *Nutrition and fitness:* Public health strategies prevent chronic ailments by championing balanced diets and regular workouts. This involves spreading knowledge about wholesome food options and fostering publicly available avenues for physical activity.
- *Disease prevention*: Informative public health campaigns on topics from vaccinations to safe sex practices empower individuals to take control of their health and make informed choices.

1.4.3   Prevention and Wellness

Public health prioritizes prevention and wellness as cornerstones of community and individual health. A brief breakdown includes:

- *Chronic disease prevention:* Includes conditions like cancer, cardiovascular diseases, and obesity that aren't typically preventable via vaccinations. Public health encourages healthful behaviors and interventions to forestall these conditions (Schmidt, 2016).
- *Infectious disease control:* Curtailing the spread of infectious diseases is central to public health. The goal is to manage and reduce transmission risks by emphasizing vaccinations, hygiene practices, clean water, and early disease detection (Rodrigues & Plotkin, 2020).
- *Environmental health:* Activities range from monitoring air and water purity to tackling pollution and ensuring safe work and living conditions. Environmental health also encompasses occupational safety (Manisalidis et al., 2020; Fuller et al., 2022).
- *Health screenings:* By advocating routine health check-ups, public health aims to catch potential health issues early, paving the way for timely treatments. Screenings span a range of conditions, from cancers to cardiovascular diseases and infectious diseases (Organization WH, Others, 2020).

1.4.4   Health Security

Health security refers to the proactive and reactive measures taken to minimize the impact of acute public health events that endanger people's health across regions and international borders. Environmental and climate change, population growth, uncontrolled urbanization, and the rise or misuse of antimicrobials have impacted the microbial world, triggering the development of new diseases. Global travel, fragile health systems, and political instability compound these risks. Health security is crucial to strengthening global public health security and protecting lives, livelihoods, and the global economy (Rodier et al., 2007; Garg & Banerjee, 2021).

1.4.5   Healthcare Insurance

Public health insurance programs exist in various countries worldwide, aiming to ensure access to healthcare services for their populations. The specifics of these programs vary significantly between countries. Still, the overarching goal is to provide affordable and comprehensive healthcare coverage and outcomes, especially for vulnerable populations, such as low-income individuals, elderly individuals, and those with disabilities.

1.5   Areas of Higher Risk

Healthcare entities often struggle to balance limited resources and mounting threats. Internal audits and compliance teams align risk evaluations with overarching goals and regulations. Organizations can concentrate on high-risk areas and minimize efforts elsewhere by adopting a risk-focused strategy.

They face diverse risks: clinical, financial, operational, legal, and technological (Ferdosi et al., 2020; World Health Organization, 2021). Efficiently handling these necessitates prioritized resources, robust risk assessments, clear guidelines, and fostering a risk-aware culture. Such initiatives bolster patient safety, financial health, regulatory compliance, and overall resilience in a complex healthcare environment.

1.5.1   Clinical Risks

Patient safety and quality of care are paramount concerns for healthcare organizations. Clinical risks involve potential patient harm, medical errors, infections, adverse drug events, and other issues impacting patient outcomes. Healthcare providers must implement robust protocols, training programs, and monitoring systems to mitigate clinical risks and ensure patient safety.

1.5.2   Financial and Operational Risks

Healthcare organizations must manage financial resources and operational processes effectively to maintain stability and sustainability. Financial risks may include revenue cycle management, reimbursement challenges, budgetary constraints, and rising costs. Operational risks encompass supply chain management, facility management, staffing, and workflow optimization. Organizations can enhance financial performance and operational efficiency by identifying and addressing these risks.

1.5.3   Legal and Regulatory Compliance Risks in Healthcare

The healthcare industry is subject to complex laws, regulations, and compliance requirements. Non-compliance can result in legal consequences, financial penalties, reputational damage, and compromised patient care. Healthcare organizations must stay updated on evolving regulations, such as privacy and data security laws, and implement robust compliance programs to mitigate legal and regulatory risks.

1.5.4   Emerging Risks

Healthcare organizations must also anticipate and address emerging risks, such as public health emergencies, infectious disease outbreaks, natural disasters, and geopolitical factors. These risks can significantly impact care delivery, supply chain operations, and organizational resilience. By developing contingency plans, disaster response strategies, and proactive risk mitigation measures, healthcare organizations can better navigate unforeseen challenges.

1.5.5   Technology Risks in Healthcare

The rapid advancement of technology in healthcare brings both opportunities and risks. Adopting electronic health records, telehealth services, and connected medical devices introduces potential vulnerabilities related to data breaches, cyber threats, system failures, and privacy breaches. Healthcare organizations must implement robust cybersecurity measures, perform regular risk assessments, and ensure the integrity and security of their technology infrastructure.

1.6   Chapter Summary

The world of healthcare is vast and constantly changing, with a diverse mix of participants, from medical professionals to policymakers. Throughout this chapter, we've navigated its many layers, emphasizing the commitment to affordable, quality care and the significance of a patient-centered approach. We've broken down the system's structure, the variety of facilities, key stakeholders, and the challenges they face. A notable challenge in today's digital age is cybersecurity. As healthcare becomes increasingly interconnected, the risks of data breaches and unauthorized data access grow. Ensuring robust cybersecurity measures is no longer optional but a crucial aspect of maintaining patient trust and safety. We've touched upon the importance of safeguarding information in healthcare, setting the stage for more detailed exploration in subsequent chapters.

After understanding all the fundamental concepts, the following questions are addressed in this chapter:

- What are the main categories within the healthcare industry, and how do they reflect the diverse health needs of individuals and communities?
- How do public and private healthcare sectors differ in terms of features, funding strategies, and challenges?
- What are the three main levels of care in the healthcare system, and how do they vary in terms of range and specialization?

- How do different types of hospitals (public, private, and academic) and their services contribute to healthcare delivery?
- What roles do various stakeholders, including external, internal, and interface stakeholders, play in shaping the healthcare system?
- How do public healthcare programs and services, such as health education, disease prevention, and health security, aim to improve overall health outcomes?
- What are the key strategies for managing risks in healthcare, including clinical, financial, operational, legal, and technological risks?
- Why is it important to recognize and manage stakeholder relationships in healthcare, and how can this improve healthcare delivery?
- What is the impact of technological innovations on healthcare, especially in terms of treatment capabilities and operational efficiency?
- What is the significance of patient-centered care, and how does it contribute to the overall quality and accessibility of healthcare services?

References

Ahmed, T. M. F., Rajagopalan, P., & Fuller, R. (2015). A classification of healthcare facilities: Toward the development of energy performance benchmarks for day surgery centers in Australia. *HERD, 8*, 139–157. https://doi.org/10.1177/1937586715575910

Andermann, A. (2016). CLEAR collaboration. Taking action on the social determinants of health in clinical practice: A framework for health professionals. *CMAJ, 188*, E474–E483. https://doi.org/10.1503/cmaj.160177

Bonawitz, K., Wetmore, M., Heisler, M., Dalton, V. K., Damschroder, L. J., Forman, J., et al. (2020). Champions in context: Which attributes matter for change efforts in healthcare? *Implementation Science, 15*, 62. https://doi.org/10.1186/s13012-020-01024-9

Culyer, T., & Jonsson, B. Public and private health services: Complementarities and conflicts. 1986. Available: https://pure.york.ac.uk/portal/en/publications/public-and-private-health-services-complementarities-and-conflict

Das, J., Woskie, L., Rajbhandari, R., Abbasi, K., & Jha, A. (2018). Rethinking assumptions about delivery of healthcare: Implications for universal health coverage. *BMJ, 361*, k1716. https://doi.org/10.1136/bmj.k1716

Edemekong, P. F., & Tenny, S. (n.d.). *Issues of concern*. Available: https://europepmc.org/books/n/statpearls/article-27995/?extid=32310501&src=med

Ferdosi, M., Rezayatmand, R., & Molavi, T. Y. (2020). Risk management in executive levels of healthcare organizations: Insights from a scoping review (2018). *Risk Manag Healthc Policy., 13*, 215–243. https://doi.org/10.2147/RMHP.S231712

Fuller, R., Landrigan, P. J., Balakrishnan, K., Bathan, G., Bose-O'Reilly, S., Brauer, M., et al. (2022). Pollution and health: A progress update. *Lancet Planet Health., 6*, e535–e547. https://doi.org/10.1016/S2542-5196(22)00090-0

Gann, C. (1997). Risk Management in Nonhospital Settings: Impact of managed care. *Home Health Care Management and Practice, 10*, 10–18. https://doi.org/10.1177/108482239701000105

Garg, S., & Banerjee, B. (2021). One world, one health. *Indian Journal of Community Medicine, 46*, 581–583. https://doi.org/10.4103/ijcm.ijcm_1230_21

Glazier, R. H. (2007). Balancing equity issues in health systems: perspectives of primary healthcare. *Healthc Pap, 8*, 35–45. https://doi.org/10.12927/hcpap.2007.19218

Gupta, N., Maliqi, B., França, A., Nyonator, F., Pate, M. A., Sanders, D., et al. (2011). Human resources for maternal, newborn and child health: From measurement and planning to performance for improved health outcomes. *Human Resources for Health, 9*, 16. https://doi.org/10.1186/1478-4491-9-16

Hahn, R. A., & Truman, B. I. (2015). Education improves public health and promotes health equity. *International Journal of Health Services, 45*, 657–678. https://doi.org/10.1177/0020731415585986

Horwitz, J. R. (2005). Making profits and providing care: Comparing nonprofit, for-profit, and government hospitals. *Health Affairs, 24*, 790–801. https://doi.org/10.1377/hlthaff.24.3.790

Jofre-Bonet, M. (2000). Health care: Private and public provision. *European Journal of Political Economy, 16*, 469–489. https://doi.org/10.1016/S0176-2680(99)00063-4

Kaabi, S. A. L., Varughese, B., & Singh, R. (2022). Public and private healthcare system in terms of quality and cost: A review. *Journal of Clinical and Diagnostic Research, 16*. Available: https://www.researchgate.net/profile/Rajvir-Singh-4/publication/362756444_Public_and_Private_Healthcare_System_in_Terms_of_both_Quality_and_Cost_A_Review/links/63035af9aa4b1206facd29ef/Public-and-Private-Healthcare-System-in-Terms-of-both-Quality-and-Cost-A-Review.pdf

Kaur, A., & Victoria, E. L. (2011). Major stakeholders in health care system: Government, non-government & other professionals. *Global Journal Of Business & Management., 2*, 2455. Available: https://www.researchgate.net/profile/Amandeep-Kaur-136/publication/344302523_Major_Stakeholders_in_Health_Care_System_Government_Non-government_Other_Professionals/links/5f64f38ca6fdcc00862d01d9/Major-Stakeholders-in-Health-Care-System-Government-Non-government-Other-Professionals.pdf

Kumar, S., & Preetha, G. (2012). Health promotion: An effective tool for global health. *Indian Journal of Community Medicine, 37*, 5–12. https://doi.org/10.4103/0970-0218.94009

Leslie, H. H., Sun, Z., & Kruk, M. E. (2017). Association between infrastructure and observed quality of care in 4 healthcare services: A cross-sectional study of 4,300 facilities in 8 countries. *PLoS Medicine, 14*, e1002464. https://doi.org/10.1371/journal.pmed.1002464

Liu, J. B., & Kelz, R. R. (2018). Types of hospitals in the United States. *Journal of the American Medical Association, 320*, 1074. https://doi.org/10.1001/jama.2018.9471

Mäkelä, M., Banerji, D., Lankinen, K. S., Bergström, S., Mäkelä, P. H., & Peltomaa, M. (1994). *Levels of health care* (pp. 393–401). Macmillan.

Manisalidis, I., Stavropoulou, E., Stavropoulos, A., & Bezirtzoglou, E. (2020). Environmental and health impacts of air pollution: A review. *Frontiers in Public Health, 8*, 14. https://doi.org/10.3389/fpubh.2020.00014

Merviö, M. M. (2013). *Healthcare management and economics: Perspectives on public and private administration: Perspectives on public and private administration*. IGI Global. Available: https://play.google.com/store/books/details?id=wNGeBQAAQBAJ

on Population Health HDTG of TFAC, Security H. (2004). *Reducing health disparities–roles of the health sector: a discussion paper*. Public Health Agency of Canada Ottawa.

Organization WH, Others. (2020). *Screening programmes: A short guide. Increase effectiveness, maximize benefits, and minimize harm*. Available: https://apps.who.int/iris/handle/10665/330829

Petkovic, J., Riddle, A., Akl, E. A., Khabsa, J., Lytvyn, L., Atwere, P., et al. (2020). Protocol for the development of guidance for stakeholder engagement in health and healthcare guideline development and implementation. *Systematic Reviews, 9*, 21. https://doi.org/10.1186/s13643-020-1272-5

Rodier, G., Greenspan, A. L., Hughes, J. M., & Heymann, D. L. (2007). Global public health security. *Emerging Infectious Diseases, 13*, 1447–1452. https://doi.org/10.3201/eid1310.070732

Rodrigues, C. M. C., & Plotkin, S. A. (2020). Impact of vaccines; health, Economic and Social Perspectives. *Front Microbiol., 11*, 1526. https://doi.org/10.3389/fmicb.2020.01526

Schmidt H. Chronic disease prevention and health promotion. In: H. Barrett D, W. Ortmann L, Dawson A, Saenz C, Reis A, Bolan G, editors. Public health ethics: Cases spanning the globe. : Springer; 2016. doi:https://doi.org/10.1007/978-3-319-23847-0

Shaw, E. K., Howard, J., West, D. R., Crabtree, B. F., Nease, D. E., Jr., Tutt, B., et al. (2012). The role of the champion in primary care change efforts: From the state networks of Colorado ambulatory practices and partners (SNOCAP). *Journal of American Board of Family Medicine, 25*, 676–685. https://doi.org/10.3122/jabfm.2012.05.110281

Starfield, B., Shi, L., & Macinko, J. (2005). Contribution of primary care to health systems and health. *The Milbank Quarterly, 83*, 457–502. https://doi.org/10.1111/j.1468-0009.2005.00409.x

Turea, M. How the big four tech companies are leading innovation. *Healthcare Weekly.*

Van Lerberghe, W., Evans, T., Rasanathan, K., et al. (2008). *The world health report 2008: Primary health care: Now more than ever*. World Health Organization. Available: https://play.google.com/store/books/details?id=q-EGxRjrIo4C

World Health Organization. (2021). *Global patient safety action plan 2021-2030: towards eliminating avoidable harm in health care*. World Health Organization. Available: https://play.google.com/store/books/details?id=csZqEAAAQBAJ

Chapter 2
The Basic of Cybersecurity Concept

2.1 Introduction

Digital technologies have changed our lives drastically, and we rely on Internet services and their applications for banking, healthcare, and other governmental services. Increased use of digital technology in the health sector industry maintains health-related information, including patient, doctor, and staff personal and health record databases. Digital technologies are becoming essential to our daily lives as new developments potentially raise security concerns. Cyberattacks on any healthcare system can result in severe disruption of services and losses. Attackers target hospitals and healthcare systems because it impacts human life and safety. In recent years, it has been growing. The healthcare sector is the top-ranked sector in the average data breach cost (Statista, 2022), with an average price of 10 million US dollars. The second is the financial industry, which averages 5.97 million US dollars per breach. Figure 2.1 shows the industry-wise cost of data breaches worldwide from May 2020 to March 2022. Cybersecurity in healthcare aims to protect personally identifiable and protected health information by securing devices, electronic systems, networks, and data from cyberattacks. Patient's protected health information is valuable and applicable to various cybercrimes, including identity theft, medical fraud, and many more. Therefore, cybersecurity awareness is essential for all health sector stakeholders, including patients, doctors, and staff. Cybersecurity is a set of techniques to protect networked systems, software programs, and data from cyberattacks, data breaches, identity theft, loss, damage, unauthorized access, and risk mitigation.

Security Threat
Drawing from the Internet Security Glossary (Shirey, 2007), cybersecurity in healthcare hinges on understanding several vital concepts: security threats, attacks, vulnerabilities, and countermeasures.

© The Author(s), under exclusive license to Springer Nature
Switzerland AG 2024
D. P. Sharma et al., *Understanding Cybersecurity Management in Healthcare*,
Progress in IS, https://doi.org/10.1007/978-3-031-68034-2_2

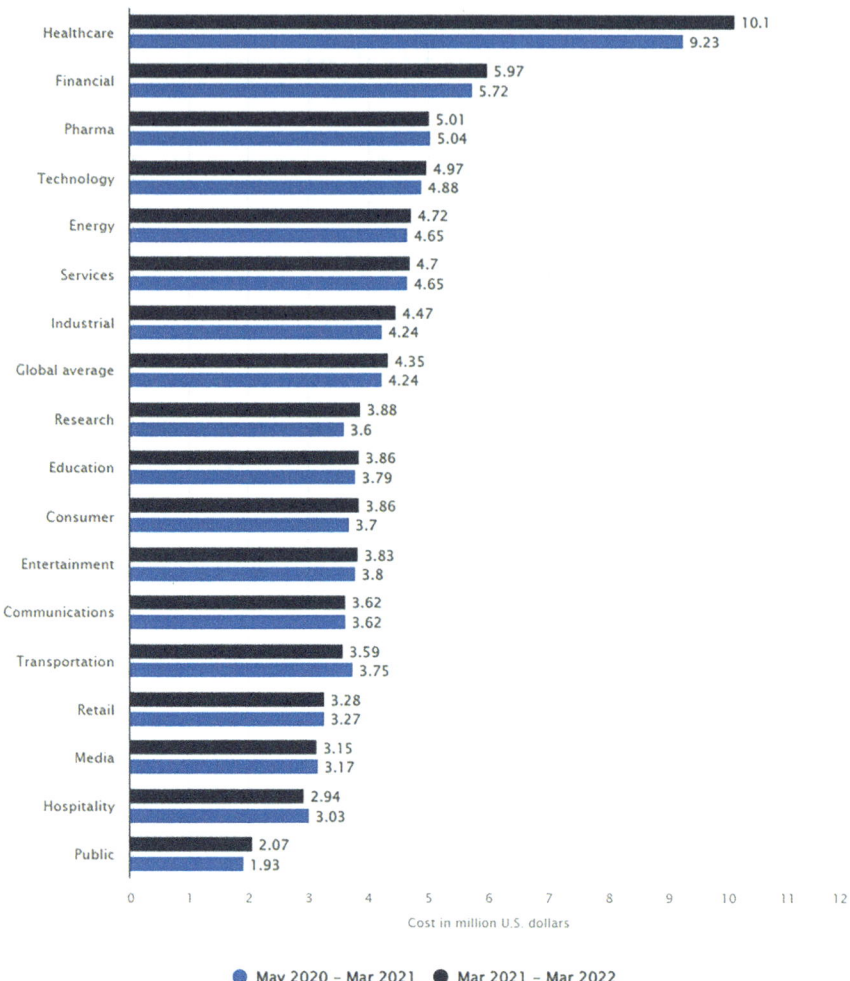

Fig. 2.1 Average cost of a data breach worldwide from May 2020 to March 2022, by industry in million US dollars (Statista, 2022)

A *Security Event* is any event or danger that could compromise an organization's security, potentially leading to financial or data losses, denial of service, fraud, or other undesirable outcomes. Its main goal is to exploit vulnerabilities. A few primary security threats are:

- *Interception:* Unauthorized access to systems or services, such as an outsider illicitly copying data or programs.
- *Interruption:* Damaging or making system assets unavailable. This could be through the malicious destruction of hardware or even cutting off communication channels.

- *Modification:* A threat where intruders gain access and alter data. This can involve changing data values or even modifying a program's functions.
- *Fabrication:* Unauthorized entities introduce counterfeit items into the system with the intention of misleading or causing harm.

In addition to these tech-centered threats, healthcare systems face risks from physical incidents or natural disasters, like hurricanes or fires, which can disrupt services and operations.

Attack

System security is perpetually threatened by deliberate attempts, termed *attacks*, which aim to bypass security measures and contravene a system's security policy. Broadly, attacks can be categorized into active and passive types. Figure 2.2 depicts the generic classification of cyberattacks.

Active Attacks are the more aggressive attacks that aim to alter or disrupt a system's operations. Key characteristics and examples include:

- *Masquerade:* Here, an attacker poses as another user or entity, often as a stepping stone for other active attacks.
- *Replay:* Capturing data and then re-sending it, tricking a system into unauthorized operations.
- *Modification of messages:* Altering, delaying, or reordering messages to affect system operations illicitly.
- *Denial of service (DoS):* Overwhelming a system or service, making it unavailable to users.

Passive Attacks are more discreet, focusing on collecting information without modifying data. Their stealthy nature makes them harder to detect. They encompass:

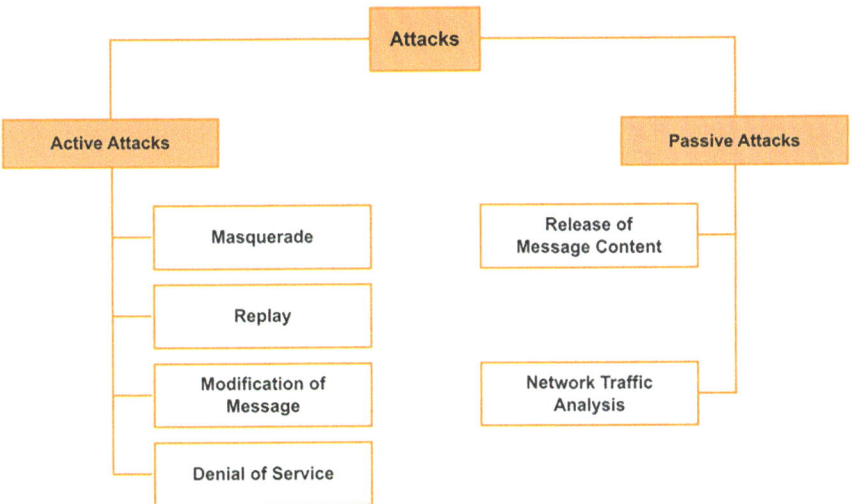

Fig. 2.2 Generic classification of attacks

- *Release of message contents:* This involves capturing sensitive information being transferred, like emails or phone calls.
- *Traffic analysis:* Beyond just capturing messages, attackers analyze patterns for more extensive insights.

While active attacks visibly impact system functionality, passive attacks silently gather information, making it imperative to guard against both.

Vulnerability

Vulnerability refers to the inherent weaknesses in a system's structure, execution, or administration that can be exploited, leading to a potential security breach. These vulnerabilities can manifest in managing patient records, hospital operations, or decision-making support systems in healthcare. Simply put, the system's Achilles' heel could be misused to cause damage or unauthorized access.

In healthcare, vulnerabilities could range from simple human errors or hardware design shortcomings to complex software malfunctions. External factors like natural disasters, such as a data center flood or earthquake damage, can also expose these vulnerabilities.

But vulnerabilities don't just expose a system to natural disasters. They can also be exploited by malicious intent. Someone with the proper knowledge and intent can leverage these weak points to instigate attacks. For instance, a system could be overwhelmed by an influx of messages from another system, causing it to shut down.

Countermeasures

Countermeasures, often termed controls, safeguard our digital assets by either thwarting potential cyber threats or reducing their potential damage. By understanding vulnerabilities, we can establish specific controls that deter threats from exploiting them, especially in critical sectors like healthcare.

Contemporary Cyberattacks and Controls:

1. *Malware attacks:* These involve malicious software performing unauthorized actions. This includes ransomware, Trojans, and viruses. To prevent malware attacks, regularly update software and devices, limit the use of administrator accounts, and exercise caution with emails and attachments from unfamiliar sources.
2. *DoS/DDoS Attacks:* These attacks overload a network with excessive traffic, making it inoperable. Avoid DDoS attacks by changing router passwords from the default, monitoring network traffic to identify suspicious trends, and using application monitoring tools.
3. *Ransomware attacks:* Hackers encrypt your data, making it inaccessible until a ransom is paid. Regularly backup data and promptly change all user credentials if a breach is suspected.
4. *Phishing and social engineering attacks:* These manipulative attacks target human behavior, luring individuals to disclose sensitive information or execute malicious actions. Train healthcare professionals with simulated phishing scenarios to enhance their ability to recognize and respond to real-life threats.

5. *Insider threats:* These threats arise from within the organization — current or former employees, contractors, or associates with access to systems. Implement policies and technologies that prevent misuse of privileges. Conduct continuous risk assessments and employ automatic monitoring.

2.2 Cybersecurity Design Principles

Saltzer and Schroeder's (Jerome & Saltzer, 1975) paper presented the mechanics of protecting computer-stored information from unauthorized use or modification. The paper presented eight design principles for computer security and examples of elementary protection and authentication mechanisms. Listed are the eight design principles for computer security:

- *Continuous improvement:* This principle emphasizes evaluating and enhancing security measures. Today's information security standards, like ISO 27001, advocate for iterative assessment and improvement.
- *Least privilege:* Users or systems should only have the minimum privileges necessary to execute their tasks. This principle restricts attacker access during an attack.
- *Defense in depth:* Systems should be built with multiple, independent layers of security. This multi-tiered approach ensures that if one layer is breached, others will still prevent an attacker from gaining access.
- *Open design:* A security system's efficacy should not rely on its design being kept secret. The underlying principle is that even if attackers know how the system works, they still shouldn't be able to breach it.
- *Chain of control:* This principle ensures that software can be trusted. It emphasizes the importance of validating software's authenticity and integrity before execution.
- *Deny by default:* In the absence of explicit permissions, all access attempts should be denied. This principle safeguards against unintentional permissions and unauthorized access.
- *Transitive trust*: This principle underscores the interconnectedness of trust relationships. If Entity A trusts Entity B, and Entity B trusts Entity C, it implies that Entity A indirectly places trust in Entity C.
- *Separation of duty:* Critical operations should be split into components, with each part being the responsibility of a different individual or entity. This ensures that no single entity has complete control, reducing the risk of insider threats.

2.3   Cybersecurity Basic Principles (CIAAA)

NIST Standards for Security Categorization of Federal Information and Information System (NIST-FIPS199., 2004) lists confidentiality, integrity, and availability as the three security objectives for data and information systems. NIST-FIPS199 provides a helpful characterization of these three objectives regarding security requirements and the definition of a loss of security in each category. The CIA triad includes these three concepts (confidentiality, integrity, and availability). Figure 2.3 shows the CIA triad for healthcare data and services. Cybersecurity in healthcare seeks to prevent unauthorized viewing (confidentiality) or modification (integrity) of healthcare data while preserving access (availability). These three concepts represent the fundamental security objectives for healthcare data and services.

2.3.1   Confidentiality

Confidentiality ensures that the authorized party only has access to computer-related assets. Only those who should have access to something will get that access. Confidentiality is also called secrecy or privacy, as it ensures that private or confidential information is not made available or disclosed to unauthorized individuals or organizations. A loss of confidentiality is the unauthorized disclosure of information by any individual or organization.

Privacy is the ability of an individual (or organization) to decide whether, when, and to whom individual (or organizational) information is released. It assures that individuals (patients, doctors, personnel, etc.) or organizations control or influence what information related to them may be collected, stored, and processed by whom and to whom that information may be disclosed. One of the mechanisms for preserving confidentiality is cryptography, which encrypts the data. It uses a cryptographic algorithm to encrypt data using the keys. If you need to see the original data, it must be deciphered using the duplicate keys.

Fig. 2.3 CIA triad for healthcare data and services

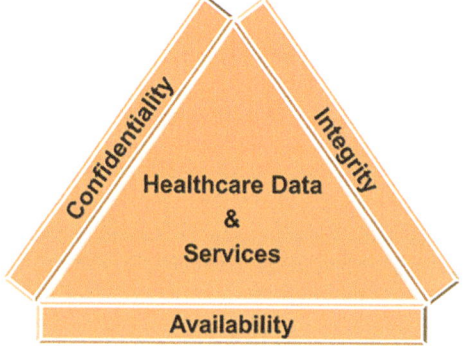

Let us consider a simple attack scenario to demonstrate how an attacker attacks confidentiality. Suppose user1 and user2 are authorized users (doctors, patients, staff, or any authorized users/stakeholders of the healthcare system); A is an attacker or opponent who tries to gain unauthorized access or attack the system. In this attack, A intercepts by reading or listening to the messages from user1 to user2. Each user (user1 and user2) can be a doctor, patient employee, or any other authorized agency or organization. A can use this information to plan and attack them later.

2.3.2 Integrity

Integrity pertains to maintaining the authenticity and consistency of data and systems. It's about ensuring that only authorized parties make modifications and do so in the proper ways.

- *Data integrity*: This focuses on ensuring data remains unchanged and consistent during usage. Whether it's a file, a dataset, or a patient's medical record, data integrity ensures that it's kept accurate and not altered maliciously or accidentally.
- *System integrity:* Beyond just data, the systems or software that process, store, or retrieve that data must be trustworthy. System integrity ensures these systems function correctly and aren't compromised by external hackers or internal errors.

Prevention mechanisms are proactive measures that protect integrity, including strict access controls, encryption, and secure coding practices that actively prevent unauthorized changes. If something goes wrong, *detection tools* like intrusion detection systems and integrity checkers can identify and alert about any breaches.

2.3.3 Availability

Availability ensures that data, systems, or services are consistently accessible to authorized users when needed. Any disruption can hamper operations, especially in sectors like healthcare, where service interruptions can have dire consequences.

Denial-of-service attacks are meant to overwhelm systems, deliberately making them unavailable to users. This could be done by flooding a network with excessive requests or exploiting system vulnerabilities.

While the traditional CIA (confidentiality, integrity, availability) triad is foundational in cybersecurity, Fig. 2.4 shows that the extended CIAAA model incorporates authenticity and accountability for a more comprehensive approach to securing data, especially critical in healthcare.

Fig. 2.4 CIAAA model
for protecting healthcare
data and services

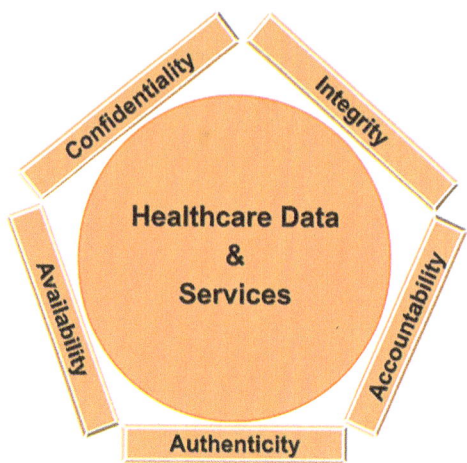

2.3.4   *Authenticity*

Authenticity is the assurance that a person, system, or organization's identity involved in a digital interaction is genuine and trustworthy. It's pivotal in establishing trust in digital engagements and safeguarding against fraudulent or malicious actions.

Various methods confirm an entity's authenticity, ranging from user IDs, passwords, and biometric data to intelligent cards, email verifications, and hardware tokens. While passwords are commonly used, there's a growing shift toward more secure methods like multi-factor authentication and biometrics.

2.3.5   *Accountability*

Accountability in security ensures that actions can be uniquely traced to an entity. It's like keeping a detailed record linking actions to specific individuals or systems. This principle supports nonrepudiation, meaning neither party can deny an action or transaction. It acts as a deterrent against unauthorized actions. If people know their actions are traceable, they're less likely to misbehave. Accountability helps in fault detection, intrusion management, and understanding security breaches. While audit logs might not prevent threats, they're vital for analyzing and understanding security issues.

2.4 Regulation

Over the years, the landscape of cybersecurity regulations has significantly transformed. In 2016, the European Union (EU) introduced the *General Data Protection Regulation (GDPR)*, updating its prior rules. The GDPR outlines guidelines for safeguarding all EU citizens' health data, including stipulations for breach notifications and penalties (GDPR, 2018). On the other side of the Atlantic, the USA enacted the *Health Insurance Portability and Accountability Act (HIPAA)* in 1996, which mandates the secure handling, storage, and transmission of health-related information (HIPAA, 1996).

In addition to these, other frameworks and standards, such as FISMA, the NIST Cybersecurity Framework, ISO/IEC 27001, and PCI-DSS, are also shaping cybersecurity measures across various sectors.

2.4.1 Cybercrime

Cybercrimes or computer crimes are criminal or illegal activities committed using the Internet and information technology with computers, smartphones, tablets, or personal digital assistants. For example, cybercriminals steal someone's personal or corporate information or infect their computers or any target devices with a virus and other malicious software. Cybercriminals also attack the information, systems (computers and software), and services of individuals, organizations, or governments. These attacks occur virtually on the personal or corporate level using the Internet and information technology.

Cybercrimes relevant to the healthcare system can be divided into two broad categories: technology as a target and an instrument.

Technology-as-Target
Technology-as-target is a criminal offense that targets computers and information technologies such as software, systems, data, or services. This offense includes unauthorized use of computers, data, software, or services. They focus on exploiting vulnerabilities or compromising the technology to gain unauthorized access, disrupt critical healthcare services, or steal patient-sensitive information. Criminals attack healthcare networks or systems to access patient records, personal information, or financial and payment information. Some of the common examples of technology-as-target cybercrimes in healthcare are:

- Attacking healthcare networks or systems to access patient records and personal information.
- Installing malicious software (malware or ransomware) on healthcare systems to disrupt services, operations, and demand ransoms.
- Exploitation of vulnerabilities in medical devices connected to healthcare systems to gain control.

- Attacking electronic health record (EHR) systems or healthcare databases to steal patient information for identity theft.

Technology-as-Instrument

Technology-as-instrument is a criminal offense where the Internet and information technologies are instrumental in the crime. Criminals use technology to commit crimes, often involving the compromise or misuse of patient's sensitive information. The crimes involve fraud, identity theft, organized crime activities, intellectual property infringements, money laundering, drug trafficking, human trafficking, child sexual exploitation, or cyberbullying. Common examples of technology-as-instrument cybercrimes in healthcare are:

- Phishing attacks target patients or healthcare employees to obtain login credentials or personal information.
- Online fraud or scams targeting patients.
- Unauthorized access or sharing of patients' protected health information for malicious purposes.
- Data theft and selling stolen patient data on the black market or dark web.

There are different types and scopes of cybercrime that impact people.

- *Personal level:* At this level, cybercriminals target individuals through online scams or any other deception or attack techniques. Cybercrime at these levels includes social costs and devastating forms of victimization, such as online child sexual exploitation and cyberbullying. Organized crime networks sometimes facilitate these threats and may cause significant economic losses.
- *Commercial or business level:* The cybercrimes of this level target banking and financial institutions, businesses and retailers, and other organizations to steal personal or corporate credential information such as passwords, credit card and payment information, information of intellectual property or trade secrets, and privacy.
- *National level:* National security cybercrimes are state-sponsored, and other criminal actors use intelligence and sophisticated and covert cyber capabilities and tools to perform espionage and steal sensitive information to conduct more disruptive attacks against the nation's critical infrastructure, such as healthcare systems, transportation, and power grids.

A list of some common cybercrimes relevant to healthcare systems is as follows:

- Phishing and social engineering attacks
- Data breaches
- Ransomware attacks
- Insider threats
- Malware attacks
- Medical device hacking or compromise
- Distributed denial-of-service (DDoS) attacks
- Identity theft
- Pharming

2.4.2 Cybersecurity Laws and Regulations

Many cyber laws and frameworks exist to curtail cybercriminal activities across various digital environments, including the Internet and email. The European Union's General Data Protection Regulation (GDPR) and the US Insurance Portability and Accountability Act (HIPAA) stand out. Both aim to shield individuals' personal and health-related data.

General Data Protection Regulation (GDPR)

The GDPR, established in 2018, outlines the dos and don'ts of personal data processing within the European Union and during external transfers. It revolves around seven central principles:

- *Lawfulness, fairness, and transparency:* Personal data should be handled lawfully, clearly, and fairly, relying on consent and legal obligations.
- *Purpose limitation:* Collection and processing should strictly align with specific and legitimate purposes, and any deviation requires fresh consent.
- *Data minimization:* Only gather essential data for the designated purpose.
- *Accuracy:* Data should be current and accurate, committed to rectifying inaccuracies.
- *Storage limitation:* Store data only for the necessary duration.
- *Integrity and confidentiality:* Data handling must ensure security and confidentiality, utilizing measures like encryption.
- *Accountability:* Data controllers must adhere visibly to the GDPR principles, maintain thorough records, and possibly assign a dedicated data protection officer.

Health Insurance Portability and Accountability Act (HIPAA)

The Health Insurance Portability and Accountability Act (HIPAA, 1996) is pivotal US legislation aiming to protect patients' healthcare information from unauthorized disclosure. It mandates national standards for the privacy and security of such information. The act primarily targets health plans, healthcare clearinghouses, and providers that electronically handle healthcare data.

Two main rules under HIPAA are:

- *Privacy rule:* Introduced by the US Department of Health and Human Services, the Privacy Rule formulates standards to shield individuals' health details, targeting entities like health plans and electronic transaction-conducting healthcare providers.
- *Security rule:* This rule underscores the need to safeguard electronically held health information, focusing on administrative, technical, and physical safety measures. It intends to simultaneously protect individuals' health data privacy and let entities embrace technology advancements to enhance patient care.

Entities required to adhere to HIPAA are:

- *Healthcare providers:* This encompasses many professionals, from doctors and dentists to clinics and nursing homes.
- *Health plans:* This covers insurance firms, company health schemes, and specific government programs.
- *Healthcare clearinghouses*: These intermediaries convert received health information into a standardized electronic format.

Lastly, the National Institute of Standards and Technology (NIST) offers guidance that aligns with HIPAA's security provisions. It's designed to aid organizations in safeguarding electronic health data, aligning the HIPAA rules with NIST's cybersecurity guidelines. This framework ensures the confidentiality, integrity, and accessibility of digital health records and related data.

Health Information Technology for Economic and Clinical Health act
The Health Information Technology for Economic and Clinical Health (HITECH) Act, introduced in 2009 as part of the American Recovery and Reinvestment Act (ARRA), focuses on the electronic management of health data, particularly electronic health records (EHRs). The act enhances the privacy and security measures for EHRs and other health technologies. HITECH also bolsters civil and criminal enforcement of HIPAA regulations, particularly breach notifications.

Federal Information Security Modernization Act (FISMA)
The Federal Information Security Modernization Act (FISMA, 2014) is a US law designed to enhance information security across federal agencies. FISMA offers a structured approach to safeguard federal operations and assets by emphasizing the importance of adequate security controls.

The act is tailored to address the unique landscape of the federal computing environment—promoting a coordinated effort across civilian, national security, and law enforcement sectors to manage information security risks. FISMA mandates that all federal agencies establish security measures in line with the potential risks and consequences of unauthorized actions, ranging from access to system disruptions.

NIST Cybersecurity Framework
The National Institute of Standards and Technology Cybersecurity Framework is a risk-based approach for assessing cybersecurity risk for various organizations. It is a cyber risk assessment used to identify, estimate, and prioritize risk to organizational operations, organizational assets, individuals, other organizations, and the Nation, resulting from the operation and use of information systems (NIST, 2018).

NIST initially produced the Framework in 2014 and updated it in April 2018 with CSF 1.1. Based on stakeholder feedback, reflect the ever-evolving cybersecurity landscape and help organizations manage cybersecurity risks more efficiently and effectively. Cybersecurity risk assessment process is concerned with answering the following questions:

- What are our organization's most crucial information technology assets?
- What are the potential cybersecurity threats (attacks) that mainly impact the business?

- What is the level (high/medium/low) of the potential impact of each identified threat?
- What are the vulnerabilities of the systems?
- What is the impact (high/medium/low) if those vulnerabilities are exploited?
- What is the likelihood (probability) of exploitation?

ISO/IEC 27001

The International Organization for Standardization/International Electrotechnical Commission (ISO/IEC 27001) is a part of the large ISO/IEC 27000 family of cybersecurity standards. The ISO/IEC 27001 standard provides a framework for an information security management system (ISMS) for all companies of any size and from all sectors of activity with guidance for establishing, implementing, maintaining, and continually improving an information security management system (ISO/IEC-27001, 2022).

Payment Card Industry Data Security Standard

Payment Card Industry Data Security Standard (PCI-DSS) is a global information security standard to prevent credit card fraud and cardholder data protection (PCI-DSS, 2022). PCI-DSS specifies requirements for secure processing, storing, and transferring payment card data. All the stakeholders (e.g., organizations, merchants, payment gateway) must comply with PCI-DSS. Although it is not specific to the healthcare industry, each healthcare organization that uses payment card information must comply with PCI-DSS requirements. These standards ensure the secure handling of credit card data to prevent unauthorized access or fraud.

2.5 Training and Development

Cybersecurity training and development for healthcare professionals are essential to mitigate the risks associated with cyber threats in healthcare. There are different training methods available for cybersecurity training and development. Figure 2.5 shows the cybersecurity training and development methods in the healthcare sector. These methods are described as follows:

- *General cybersecurity awareness training:* Basic cybersecurity awareness training focuses on raising employee awareness of potential cyber threats. It provides comprehensive training to healthcare personnel about cybersecurity fundamentals, including best practices for password management, email security, safe web browsing, and data protection. This awareness training helps them to maintain the confidentiality, integrity, and availability of patient data.
- *Specialized (role-based) training:* It is essential to provide tailored cybersecurity training programs to specific roles within the healthcare organization because different people have different roles with distinct cybersecurity responsibilities and requirements. These are more advanced training that could be ideal for information technology (IT) teams and roles like security analysts and help them gain

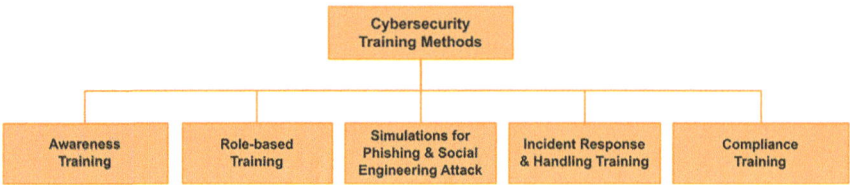

Fig. 2.5 Cybersecurity training and development methods in healthcare

a deeper understanding of cybersecurity skills to build and apply. For example, training for IT administrators might focus on network security, while training for doctors and other staff could concentrate on securing patient records and recognizing various attacks, including scams and social engineering attacks.

- *Simulation of phishing and social engineering attacks training:* This training method educates people about phishing and social engineering attacks. In this method, simulated phishing campaigns and social engineering exercises have been conducted to train healthcare staff on identifying and responding to suspicious emails, links, and phone calls. These simulations help raise awareness of common attack vectors and teach employees to exercise caution before sharing sensitive information or clicking on malicious links.
- *Incident response and handling training:* This training educates healthcare professionals on the proper procedures and protocols to follow and report a cybersecurity incident or data breach. It covers incident detection, reporting, containment, and communication to minimize the impact of an incident.
- *Compliance training:* This is training for healthcare professionals and staff on regulations and compliance standards in the healthcare industry, such as the Health Insurance Portability and Accountability Act (HIPAA) and the General Data Protection Regulation (GDPR). It helps healthcare professionals understand their responsibilities in protecting patient privacy and maintaining compliance with applicable laws and regulations.

Continuous education and training with regular workshops, seminars, or webinars enhances the cybersecurity knowledge and awareness of evolving cyber threats among healthcare staff and helps reduce the risk of cyber incidents.

2.6   Chapter Summary

This chapter introduces the basic concept of cybersecurity relevant to the healthcare system, including threats, attacks, vulnerabilities, and countermeasures for preventing cyberattacks and protecting the data. Contemporary cyberattacks such as malware, phishing and social engineering, ransomware, DDoS, and insider threats and best practices to reduce these attacks are discussed. The CIA model ensures confidentiality, integrity, and availability of data. It is extended by adding two more principles of accountability and authenticity with the CIAAA model. Cybersecurity regulations and laws (e.g., GDPR, HIPAA, etc.) applicable to their jurisdiction and necessary steps to comply with the requirements are presented. Finally, various cybersecurity training and development methods for healthcare professionals are discussed at the end of the chapter.

After understanding all the fundamental concepts, the following questions are addressed in this chapter:

- What are the motivations to launch a cybersecurity attack in the healthcare industry?
- What are security threats, vulnerabilities, attacks, and countermeasures for cyberattacks?
- What are the cybersecurity design principles in the healthcare system?
- What are the essential elements of the CIAAA principle and how does this help to protect healthcare data and services?
- What is the importance of cybersecurity in healthcare?
- What are the contemporary cyberattacks in the healthcare sector?
- What are cybercrimes in the healthcare system?
- How do cybercriminals target the healthcare system?
- What are the regulations and cyber laws for protecting healthcare data?
- What are the methods of cybersecurity training and development of healthcare professionals?

References

FISMA. (2014, December 18). Federal information security modernization act of 2014. Senate Reports: No. 113-256 (Comm. on Homeland Security and Governmental Affairs). *Congressional Record, 160*(2014).

GDPR. (2018). *Corrigendum to regulation (EU) 2016/679 of the European parliament and of the council of 27 April 2016 on protecting natural persons about the processing of personal data and on the free movement of such data, and repealing directive 95/46.* European Union. Accessed May 14, 2023, from http://data.europa.eu/eli/reg/2016/679/corrigendum/2018-05-23/oj

HIPAA. (1996, August 21). *H.R.3103-104th congress (1995–1996): Health insurance portability and accountability act of 1996.* https://www.congress.gov/bill/104th-congress/house-bill/3103

ISO/IEC-27001. (2022). *Information security management systems.* International Organization for Standardization. Retrieved from https://www.iso.org/standard/27001

Jerome, H., & Saltzer, M. D. (1975). *The protection of information in computer systems* (Vol. 63, p. 1278).

NIST. (2018). *Cybersecurity framework V1.1.* National Institute of Standards and Technology (NIST). Accessed from https://www.nist.gov/cyberframework/framework

NIST-FIPS199. (2004). *Standards for security categorization of federal information and information systems.* NIST.

PCI-DSS. (2022). *Payment card industry data security standards (PCI DSS) Version 4.0.* PCI Security Standards Council. Accessed from https://listings.pcisecuritystandards.org/documents/PCI-DSS-v4-0-SAQ-A.pdf

Shirey, R. (2007). *Internet security glossary, version 2, RFC 4949.* https://www.rfc-editor.org/info/rfc4949

Statista. (2022). *Average total cost per data breach worldwide 2020–2022, by industry.* Statista. Accessed May 14, 2023, from https://www.statista.com/statistics/387861/cost-data-breach-by-industry/

Chapter 3
Defining Cybersecurity in Healthcare

3.1 Introduction

In the previous chapter, we explained that cybersecurity prevents information leakage, data theft, and damage to computer systems and networks and ensures uninterrupted service delivery. Cybersecurity has evolved significantly over the past few decades in response to the increasing concerns posed by attackers (Kruse et al., 2017; Wasserman & Wasserman, 2022). Healthcare is a notable target for cybercrime, making it a critical concern for digital-centric companies. Concurrently, the healthcare industry has experienced a paradigm shift, with technology playing an increasingly pivotal role. Technology has brought many innovations to the healthcare sector, from storing patient data in cloud platforms to integrating artificial intelligence into medical processes such as radiology screening (Javaid et al., 2023). However, many healthcare organizations lack effective risk management and incident reporting, making monitoring cyberattacks challenging. Due to the increase in cyberattacks in the healthcare industry, which accounted for 24% of all attacks in 2019, vulnerabilities have come to the forefront (Martignani, 2019). The evaluation and comprehension of threat data can help reduce damage and vulnerabilities. In the healthcare industry, cybersecurity risks are significant due to the potentially life-threatening consequences of data breaches.

This chapter outlines the critical role of cybersecurity in healthcare by safeguarding patient data, maintaining medical system integrity, and ensuring patient safety. It highlights the industry's growing cyber threats due to technological integration and emphasizes the imperative for robust cybersecurity measures to counteract potential breaches and vulnerabilities. It also discusses the necessity and various applications of cybersecurity, design considerations, and the development of healthcare security systems.

D. P. Sharma et al., *Understanding Cybersecurity Management in Healthcare*, Progress in IS, https://doi.org/10.1007/978-3-031-68034-2_3

3.2   Basic Rationale of Cybersecurity in Healthcare

The fundamental purpose of cybersecurity in healthcare is to safeguard sensitive patient data, maintain the integrity of essential medical systems, and ensure patient safety and quality. Cyber threats are becoming more prevalent with the increasing reliance on technology in healthcare.

3.2.1   The Necessity of Cybersecurity in Healthcare

The widespread use of electronic healthcare technology worldwide presents significant opportunities for enhancing clinical outcomes and revolutionizing care delivery. However, as technology evolves, concerns over the security of healthcare data and devices are growing. Healthcare organizations handle sensitive information regularly, and increased integration with computer networks has created new cybersecurity vulnerabilities for this data.

Using medical devices to provide efficient patient care has also introduced multiple points of entry for attackers. The ease of access to these devices increases the likelihood of breaches. Therefore, ensuring robust cybersecurity is essential for patient safety. Furthermore, as the industry focuses on proactive patient care, continuous monitoring outside clinical settings has become more common (Coventry & Branley, 2018). While this approach has numerous benefits for patients, it also increases the attack surface, making healthcare systems more vulnerable to breaches. Cybersecurity breaches can erode patient trust, disrupt health systems, and thus threaten human life.

The rapid adoption of electronic health records and interconnected devices, combined with a lack of expertise and funding for cybersecurity initiatives, leaves the healthcare sector alarmingly vulnerable to cyberattacks (Cartwright, 2023). As cyber threats become more prevalent, healthcare organizations must recognize this vulnerability and take proactive measures to address it.

3.2.2   Applications of Cybersecurity in Healthcare

The healthcare industry is particularly vulnerable to cyberattacks due to the importance and value of its data, including clinical records, financial data, and patient health histories. In healthcare, a complex network of devices is supported by cybersecurity measures to handle vast amounts of data and equipment. Large organizations' interconnected networks, often linked to vital servers, present potential entry points for hackers (Anderson Jr, 2018; Frumento, 2019). The healthcare industry needs to ensure that cybersecurity measures are in place to prevent email account compromises, breaches, and other cyber threats (Javaid et al., 2023). The following are some of the main applications of cybersecurity in healthcare (Fig. 3.1):

- *Data protection, privacy, and data breach prevention:* Healthcare organizations handle a vast amount of sensitive patient data, making them prime targets for cybercriminals. Robust cybersecurity measures can help prevent data breaches and protect electronic health records, keeping patient information confidential and secure. It plays a crucial role in detecting anomalies and warning of potential risks while maintaining patient safety and privacy (Skierka, 2018; Quasim et al., 2020; Nyakasoka & Naidoo, 2022).
- *Medical equipment security and linked medical devices security:* As the Internet of Things (IoT), including Internet of Health Things (IoHT) and Internet of Medical Things (IoMT) devices, become more prevalent in healthcare, such as connected medical devices, new security risks arise. Cybersecurity measures can help ensure these devices' proper functioning and data integrity (Williams & Woodward, 2015; Sparrell, 2019; Radoglou-Grammatikis et al., 2021).
- *Attack prevention, detection, and response to cyber threats:* Healthcare cybersecurity protects patient data from unauthorized access. Cyberattacks can vary in severity, and advanced technology disruptions are a concern. The hospital industry requires modern security technology and automation to combat escalating threats, but gaps persist. With healthcare digitization growing, cybersecurity's importance rises as threats increase and vulnerabilities evolve. Healthcare organizations can also detect and respond to cyber threats more promptly by implementing cybersecurity measures, such as using threat intelligence tools, conducting regular vulnerability assessments, and implementing incident response plans (Quasim et al., 2020; Sam et al., 2022).
- *Compliance with data protection regulations:* Cybersecurity measures in healthcare are essential for complying with data protection regulations. Healthcare organizations are subject to various rules and standards, such as the US Health

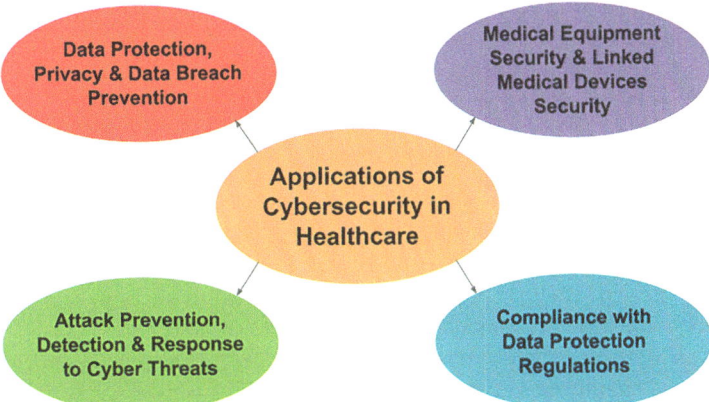

Fig. 3.1 Applications of cybersecurity in healthcare

Insurance Portability and Accountability Act (HIPAA), the General Data Protection Regulation (GDPR) in the European Union, and others specific to different regions. Compliance with these regulations is essential to avoid legal consequences, maintain patient trust, and protect patient information (Akinsanya et al., 2019; Swede et al., 2019).

3.3   Categories of Cybersecurity in Healthcare

Healthcare sectors are vulnerable to data breaches, identity theft, and cyberattacks, underscoring robust cybersecurity's imperative. Strengthening authentication methods and staff training to reduce breach risks is crucial, while healthcare networks and supplier relationships require enhanced security strategies. As healthcare technology advances, the risk of cybercrime escalates, requiring vigilance against both external and internal threats. Security challenges arise when collaborative partnerships require balancing patient data protection with operational requirements. Here, we explore the categories of cybersecurity applications in healthcare.

3.3.1   Common Cybersecurity Vulnerabilities in Healthcare Data

Healthcare database systems generally use simple encryption and user connections, which are vulnerable to unauthorized access and data breaches (Razaque et al., 2019). Cybersecurity is required at every step of the medical data flow, from collecting the patient's information to storing it and finally using it for practical purposes (Mohan, 2014). For example, wearable and IoT-enabled medical devices can be prone to data transmission vulnerabilities when attacked, which can result in data disruption and health information theft. Internet access security is also crucial for data transmission, but various network access technologies pose authentication and access control issues (Razaque et al., 2019). The following are the two principal cybersecurity vulnerabilities in healthcare (Fig. 3.2):

- *Information storage:*

  - *Insecure data disposal:* Medical data storage practices pose significant threats to patient privacy and security, particularly when data is stored on cloud platforms (Widjaja et al., 2019).
  - *Insecure IoT devices:* IoT accessibility provides hackers access to breach passwords and access medical data (Arfaoui et al., 2019).
  - *Weak authentication and password practices:* Inadequate authentication poses a significant security threat to devices like sensor nodes (Masdari & Ahmadzadeh, 2017).

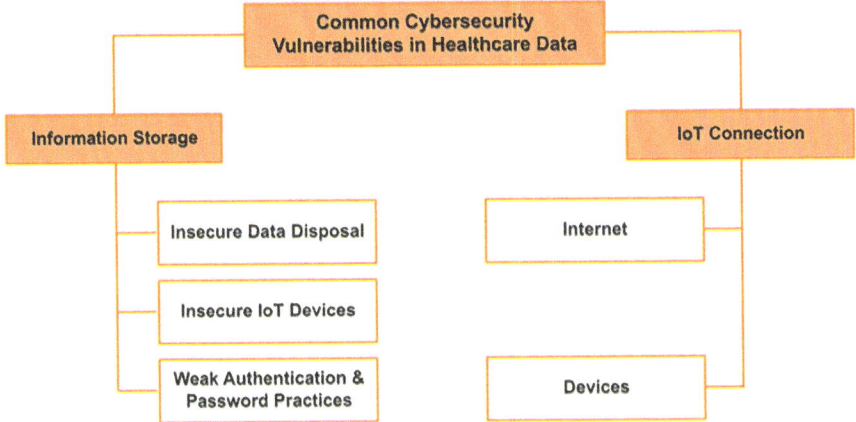

Fig. 3.2 Main cybersecurity vulnerabilities in healthcare

- *IoT connection:*
  - *Internet:* Connectivity to the Internet and carriers like Wi-Fi, Bluetooth, and cellular networks can affect IoT connections (Yeole et al., 2019).
  - *Devices:* Insecure IoT-enabled medical devices, such as internally embedded medical devices, wearables, external medical devices, and consumer products for health monitoring, can expose patient information or gain unauthorized access to networks (Azeez & Van der Vyver, 2019).

3.3.2   Common Cybersecurity Threats to Healthcare Data

As mentioned, healthcare data is vulnerable to various security threats due to its sensitive nature and increasing reliance on technology. Implementing effective cybersecurity measures requires healthcare organizations to understand these threats. The following are some of the most common security threats to healthcare data (Bartholomeusz Sarah, 2023; Javaid et al., 2023) (Fig. 3.3):

- *Data breaches:* Data breaches occur when unauthorized individuals gain access to sensitive healthcare information. Cyberattacks, weak security controls, insider threats, lost or stolen devices, and human errors can all result in breaches.

  - *Cyberattacks:* Data breaches can result from various cyberattacks, including ransomware, targeting healthcare organizations, encrypting data, and demanding a ransom for its release. Also standard are phishing attacks, which use deceptive emails or messages to trick employees into divulging sensitive information. However, some cyberattacks focus on other attack objectives, such as disrupting operations or causing financial harm without necessarily involving data exposure.

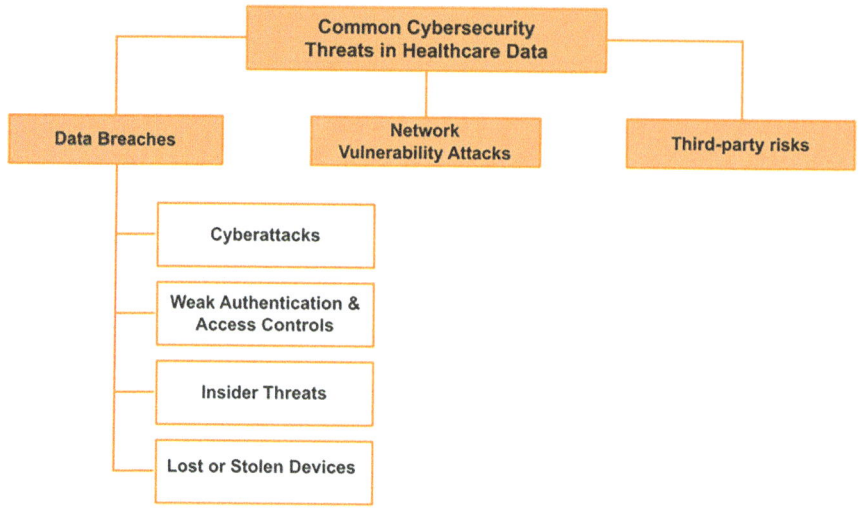

Fig. 3.3 Main cybersecurity threats in healthcare

- *Weak authentication and access controls:* Data breaches can easily occur due to inadequate password protection, a lack of multi-factor authentication, and improper access controls.
- *Insider threats:* Employees who lack cybersecurity training and awareness and misuse access privileges can pose significant risks to healthcare data. Insider threats may intentionally or accidentally disclose sensitive information, leading to data breaches.
- *Lost or stolen devices:* Misplaced, lost, or stolen mobile devices, laptops, or portable storage media containing sensitive healthcare data can lead to data breaches.

• *Network vulnerability attacks:* Data transmitted over insecure networks may be intercepted by attackers, compromising patient privacy and confidentiality. Poorly secured medical devices and outdated software and operating systems can introduce security vulnerabilities and allow hackers to access sensitive data and networks.
• *Third-party risks:* Healthcare organizations often work with third-party vendors and partners who may have access to sensitive data. These third parties can pose data security risks if they do not implement robust security measures.

3.3.3 *Common Cybersecurity Attacks on Healthcare Data*

Cybersecurity attacks on healthcare data are becoming more prevalent, posing significant risks to patient privacy, healthcare providers, and the entire healthcare system. These attacks target vulnerabilities in technology, human behavior, and organizational practices to obtain unauthorized access to sensitive information, disrupt healthcare services, or extort funds from healthcare providers (Yang, 2015). The following are some of the most prevalent cybersecurity attacks on healthcare data (Razaque et al., 2019; Javaid et al., 2023) (Fig. 3.4):

- *Information collection attacks:* Due to digitization of patient information and procedures in digital healthcare, healthcare systems are increasingly vulnerable to malicious attacks.

  - *Data interception:* A healthcare device or system that intercepts data transmissions can lead to the theft of sensitive patient information.
  - *Malware infections:* Malicious software, such as viruses, worms, Trojans, and ransomware, can infiltrate systems and compromise patient data, disrupting healthcare services. It can also lead to healthcare system or service outages and unauthorized control of medical devices.
  - *Man-in-the-middle (MitM) attacks:* The MitM attacks intercept and manipulate communications between devices or networks, potentially stealing sensitive data and compromising privacy and confidentiality.
  - *Phishing:* False emails or messages entice healthcare employees to reveal sensitive information. They can also lead to the installation of malware on systems.

- *Database attacks:* Unauthorized access to patient records can lead to potential identity theft, financial fraud, and breaches of patient confidentiality.

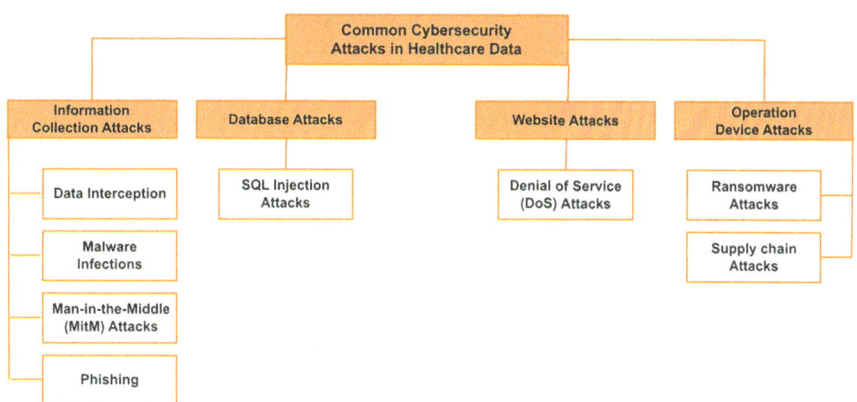

Fig. 3.4 Main cybersecurity attacks in healthcare

- *SQL injection attacks:* Executing malicious SQL queries into web applications is a type of database attack that can result in gaining access to sensitive databases. Hackers can alter, steal, or erase application data in a database using SQL injection techniques.

• *Website attacks:* In digital healthcare systems, doctors use websites linked to databases for patient information and prescriptions. However, website attacks could lead to them receiving incorrect information.

- *Denial of service (DoS) attacks:* These are malicious, targeted website attacks that disrupt services, patient care, or operations by overloading systems and networks.

• *Operation device attacks:* Despite technological advancements promising more precise medical treatment, Internet-connected medical devices expose operational devices to potential Internet-based attacks, putting patient safety at risk. The American Hospital Association (AHA) has warned about the danger of interrupted communication between pacemakers, emphasizing its critical implications (Javaid et al., 2023).

- *Ransomware attacks:* Ransomware, a type of malware, damages devices and encrypts data, complicating patient management. Its easy installation via phishing emails highlights the need for gateway protection and user education on best practices for email security. Encrypting critical healthcare data and the demand for payment disrupt operations and jeopardize patient safety.
- *Supply chain attacks:* Supply chain attacks are another type of operation device attacks that target trusted third-party vendors in the supply chain, either by injecting malicious code into software applications or by compromising physical components to infect users. These attacks exploit the reliance on off-the-shelf components, making software supply chains especially vulnerable due to the integration of third-party APIs, open-source code, and proprietary software.

Healthcare organizations must implement a comprehensive cybersecurity strategy, discussed in the next chapter, to protect against cybersecurity threats and attacks. Proactive cybersecurity measures are essential to ensuring patient safety and trust in healthcare.

3.4 Cybersecurity Objectives in Healthcare

The cybersecurity strategy in healthcare aims to secure information, including protecting the confidentiality, integrity, and availability (CIA) of data and technology-based services. It is intended to ensure a robust security framework for the healthcare industry. Attaining robust security involves establishing secure infrastructure, securing medical endpoints, adhering to consistent standards, and providing user-friendly security measures.

3.4.1   Building a Secure Infrastructure

By accurately identifying and categorizing sensitive patient data within a healthcare organization's framework and recognizing its locations, targeted security measures can be implemented to ensure the CIA of data. Data confidentiality emerges as a critical principle enabling secure exchange of information within a broader context while safeguarding research integrity as medical research increasingly relies on shared data (Williams & Pigeot, 2017). Data integrity remains a persistent concern in healthcare, as errors can lead to health risks, fraud, misconduct, inadequate treatment, and data breaches (Zarour et al., 2021). Although privacy-enhancing techniques are essential for trust-building and regulatory compliance, they can constrain the depth and breadth of analyses on shared data (Wirth et al., 2021). As cyber threats affect these aspects, prioritizing secure access to healthcare data is imperative to prevent unauthorized access, exposure, and manipulation, involving practices such as data inventory, flow mapping, access controls, encryption, and secure storage (Rizwan et al., 2022).

3.4.2   Securing Medical Endpoints

Integrating advanced technologies like sensors, networks, and cloud computing has transformed healthcare systems, but security concerns have arisen. Endpoint security is a concept that has evolved to encompass a wide range of digital devices connected to networks. Medical endpoints, such as IoT devices and medical equipment, must be protected to prevent unauthorized access and potential breaches. Enhancing endpoint security involves safeguarding sensitive data input and enveloping security around data-handling applications. This additional layer of protection helps mitigate risks associated with various endpoint devices in today's interconnected landscape (Waterson, 2020).

Endpoint security tools are crucial in safeguarding organizations against cyber threats originating from network-connected devices. Cyberattacks targeting endpoints can be effectively mitigated using these tools in combination with network security measures, robust incident response plans, and employee cybersecurity training. Investing in and implementing these tools to enhance cybersecurity posture is essential for healthcare organizations as endpoints increase (Waterson, 2020; Gioulekas et al., 2022).

3.4.3   Implementing Consistent Security Standards

In healthcare, the effectiveness of common security approaches within controlled environments is assessed to determine awareness, confidence, and adherence to relevant standardization. Due to the sensitivity of patient information, healthcare organizations should implement consistent security standards across all systems, applications, and processes to ensure a cohesive and effective cybersecurity approach. Mobile devices are a significant focus for advanced information security, especially in healthcare settings. Their increasing prevalence poses challenges for securing sensitive health information. Mobile functionality is essential across healthcare, including emergency treatments, rehabilitation, and home care. Unfortunately, outdated and insecure communication practices persist, risking sensitive data. The security awareness among users, patients, and care professionals is often insufficient, leaving potential threats unaddressed and weakening information security management. Internationally recognized security standards like ISO/IEC 27000 ISMS family, ISO/IEC 27799 guidelines, and regulatory compliance frameworks like HIPAA offer solutions to enhance healthcare information security (Orel & Bernik, 2013).

3.4.4   Making Security Easy for End-Users

One of the challenges in healthcare cybersecurity is ensuring that end-users, including healthcare professionals, adhere to security protocols. This objective aims to simplify end-user security practices by providing user-friendly interfaces, clear guidelines, and ongoing training. When security practices are intuitive and user-friendly, compliance is more likely, reducing the risk of human error. At the user level, responsibilities are defined based on the type of user category, determining their role in adhering to security measures. User categories encompass management, end-users, and all users. Management entails top-level personnel like CEOs, directors, managers, and officers responsible for implementing and overseeing healthcare security practices. End-users cover employees, consultants, suppliers, and others with system access. All user-level categories encompass responsibilities that intersect management and end-user roles, emphasizing the shared responsibility for maintaining security measures (Yeng et al., 2022). End-users ensure access control and security by managing their access-related actions, including password management. This level comprises healthcare professionals granted system access according to their therapeutic requirements and responsibilities (Yeng et al., 2022).

3.5   Cybersecurity Design Considerations for Healthcare

In the healthcare industry, maintaining robust cybersecurity is critical to patient safety. Keeping medical devices secure and protecting patient data requires a convergence of global principles and practices as the digital landscape evolves. However, disparate regulations across governments pose challenges. By encompassing essential aspects, from leadership and human factors to technology integration and third-party provider security, healthcare organizations can pave the way for a safer and more secure healthcare environment through pivotal cybersecurity design considerations.

3.5.1   Principles of Safety Systems Design in Healthcare Organizations

Ensuring patient safety and medical device performance requires converging global healthcare cybersecurity principles and practices. However, the current alignment of regulations across different governments hampers this effort. The following general principles for medical device cybersecurity are crucial for enhancing security across all stakeholders' activities, aiming to improve patient safety (Institute of Medicine (US) Committee on Quality of Health Care et al., 2000; Dixit et al., 2023; Zhang & Zhang, 2023) (Table 3.1):

- *Providing leadership:* Patient safety must be a central focus of healthcare institutions, cultivating a safety culture with active leadership participation. Safety measures should be implemented throughout the product life cycle, involving shared responsibility, information exchange, and resources for error analysis and improvement. It is essential to address unsafe practitioners and emphasize safety in system design, coupled with efficient protocols to deal with incompetence and avoid harm to patients.
- *Respecting human limits in process design:* Human cognitive strengths and limitations shape the approach to healthcare design. While human abilities include creativity, adaptability, and memory, limitations involve multitasking difficulties and computational shortcomings. To integrate human factors, employers can design jobs for safety, minimize reliance on memory and vigilance, apply constraints and forcing functions, and simplify critical processes. These principles create a safety-focused culture, recognizing strengths while minimizing weaker traits and ensuring accountability and transparency in patient care.
- *Promoting effective team functioning:* Effective teamwork and including patients in healthcare are vital for patient safety. A team training program should be adopted in critical care areas to improve collaboration and reduce errors. Patients should also play an active role, involving their preferences, knowledge, and

Table 3.1 Principles of safety systems design in healthcare organizations

- **Providing leadership:**
- Prioritizing patient safety with active leadership involvement.
- Implementing safety measures throughout the product's life cycle.
- Sharing responsibility and resources for error analysis.
- Addressing unsafe practitioners and emphasizing safety in design.
- **Respecting human limits in process design:**
- Designing processes acknowledging human cognitive abilities and limitations.
- Minimizing reliance on memory and simplifying processes.
- Applying constraints to enhance safety.
- Considering multitasking difficulties and computational limitations.
- **Promoting effective team functioning:**
- Enhancing safety through effective teamwork and patient involvement.
- Team training in critical care should be adopted for improved collaboration and error reduction.
- Involving patients in their care, considering preferences and knowledge.
- Providing clear information about medications and therapies for patient understanding.
- **Anticipating unexpected system threats:**
- Enhancing patient safety by proactively examining care processes.
- Integrating technology to anticipate and prevent errors.
- Creating recoverable systems with visible and reversible errors.
- **Creating a learning environment:**
- Enhancing training through essential simulations for novices and crisis management.
- Encouraging error reporting in nonpunitive environments to foster a safety culture.
- Promoting open communication to share information without fear.
- Learning from mistakes and establishing feedback mechanisms for improvement.

understanding of their treatments and receiving clear information about their medications and therapies.

- *Anticipating unexpected system threats:* To enhance patient safety, healthcare organizations should adopt a proactive approach by examining care processes for potential safety threats and redesigning them before accidents occur. Technology integration demands careful attention, as it can introduce new errors. Organizations should adopt technology thoughtfully, anticipate issues, and consistently revise systems to reduce mistakes. Creating systems that allow recovery is also vital, making errors visible, reversible, and easily detectable. Simulation training and access to accurate, timely information enhance patient safety.
- *Creating a learning environment:* When introducing new procedures or equipment in healthcare, simulations are essential for training novice practitioners and crisis management. Fostering a safety culture entails encouraging error and hazard reporting through nonpunitive environments. Open communication at all levels is crucial, allowing information to be shared without fear. Learning from mistakes and establishing feedback mechanisms are critical for enhancing patient safety. Analyzing errors, developing recommendations, implementing changes, and tracking results are all part of continuous improvement. Moreover, collaborative efforts, benchmarking, and voluntary reporting systems contribute to shared learning and ongoing enhancement.

3.5.2 Sufficient Risk Assessments

According to ISO standards [ISO 31000; ISO 27005], risk refers to the impact of uncertainty on objectives, encompassing positive and negative deviations from expectations. It is often quantified by evaluating consequences, costs, impacts, and likelihood of occurrence (ISO, 2009). ISO 31000 defines risk assessment as identifying, analyzing, and assessing risks:

- *Risk identification* involves recognizing and describing hazards and risk factors.
- *Risk analysis* entails understanding the nature of hazards, determining risk levels, and estimating associated risks.
- *Risk evaluation* involves comparing estimated risks against predefined criteria to ascertain their significance.

These assessments can be conducted using qualitative, quantitative, or hybrid approaches (Ksibi et al., 2022).

3.5.3 Compliance before Security

It is becoming increasingly challenging to safeguard sensitive data and protect patient privacy during an evolving cyber threat landscape. The healthcare industry faces the challenge of maintaining robust security measures while adhering to strict regulatory standards. Fortifying healthcare systems is a priority to prevent breaches and data compromises. Establishing a cohesive communication network among stakeholders is crucial to fostering a unified response to potential threats. Stakeholder communication, risk assessment, and mitigation tactics are also essential. As healthcare continues to evolve digitally, it is necessary to maintain operational continuity, ensure patient data security, and maintain patient trust through secure practices and regulatory alignment (Kwon & Johnson, 2013).

3.5.4 Considering Security of Third-Party Providers

The more organizations engage with external partners and vendors, the more vulnerable they become to cyber threats. Organizations can use non-intrusive risk-scoring reports to understand the cybersecurity risks linked to third-party providers without compromising their systems. This method allows for a thorough evaluation of cyber risks while maintaining the privacy and security of external entities. Overall, cyber third-party risk management strategies in healthcare need to integrate collaboration with security in today's digitally interconnected world (Caramancion et al., 2021).

3.6   Developing the Healthcare Security System

In the healthcare system, controlling access to sensitive information and strategies to maintain patient data privacy and integrity is essential. Health records databases play a pivotal role, requiring a balance between digitization, patient privacy, and robust access control mechanisms. A comprehensive healthcare cybersecurity strategy involves continuous risk assessments, user education, backup and recovery plans, and a zero-trust security model. It requires authentication protocols, role-based access permissions, encryption strategies, and user activity monitoring to adapt to an evolving digital landscape.

3.6.1   Controlling Access to Sensitive Healthcare Information and Systems

In the dynamic landscape of healthcare information management, a pressing concern revolves around effectively controlling access to sensitive data and systems. This concern addresses the need to protect patient privacy and the integrity of critical healthcare information. Organizations strive to establish stringent access control mechanisms to prevent unauthorized access and potential cyber threats (Edemacu et al., 2019).

Health records databases are pivotal in storing vital patient information (Keshta & Odeh, 2021). The interplay between digitization, patient privacy, and access control is crucial. Healthcare entities must maintain a delicate balance between enabling authorized personnel to retrieve essential information and ensuring their confidentiality and integrity (Chenthara et al., 2019; Basil et al., 2022).

Healthcare organizations use various methods to enforce effective access control. These include authentication protocols, role-based access permissions, encryption strategies, and real-time user activity monitoring (Basil et al., 2022). Access control frameworks must constantly adapt to emerging cyber threats as the digital landscape evolves.

Healthcare access control limits the operation and access of documents in the healthcare system to protect data privacy (Chenthara et al., 2019). The intersection of access control, healthcare information systems, and security concerns is of utmost importance. With technological advancements continuing, protecting patient data is becoming increasingly important. Considering both theoretical and practical constructs, this field contributes significantly to the discussion of how healthcare institutions navigate the complex realm of access control. Ultimately, healthcare information and systems must maintain confidentiality and integrity, ensuring patient privacy while facilitating authorized data usage (Chenthara et al., 2019; Basil et al., 2022).

3.6.2 Performing Continual Risk Assessments

In healthcare settings, cybersecurity risks are posed by various factors. Thus, systematic continuous risk assessment and potential vulnerability evaluation are vital to maintaining the security and integrity of sensitive patient data and essential systems in healthcare cybersecurity. As mentioned in the previous sections, continuous risk assessment involves systematically identifying vulnerabilities, evaluating their potential consequences, and implementing strategies to mitigate risks. Maintaining the seamless operation of healthcare systems and strengthening the sector against evolving cyber threats require continuous risk assessment (Ksibi et al., 2022).

3.6.3 Educating Users about their Role as the First Line of Defense

With the rise of digital platforms in healthcare systems, it is essential to educate users about cybersecurity. End-users, including frontline staff, clinicians, and administrators, primarily pose cyber threats. Three crucial steps can be taken to strengthen this frontline (Walker-Roberts et al., 2018; Bhuyan et al., 2020; He et al., 2021):

- *Creating a clear cybersecurity policy:* In case of a breach, actions should be outlined in a comprehensive policy. Preparation is the key to a cohesive response under pressure, regardless of the organization's size.
- *Educating and empowering users:* A cybersecurity strategy focusing on user education is crucial. Human actions are the most common cause of breaches, so users should know how to identify and prevent them.
- *Implementing robust cybersecurity tools:* Threat protection tools should be used with education. These tools act as safety nets, detecting and mitigating threats before they reach humans.

3.6.4 Preparing for Attacks and Breaches with a Backup and Recovery Plan

With the increasing prevalence of cyber threats, healthcare organizations, particularly critical institutions such as hospitals, highlight the importance of a well-structured backup and recovery strategy. This plan's core lies in quickly restoring systems and data after a cyber incident, minimizing downtime, and preventing disruptions to patient care and medical operations. The integration of risk assessments and simulations can further enhance the efficacy of this strategy. Healthcare organizations can use these evaluations to gain insights into their vulnerabilities and susceptibilities to cyber threats and take proactive measures to improve their resilience (Ghayoomi et al., 2021).

3.6.5 *Adopting a Zero-Trust Security Model*

Zero-trust is a cybersecurity approach that emphasizes minimizing uncertainty in access decisions by enforcing strict identity verification and least privilege principles, even in the face of a potentially compromised network (Rose, 2020). Adopting a zero-trust security model is emerging as a strategic departure from traditional cybersecurity methods in the healthcare system. With this innovative approach, all users and devices are considered potentially untrustworthy, regardless of where they are on the network. Thus, patient information and system security can be significantly enhanced (Gellert et al., 2023). This approach represents a pivotal response to healthcare's ever-evolving cybersecurity challenges.

3.7 Chapter Summary

This chapter delves into the fundamental rationale behind cybersecurity in healthcare, emphasizing its role in protecting sensitive patient data, preserving medical system integrity, and ensuring patient safety and quality. It underscores the rising significance of cybersecurity in the face of increasing cyber threats resulting from integrating technology in healthcare. It outlines applications such as data protection, medical equipment security, and compliance with regulations. In the subsequent chapters, the discussion continues with a focus on different categories of security in healthcare, including data and information security, personal security, and healthcare system and infra security.

After understanding all the fundamental concepts, the following questions are addressed in this chapter:

- What is the role of cybersecurity in preventing information leakage, data theft, and damage to computer systems and networks in healthcare?
- How do healthcare organizations manage cybersecurity risks, and why is healthcare a significant target for cybercrime?
- How does cybersecurity contribute to the safety, integrity, and confidentiality of patient data in healthcare?
- What are the fundamental design considerations and objectives of cybersecurity in healthcare, and how do they address the unique challenges faced by the industry?
- How do healthcare organizations secure sensitive information, perform ongoing risk assessments, and educate users about cybersecurity?

- What strategies and tools can healthcare organizations adopt to protect themselves against cyberattacks and breaches?
- How do safety systems contribute to improving patient safety and medical device performance in healthcare organizations?
- How do healthcare organizations assess cybersecurity risks associated with third-party providers, and what measures can they take to mitigate these risks effectively?

References

Akinsanya, O. O., Papadaki, M., & Sun, L. (2019). Current cybersecurity maturity models: How effective in the healthcare cloud? *CEUR Workshop Proc.* Accessed Aug 21, 2023, from http://pearl.plymouth.ac.uk/handle/10026.1/20912

Anderson, R. E., Jr (2018). *Low-cost strategies to strengthen cybersecurity: Low-cost strategies can help healthcare organizations avoid the high price of a data breach. https://go.gale.com › i.do https://go.gale.com › i.do* 72, 60+. Available at: https://go.gale.com/ps/i.do?id=GALE%7CA544403401&sid=googleScholar&v=2.1&it=r&linkaccess=abs&issn=07350732&p=AONE&sw=w

Arfaoui, A., Kribeche, A., & Senouci, S.-M. (2019). Context-aware anonymous authentication protocols in the internet of things dedicated to e-health applications. *Computer Networks, 159,* 23–36. https://doi.org/10.1016/j.comnet.2019.04.031

Azeez, N. A., & Van der Vyver, C. (2019). Security and privacy issues in e-health cloud-based system: A comprehensive content analysis. *Egyptian Informatics Journal, 20,* 97–108. https://doi.org/10.1016/j.eij.2018.12.001

Bartholomeusz Sarah. (2023). Cyber threats in healthcare. *Governance Directions, 75,* 867–870. https://doi.org/10.3316/informit.013665247149702

Basil, N. N., Ambe, S., Ekhator, C., & Fonkem, E. (2022). Health records database and inherent security concerns: A review of the literature. *Cureus, 14,* e30168. https://doi.org/10.7759/cureus.30168

Bhuyan, S. S., Kabir, U. Y., Escareno, J. M., Ector, K., Palakodeti, S., Wyant, D., et al. (2020). Transforming healthcare cybersecurity from reactive to proactive: Current status and future recommendations. *Journal of Medical Systems, 44,* 98. https://doi.org/10.1007/s10916-019-1507-y

Caramancion, K. M., Keskin, O. F., Tatar, I., Raza, O., & Tatar, U. (2021). Cyber third-party risk management: A comparison of non-intrusive risk scoring reports. https://doi.org/10.3390/electronics10101168.

Cartwright, A. J. (2023). The elephant in the room: Cybersecurity in healthcare. *Journal of Clinical Monitoring and Computing, 1–10,* 1123. https://doi.org/10.1007/s10877-023-01013-5

Chenthara, S., Ahmed, K., Wang, H., & Whittaker, F. (2019). Security and privacy-preserving challenges of e-health solutions in cloud computing. *IEEE Access, 7,* 74361–74382. https://doi.org/10.1109/ACCESS.2019.2919982

Coventry, L., & Branley, D. (2018). Cybersecurity in healthcare: A narrative review of trends, threats and ways forward. *Maturitas, 113,* 48–52. https://doi.org/10.1016/j.maturitas.2018.04.008

Dixit, A., Quaglietta, J., Nathan, K., Dias, L., & Nguyen, D. (2023). Cybersecurity: Guiding principles and risk management advice for healthcare boards, senior leaders and risk managers. *Healthcare Quarterly, 25,* 35–40. https://doi.org/10.12927/hcq.2023.27019

Edemacu, K., Park, H. K., Jang, B., & Kim, J. W. (2019). Privacy provision in collaborative health with attribute-based encryption: Survey, challenges, and future directions. *IEEE Access, 7,* 89614–89636. https://doi.org/10.1109/access.2019.2925390

Frumento, E. (2019). Cybersecurity and the evolutions of healthcare: Challenges and threats behind its evolution. In G. Andreoni, P. Perego, & E. Frumento (Eds.), *m_Health current and future applications* (pp. 35–69). Springer International Publishing. https://doi.org/10.1007/978-3-030-02182-5_4

Gellert, G. A., Kelly, S. P., Wright, E. W., & Keil, L. C. (2023). Zero trust and the future of cybersecurity in healthcare delivery organizations. *International Journal of Hospitality & Tourism Administration, 12*, 1. https://doi.org/10.5430/jha.v12n1p1

Ghayoomi, H., Laskey, K., Miller-Hooks, E., Hooks, C., & Tariverdi, M. (2021). Assessing resilience of hospitals to cyberattack. *Digit Health, 7*, 20552076211059366. https://doi.org/10.1177/20552076211059366

Gioulekas, F., Stamatiadis, E., Tzikas, A., Gounaris, K., Georgiadou, A., Michalitsi-Psarrou, A., et al. (2022). A cybersecurity culture survey targeting healthcare critical infrastructures. *Healthcare (Basel), 10*. https://doi.org/10.3390/healthcare10020327

He, Y., Aliyu, A., Evans, M., & Luo, C. (2021). Health care cybersecurity challenges and solutions under the climate of COVID-19: Scoping review. *Journal of Medical Internet Research, 23*, e21747. https://doi.org/10.2196/21747

Institute of Medicine (US) Committee on Quality of Health Care, Kohn, L. T., Corrigan, J. M., & Donaldson, M. S. (2000). *Creating safety systems in health care organizations*. National Academies Press (US). Accessed Aug 29, 2023, from https://www.ncbi.nlm.nih.gov/books/NBK225188/

ISO. (2009). *International Standard: Risk management: principles and guidelines. ISO 31000. principes et lignes directrices*. ISO Available at: https://play.google.com/store/books/details?id=WqUiMwEACAAJ

Javaid, M., Haleem, A., Singh, R. P., & Suman, R. (2023). Towards insight cybersecurity for healthcare domains: A comprehensive review of recent practices and trends. *Cyber Security and Applications, 1*, 100016. https://doi.org/10.1016/j.csa.2023.100016

Keshta, I., & Odeh, A. (2021). Security and privacy of electronic health records: Concerns and challenges. *Egyptian Informatics Journal, 22*, 177–183. https://doi.org/10.1016/j.eij.2020.07.003

Kruse, C. S., Frederick, B., Jacobson, T., & Monticone, D. K. (2017). Cybersecurity in healthcare: A systematic review of modern threats and trends. *Technology and Health Care, 25*, 1–10. https://doi.org/10.3233/THC-161263

Ksibi, S., Jaidi, F., & Bouhoula, A. (2022). *A comprehensive study of security and cyber-security risk management within e-health systems: Synthesis, analysis and a novel quantified approach*. Mobile Networks and Applications. https://doi.org/10.1007/s11036-022-02042-1

Kwon, J., & Johnson, M. E. (2013). Security practices and regulatory compliance in the healthcare industry. *Journal of the American Medical Informatics Association, 20*, 44–51. https://doi.org/10.1136/amiajnl-2012-000906

Martignani, C. (2019). Cybersecurity in cardiac implantable electronic devices. *Expert Review of Medical Devices, 16*, 437–444. https://doi.org/10.1080/17434440.2019.1614440

Masdari, M., & Ahmadzadeh, S. (2017). A survey and taxonomy of the authentication schemes in telecare medicine information systems. *Journal of Network and Computer Applications, 87*, 1–19. https://doi.org/10.1016/j.jnca.2017.03.003

Mohan, A. (2014). Cyber security for personal medical devices internet of things. In *2014 IEEE international conference on distributed computing in sensor systems* (pp. 372–374). https://doi.org/10.1109/DCOSS.2014.49

Nyakasoka, L., & Naidoo, R. (2022). *Barriers to dynamic cybersecurity capabilities in healthcare software services*. Available at: https://repository.up.ac.za/handle/2263/91078

Orel, A., & Bernik, I. (2013). Implementing healthcare information security: Standards can help. *Studies in Health Technology and Informatics, 186*, 195–199. Available at: https://www.ncbi.nlm.nih.gov/pubmed/23542997

Quasim, M. T., Radwan, A. A. E., Alshmrani, G. M. M., & Meraj, M. (2020). A Blockchain framework for secure electronic health records in healthcare industry. In *2020 international conference on smart Technologies in Computing, electrical and electronics (ICSTCEE)* (pp. 605–609). https://doi.org/10.1109/ICSTCEE49637.2020.9277193

Radoglou-Grammatikis, P., Sarigiannidis, P., Efstathopoulos, G., Lagkas, T., Fragulis, G., & Sarigiannidis, A. (2021). A self-learning approach for detecting intrusions in healthcare systems. In *ICC 2021–IEEE International Conference on communications* (pp. 1–6). https://doi.org/10.1109/ICC42927.2021.9500354

Razaque, A., Amsaad, F., Jaro Khan, M., Hariri, S., Chen, S., Siting, C., et al. (2019). Survey: Cybersecurity vulnerabilities, attacks and solutions in the medical domain. *IEEE Access, 7*, 168774–168797. https://doi.org/10.1109/ACCESS.2019.2950849

Rizwan, M., Shabbir, A., Javed, A. R., Srivastava, G., Gadekallu, T. R., Shabir, M., et al. (2022). Risk monitoring strategy for the confidentiality of healthcare information. *Computers and Electrical Engineering, 100*, 107833. https://doi.org/10.1016/j.compeleceng.2022.107833

Rose, S. W. (2020). *Zero trust architecture*. U.S. Department of Commerce, National Institute of Standards and Technology Available at: https://play.google.com/store/books/details?id=rdVhzwEACAAJ

Sam, M. F. M., Ismail, A. F. M., Bakar, K. A., Ahamat, A., & Qureshi, M. I. (2022). The effectiveness of IoT-based wearable devices and potential cybersecurity risks: A systematic literature review from the last decade. *International Journal of Online Engineering, 18*, 56–73. https://doi.org/10.3991/ijoe.v18i09.32255

Skierka, I. M. (2018). The governance of safety and security risks in connected healthcare. In *Living in the internet of things: Cybersecurity of the IoT* (pp. 1–12). https://doi.org/10.1049/cp.2018.0002

Sparrell, D. (2019). Cyber-safety in healthcare IOT. In *2019 ITU kaleidoscope: ICT for health: Networks, standards, and innovation (ITU K)* (pp. 1–8). https://doi.org/10.23919/ITUK48006.2019.8996148

Swede, M. J., Scovetta, V., & Eugene-Colin, M. (2019). Protecting patient data is the new scope of practice: A recommended cybersecurity curricula for healthcare students to prepare for this challenge. *Journal of Allied Health, 48*, 148–155. Available at: https://www.ncbi.nlm.nih.gov/pubmed/31167018

Walker-Roberts, S., Hammoudeh, M., & Dehghantanha, A. (2018). A systematic review of the availability and efficacy of countermeasures to internal threats in healthcare critical infrastructure. *IEEE Access, 6*, 25167–25177. https://doi.org/10.1109/ACCESS.2018.2817560

Wasserman, L., & Wasserman, Y. (2022). Hospital cybersecurity risks and gaps: Review (for the non-cyber professional). *Frontiers in Digital Health, 4*, 862221. https://doi.org/10.3389/fdgth.2022.862221

Waterson, D. (2020). Managing endpoints, the weakest link in the security chain. *Network Security, 2020*, 9–13. https://doi.org/10.1016/S1353-4858(20)30093-3

Widjaja, A. E., Chen, J. V., Sukoco, B. M., & Ha, Q.-A. (2019). Understanding users' willingness to put their personal information on the personal cloud-based storage applications: An empirical study. *Computers in Human Behavior, 91*, 167–185. https://doi.org/10.1016/j.chb.2018.09.034

Williams, G., & Pigeot, I. (2017). Consent and confidentiality in the light of recent demands for data sharing. *Biometrical Journal, 59*, 240–250. https://doi.org/10.1002/bimj.201500044

Williams, P. A., & Woodward, A. J. (2015). Cybersecurity vulnerabilities in medical devices: A complex environment and multifaceted problem. *Medical Devices, 8*, 305–316. https://doi.org/10.2147/MDER.S50048

Wirth, F. N., Meurers, T., Johns, M., & Prasser, F. (2021). Privacy-preserving data sharing infrastructures for medical research: Systematization and comparison. *BMC Medical Informatics and Decision Making, 21*, 242. https://doi.org/10.1186/s12911-021-01602-x

Yang, H.-S. (2015). A study on attack information collection using virtualization technology. *Multimedia, 74*, 8791–8799. https://doi.org/10.1007/s11042-013-1487-8

Yeng, P. K., Fauzi, M. A., Sun, L., & Yang, B. (2022). Assessing the legal aspects of information security requirements for health care in 3 countries: Scoping review and framework development. *JMIR Human Factors, 9*, e30050. https://doi.org/10.2196/30050

Yeole, A., Kalbande, D. R., & Sharma, A. (2019). Security of 6LoWPAN IoT networks in hospitals for medical data exchange. *Procedia Computer Science, 152*, 212–221. https://doi.org/10.1016/j.procs.2019.05.045

Zarour, M., Alenezi, M., Ansari, M. T. J., Pandey, A. K., Ahmad, M., Agrawal, A., et al. (2021). Ensuring data integrity of healthcare information in the era of digital health. *Healthcare Technology Letters, 8*, 66–77. https://doi.org/10.1049/htl2.12008

Zhang, J., & Zhang, Z.-M. (2023). Ethics and governance of trustworthy medical artificial intelligence. *BMC Medical Informatics and Decision Making, 23*, 7. https://doi.org/10.1186/s12911-023-02103-9

Chapter 4
Data and Information Security

4.1 Introduction

With the digitization of medical records and the adoption of electronic health systems, healthcare organizations face tremendous cybersecurity problems, specifically in maintaining healthcare data's confidentiality, availability, and reliability. Protecting sensitive patient information and medical health records against data breaches and other cyberattacks with security and privacy regulations is critical for patient trust and quality healthcare services. A healthcare organization can create a safe and secure environment for managing and protecting patient data by implementing robust security measures and best practices throughout its lifecycle. This chapter describes various healthcare data, security threats, and protection methods that apply to healthcare organizations.

4.2 Types of Data and Information in Healthcare

4.2.1 Electronic Health Records

The electronic health record (EHR) is a repository of patient data in a digital form, stored and exchanged securely and accessible by authorized users (Häyrinen, 2008). EHR is a longitudinal collection of electronic health information about individual patients. EHRs contain patient information, including demographics, medical history, medication, laboratory tests, vital signs, and doctor's notes. The patient's EHRs can be divided into two types of information: structured information and unstructured information. Structured information refers to the fields that contain data using existing lexicons such as demographics, diagnosis, laboratory tests, medications, and procedures; unstructured information is also found in text documents

D. P. Sharma et al., *Understanding Cybersecurity Management in Healthcare*,
Progress in IS, https://doi.org/10.1007/978-3-031-68034-2_4

such as clinical notes from doctors and nurses. Unstructured data, such as clinical narratives, describe the medical reasoning behind the prescription. Figure 4.1 shows the patient's EHR data types. The description of the primary patient's EHR types is as follows:

- *Demographic information:* This includes the patient's personal information, such as name, age, gender, address, contact details, and insurance information. Demographic data help identify and distinguish patients.
- *Medical history:* A patient's medical history encompasses past and current health conditions, previous illnesses, surgeries, allergies, immunization records, family medical history, and lifestyle factors. It provides an essential context for understanding a patient's health status.
- *Medication records:* Medication records document the medications a patient takes, including the names, dosages, frequencies, and routes of administration. It helps healthcare professionals avoid potential drug interactions or allergies.
- *Laboratory and test results:* This includes data from different diagnostic tests and medical examinations, such as blood tests, urine tests, imaging (X-rays, CT scans, MRIs), pathology reports, and genetic tests. These results help diagnose and monitor patients' conditions.
- *Vital signs:* This includes measurements such as temperature, heart rate, blood pressure, respiratory rate, and oxygen saturation. These measurements help assess a patient's essential physiological functions.
- *Clinical notes:* Clinical notes are narrative summaries prepared by the doctors or nurses for a patient's hospital/clinic visit. It describes the patient's condition, assessments, diagnoses, treatments, and plans.
- *Physiologic data:* These are continuous data, typically referring to signals from processes such as electrocardiograms (EKGs) and electroencephalograms (EEGs). They are usually categorized as constant in terms of time and value.
- *Multi-omics data:* These are the various types of biological data at different molecular levels, such as genomics, transcriptomics, proteomics, metabolomics, and epigenomics. Recently, artificial intelligence (AI) technology has been used extensively in analyzing medical data, including medical images, electronic health records (EHRs), physiological signals, and multi-omics data (Wang & Preininger, 2019).

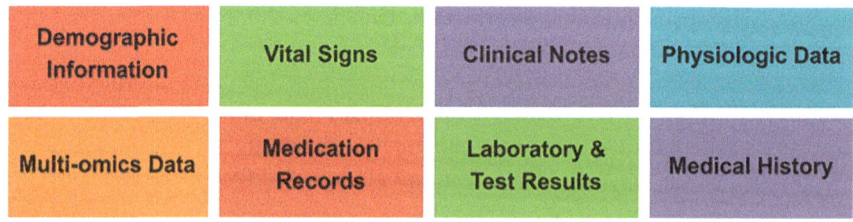

Fig. 4.1 Patient's EHR data types

4.2.2 Administrative Data

These are the healthcare operations and management-related data, including health insurance information, healthcare facilities and services information, appointments, billings, and regulatory and compliance information.

- *Health insurance information:* This includes data related to insurance coverage, policy details, claims processing, reimbursement information, etc.
- *Billing information:* This is the financial data, which typically includes information about healthcare costs, invoices, billing codes, payment records, financial transactions, etc.
- *Healthcare facility information:* This includes information about healthcare facilities and services, such as hospitals, clinics, and pharmacies, including their locations, contact details, available services, and availability of specialists or resources, etc.
- *Appointments:* These data are about patient appointments and schedule information, such as visit dates, times, duration, and the next visit.
- *Regulatory and compliance information:* These are the regulatory, standards, and compliance information, for example, regulatory requirements, compliance with healthcare standards, and legal documentation.

4.2.3 Claims Data

Claims data refer to the information obtained from the claims submitted by hospitals, clinics, doctors, or pharmacies to insurance companies or other payers for payments. These data contain detailed records of patient services, including diagnoses, procedures, medications, costs, and other relevant information. The claims data include the following information:

- *Patient identifiers:* These include patient identifiers, such as name, age, gender, and insurance information.
- *Diagnosis and procedure codes:* Claims data contain diagnosis codes representing the patient's medical conditions or reasons for seeking healthcare services. Similarly, the procedure codes indicate what medical procedures or interventions are performed during a patient's healthcare visit.
- *Service dates and durations:* It contains information about the dates of service, including the start and end dates of a particular healthcare visit.
- *Healthcare provider* information concerns the healthcare providers providing patient services. This includes the names, addresses, and unique identification numbers of the healthcare facilities and individual providers involved in the patient's care.
- *Cost and billing information:* It is financial information that includes billed charges related to healthcare services, paid amounts, etc.

4.2.4   Patient/Disease Registries

Disease registries are clinical information systems that track critical data for certain chronic diseases such as cancer, diabetes, heart disease, asthma, and Alzheimer's disease. These registries often provide crucial information for managing patient conditions (Library, 2023). The primary purpose of disease registries is to gather comprehensive and standardized data about individuals with a specific disease or condition. The data collected in registries often include demographic, clinical, treatment details, etc. Some common examples of disease registries are as follows.

- The Global Alzheimer's Association Interactive Network is a repository for Alzheimer's disease research data and analytical tools.
- The National Cardiovascular Data Registry (NCDR) is the cardiology data registry.
- National Program of Cancer Registries for cancer data.
- National Trauma Data Bank for trauma registry.

4.2.5   Health Surveys

Health survey data are collected via national health surveys. These surveys can be conducted face-to-face, by telephone, online, or through self-administered paper questionnaires. They provide valuable information about a population's health status. Medicare Current Beneficiary Survey, National Health and Nutrition Examination Survey, and National Medical Expenditure Survey are typical examples of health surveys (Library, 2023).

4.2.6   Clinical Trials Data

Clinical trial data are collected during the clinical trial. A clinical trial is a research study that prospectively assigns human participants or groups of humans to one or more health-related interventions to evaluate the effects on health outcomes. It evaluates the safety, efficacy, and effectiveness of new medical treatments, interventions, and therapies. The clinical trial data include details about the study design, such as the research question, objectives, eligible participant eligibility criteriaization procedures, treatment interventions, and outcome measures. These data are typically used to assess the benefits and risks of investigational products and information, clinical practice guidelines, and healthcare interventions. WHO's International Clinical Trials Registry Platform maintains the trial registration for designing, designing, conducting, and administering. These details are published on a publicly accessible website managed by a registry conforming to WHO standards

(WHO, 2023). ClinicalTrials.gov and the European Union Clinical Trials Database are two everyday clinical trials databases of the y.

4.3 Information Security Methods

4.3.1 Authentication and Authorization

Authentication is verifying a user's or entity's identity to grant them access to specific resources, systems, or services. The authentication can be user-based and node-based authentications (Bahache et al., 2022). There are several authentication methods, which are as follows:

- *Password-based authentication:* A password is information associated with a user or entity that confirms the entity's identity. Passwords are the most common form of authentication. Users provide a unique combination of characters (passwords) they know, and the system compares it with the stored password associated with the account. It is a simple and widely used method but can be vulnerable to attacks. The most straightforward attack against a password-based system is to guess passwords. A dictionary attack is guessing a password by repeated trial and error. The dictionary may be a set of strings in random order or decreasing order of probability of selection.
- *Multi-factor authentication (MFA):* MFA requires users to provide two or more authentication factors to gain access. For example, passwords, PINs, tokens, smart cards, fingerprints, facial recognition, etc., are the factors used in multi-factor authentication. MFA adds another layer of security to your password by asking for other information in real time so that intercepted login credential information cannot be sufficient to log in to the system. MFA significantly enhances security compared to single-factor authentication, as even if one factor is compromised, an attacker would still need access to the other factors to gain access.
- *Biometric-based authentication:* It uses an individual's unique physical characteristics to verify their identity. Standard biometric methods include fingerprint scanning, facial recognition, iris or retinal scanning, and voice recognition.
- *Token-based authentication* involves using physical devices or software applications that generate one-time passwords (OTP) or access codes. These tokens can be hardware tokens or software-based tokens. During the authentication process, users must provide their current OTP and password.
- *Certificate-based authentication:* This authentication mechanism uses digital certificates issued to users by a trusted third authority. These unique certificates prove the user's identity, and the system verifies the certificate's authenticity to grant access.

- *Smart card-based authentication:* This method uses data stored in smart cards, which are physical cards with embedded integrated circuits that store authentication information.
- *Single sign-on (SSO)-based authentication:* SSO allows users to access multiple applications or systems using a single set of credentials such as username and password. Once a user is authenticated to the system, they don't need to re-enter their credentials for other linked applications.

Authorization grants or denies access to specific resources, data, or services and the user's identity and permissions. Authorization determines what actions or operations the user can perform and what data they can access. It is based on the organization's access control policy, which defines what permits or denies a particular user's use of a specific resource. Four types of access control models that can be used in the authorization process are as follows:

- *Identity-based access control (IAM): An individual user sets an* access control mechanism to allow or deny access to an object.
- *Mandatory access control or rule-based access control (MAC or RAC):* A system mechanism controls access to objects (resources), and an individual cannot alter that access based on a rule.
- *Originator access control (OAC):* Controlled by the originator (creator) of information controls who can access information.
- *Role-based access control (RBAC):* This type of access control is based on the user's roles or job functions. RBAC simplifies security administration by using roles, hierarchies, and constraints to organize privileges (Ferraiolo, 2003).

In the healthcare organization, authorization refers to granting or denying access to patient data, medical records, and other healthcare resources based on the identity and permissions of the individuals or entities requesting access. Role-based access control model is commonly used in the healthcare industry to manage authorization because it assigns specific roles to healthcare professionals (doctors, employees, and other associates) based on their job responsibilities. Each role is associated with a predefined set of permissions that determine what data and functionalities or services the user can access.

4.3.2   Encryption

Encryption or enciphering converts data from plaintext (human-readable) to ciphertext (human-readable). It is one of the fundamental security measures used to prevent unauthorized access and maintain data confidentiality and integrity. The encryption algorithm performs various substitutions and transformations on the plaintext. The original message or data fed into the encryption algorithm as input is called plaintext. The secret key is also an input to the encryption algorithm. The encryption method produces the scrambled message as output, called ciphertext. It depends on the plaintext and the secret key. The reverse process of encryption is called decryption. It restores the plaintext from the ciphertext using the same secret key. Figure 4.2 shows a general block diagram for a symmetric encryption scheme, where X denotes plaintext, Y denotes ciphertext, and K denotes a secret key shared by both sender and recipient. E and D denote encryption and decryption algorithms, respectively (Stallings, 2011).

4.3.3 Data Masking

Data masking is a method that conceals original data, susceptible ones like person-ally identifiable information (PII) or financial details, to prevent unauthorized access. Transforming the actual data while retaining its authenticity for testing or developmental purposes mitigates cybersecurity risks, especially in cloud storage. This approach allows safe data sharing with developers or testers without exposing genuine production information.

The standard data masking techniques are as follows:

- *Data randomization:* Sensitive data values are replaced with random values. For example, a person's social security number or number may be replaced with a randomly generated number.
- *Data substitution:* Sensitive data values are substituted with realistic but fictional or fake data. This technique replaces the original data with another value from a supply of credible or similar but fake values.
- *Data shuffling:* Sensitive data values are rearranged or shuffled among the obser-vations, maintaining the overall statistical properties, but individual values are unidentifiable. The shuffled data provides a high level of data utility and mini-mizes the risk of disclosure.
- *Data encryption:* Sensitive data are encrypted using encryption algorithms, and the original data are replaced with encrypted values. Encryption is the most

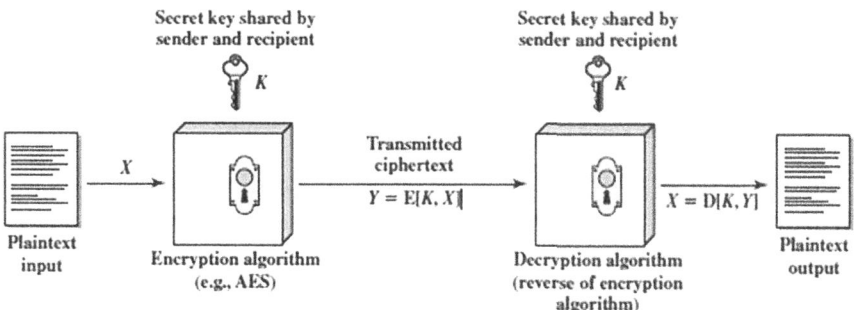

Fig. 4.2 A symmetric encryption scheme (adapted from Stallings, 2011).

complex approach to solving the data masking problem as it uses a key to encrypt and decrypt the data, and access to the encryption keys is strictly controlled.

- *Data tokenization:* Sensitive data are replaced with randomly generated tokens, and the mapping between the original data and tokens is securely maintained in a separate system.

Data Masking Types

Several types of data masking methods can be deployed in an organization. The common types of data masking are as follows:

- *Static data masking:* Static data masking creates separate masked data from a production database that can be used in non-production environments such as research and development. The masked data values must generate test and analytical results that mirror the original data and persist over time to ensure accurate and repeatable results.
- *Dynamic data masking* is applied in production systems when users require absolute data masking. This ensures that sensitive data are only revealed to authorized individuals or systems during specific operations or activities. This transforms, obscures, or blocks access to sensitive information fields in real time based on the user's role. For example, when a user handles a patient's query, sensitive fields such as date of birth and social security number will be masked unless the user has the privileges required to view those fields. It protects sensitive data without modifying the data on the disk and is transparent to the applications (Fotache et al., 2023). It is a powerful data security method with data masking to protect personal and other sensitive database information from unauthorized access.
- *Full masking:* In complete masking, all instances of sensitive data in a dataset are replaced with masked values. This method provides the highest level of data protection. Still, it may impact data analysis and processing (i.e., data utility reductions) as it does not preserve the original data or its specific characteristics. It replaces sensitive information with scrambled values so that the data analysis, pattern recognition, or testing may be affected.
- *Partial masking:* In partial masking, only a subset of sensitive data is masked, and other non-sensitive data remain unchanged. This method allows for a balance between data protection and data utility.
- *Data redaction:* Data redaction is another data masking technique that masks all alphabetic characters with "x" and all numeric characters with "n" (Fotache et al., 2023). It is a data protection technique that selectively removes or obscures sensitive information from records. This method is commonly used to safeguard sensitive legal, financial, healthcare, and government data.
- *On-the-fly data masking:* This method relies on extract-transform-load (ETL) methodology to move data from environment to environment without data touching the disk. It is like dynamic data masking but works on one record simultaneously. It provides an additional layer of protection for sensitive data as it ensures that even users with access privileges can only see the masked version of the

data. This method is most useful for environments with continuous deployments and delivery.

4.3.4 Hardware-Based Security

Hardware-based security uses specialized hardware components and methods to enhance the security of computer systems and protect against various security threats, including unauthorized access, data breaches, and tampering. It employs the hardware's intrinsic properties to enhance security (Arafin & Qu, 2021). It involves embedding the security methods directly into the hardware design and architecture and provides a strong foundation for system security. The key hardware-based security measures are as follows:

- *Trusted platform module (TPM):* A TPM is an embedded or physical security technology that uses a microcontroller in a computer's motherboard or processor. A dedicated microcontroller provides cryptographic functions and secure storage of sensitive information such as user credentials, passwords, fingerprints, digital certificates, and encryption/decryption keys. It helps to ensure the integrity of computer systems and protects against unauthorized access and tampering attacks (TCG, 2019).
- *Secure enclaves:* Secure enclaves provide CPU hardware-level isolation and memory encryption by isolating application code and data. For example, Intel Software Guard Extensions (SGX) is a set of security-related instruction codes built into some Intel CPUs that allows user-level protected private memory regions called enclaves. SGX is a hardware-isolated processor that provides a secure execution environment for sensitive computations and data with its practical guarantees of privacy and integrity for remote computation at a reasonable design cost and performance overhead (Costan et al., 2017).
- *Hardware security modules (HSMs):* HSMs are physical devices that securely generate, store, and manage cryptographic keys. HSMs, also known as tamper-resistant security modules (TRSMs), perform cryptographic functions such as data encryption/decryption and certificate management. They provide high-assurance key management, secure key storage, and cryptographic operations, making them particularly useful for applications requiring strong encryption and critical handling (Mavrovouniotis, 2014). Physical security and key management are essential to protect the confidentiality and integrity of the keys. These security requirements for cryptographic modules, including physical security, are correctly described in the report NIST-FIPS-140-3 (Cooper & Schaffer, 2019).
- *Hardware authentication:* Hardware authentication is a physical security method (i.e., hardware-based authentication mechanism) that involves using hardware tokens or physical keys for authentication. These tokens generate one-time passwords (OTP) or cryptographic keys. Several lightweight hardware intrinsic security methods are used for the authentication. Physically unclonable functions

(PUFs) are used for entity authentication. PUFs are on-chip circuitry that can extract fabrication variations to generate chip-dependent PUF data that can be used as secret keys, which are device-dependent (Arafin & Qu, 2021).

4.3.5   Data Backup and Resilience

Backups are copies of data taken at a particular time and stored in a standard format. These backups should be tracked over some period of usefulness of the data (Nelson, 2011). There are the following types of data backups:

- *Full backups: These are complete snapshots of the data intended to be protected. They provide the baseline for all other levels of backup. In addition, two different levels of backup* capture changes relative to the full backup.
- *Differential backup:* The differential backup, also known as the cumulative incremental backup, captures backups that have occurred since the last full backup. This type of backup is typically used in environments with little change.

The simplest way to protect a file system against disk failures or file corruption is to copy the entire contents of the file system to a backup device. The resulting archive is called a full backup.

4.3.6   Data Erasure

Data erasure is a software-based technique for securely and permanently removing all data from a storage device. It is also known as data clearing, wiping, or sanitization. The primary goal of data erasure is to ensure that the data on the device cannot be recovered or accessed by unauthorized individuals, even with specialized data recovery techniques. Device formatting and deleting the files through the operating system is insufficient for data erasure. These methods only remove references to the data, which are recoverable. Therefore, proper data erasure methods are necessary to ensure privacy and security. The standard data erasure methods are as follows:

- *Overwriting:* The most common data erasure method involves repeatedly overwriting the entire storage device with random data patterns or zeros.
- *Cryptographic erasure:* In this method, data are first securely encrypted with a robust cryptographic algorithm, and then the decryption key is securely deleted.
- *Physical destruction:* This method physically damages the storage medium (hard drive, solid-state drive), making data recovery impossible.

4.4   Understanding Common Data Threats and Vulnerabilities

4.4.1   Accidental Exposure

Accidental exposure is a data breach caused by inadequate security measures, human errors, or system vulnerabilities. Misaddressed emails, employee mistakes or negligence, software or system bugs and vulnerabilities, system misconfiguration, and weak access control are common causes of accidental exposures.

- *Misaddressed emails:* Sending emails to the wrong recipients is referred to as misaddressed emails. It is a common cause of accidental data exposure. It occurs when an email containing sensitive information is sent to the wrong recipient. It is often the result of a simple mistake made by the sender, a human error. It can happen due to typing errors in the email address, selecting the wrong recipient from an address book, confusion between similarly named contacts, etc. Autocomplete features, copy-paste, shared mailbox, and email forwarding are the common causes of accidental data exposure via misaddressed emails. Double-checking the recipient addresses and applying encryption methods and data loss prevention tools to sensitive emails can help minimize the risk of unintentional data exposure through misaddressed emails.
- *Employee negligence:* Employees may accidentally expose data by uploading sensitive files to public file-sharing platforms such as cloud storage, losing physical storage devices, or falling victim to social engineering attacks that result in unintentional data disclosure. Employees may lose laptops, smartphones, USB drives, or other sensitive data devices. If these devices are not adequately protected with encryption or passcodes, unauthorized individuals can access the data. Providing security training and awareness and implementing strong security measures can reduce the risk of data exposure from employee negligence.
- *Software bugs or vulnerabilities* are common reasons for accidental data exposure. Developers' insecure coding practices, insufficient input validation, weak authentication and authorization mechanisms, buffer overflows, and memory corruption mainly lead to data exposure. Following secure coding practices, regular security audits, and code reviews and promptly applying security patches and updates help to reduce the risk of accidental data exposure to software bugs or vulnerabilities.
- *Misconfiguration of the system: Misconfigurations in security settings, such as the improper configuration of firewalls and data encryption protocols,* can leave the systems more vulnerable to data exposures. Regularly updating systems and deploying robust security measures can help to reduce the risk of accidental data exposure resulting from misconfigurations.
- *Weak access controls:* Weak passwords or improper user permission settings can allow unauthorized individuals to expose sensitive data accidentally. Strengthening access controls that use multi-factor authentication and regularly

reviewing and updating permissions can reduce the risk of accidental data exposure resulting from weak access controls.

4.4.2   Insider Threats

Insiders are called employees or former employees, contractors, or business associates with inside information concerning the organization's security practices, data, software, and computer systems. These insiders may intentionally or unintentionally expose data by circumventing security measures, mishandling data, or using unauthorized tools or devices (Costa, 2017).

Insider threats can be managed by developing and deploying security policies, procedures, and technologies that help prevent privilege misuse. Continuous risk assessment, security incident management, and automatic monitoring tools can also help mitigate insider threats.

4.4.3   Ransomware

A malware assault is a prevalent digital threat where harmful software undertakes unwarranted activities in a system. There are various types of malware families, including ransomware, spyware, Trojans, worms, and viruses. Precisely, ransomware locks critical data, demanding payment to regain access. Such attacks can originate from dubious email attachments, compromised websites, or software vulnerabilities. Upon system entry, the attacker encrypts files using robust algorithms, rendering them inaccessible without the attacker's decryption key. To regain access, victims are often asked to pay in digital currencies.

Such threats increasingly target diverse entities, from fuel lines and schools to hospitals and banks. These attackers use malicious codes to encrypt and steal data. A notable instance is the WannaCry attack of May 2017, which affected approximately 230,000 computers globally, including many in UK hospitals. These hospitals were particularly vulnerable due to their reliance on older operating systems like Windows XP, primarily because some costly equipment, such as MRI machines, was compatible only with this older OS. Hence, despite governmental advice to upgrade, many healthcare institutions persisted with outmoded Windows versions (WannaCry, 2017).

Ransomware attacks can be highly disruptive and damaging. Regularly backing up your data, updating software applications, and having a robust incident response plan can help minimize the impact of ransomware attacks in the healthcare sector.

4.4.4   SQL Injection

An SQL injection attack consists of inserting or" injecting" a Structured Query Language (SQL) query into the application's input data from users. SQL is a database query language typically used in relational database management software. Successful SQL injection attacks can provide attackers with unauthorized access to the underlying systems, which may lead to further exploitation and compromise of the entire system.

SQL injection attacks allow attackers to spoof identity, tamper with existing data, cause repudiation issues such as voiding transactions or changing balances, allow the complete disclosure of all data on the system, destroy the data, or make it otherwise unavailable, and become administrators of the database server. A combination of secure coding practices (using parameterized queries, input validation, and use of stored procedures) and implementing a defense-in-depth strategy, including the use of low-privilege connections to the database servers, can help to reduce the impact of SQL injection attacks in healthcare systems (OWASP, 2023).

Defensive coding practices with vulnerability detection and runtime attack prevention methods are used to combat SQL injection attacks (Shar & Tan, 2013). Keeping database systems and web application frameworks up to date with the latest security patches and implementing web application firewalls (WAF) can detect and block SQL injection attempts in real time. WAF provides an additional layer of defense.

4.4.5   Social Engineering Attacks

Social engineering attacks exploit human behavior by tricking people into unknowingly divulging sensitive information and using it for criminal purposes. Attackers can use different social engineering attacks such as phishing, vishing, smishing, tailgating, pretexting, dumpster diving, shoulder surfing, and baiting attacks (Syafitri et al., 2022). A social engineering attacker is a person who wants access to sensitive information or money. Social engineering attacks have evolved into telephone calls, emails, and face-to-face.

Phishing is a typical social engineering attack where the attacker sends a fraudulent message using email, social media, instant messaging, SMS, or phone calls to obtain sensitive personal information from the victims.

Protecting sensitive medical data is crucial in healthcare, and it's essential to be aware of it and take measures to prevent social engineering attacks. Healthcare organizations can reduce the risk of social engineering attacks by implementing preventive measures such as strong authentication and access controls, employee education and training, and security awareness campaigns.

4.4.6   Data Loss in the Cloud

Sensitive information disclosure is protected by law or regulation and organizational policy. Sensitive information includes confidential and personally identifiable information (PII), and the loss or compromise could lead to identity theft or fraud (Photopoulos, 2008a). Figure 4.3 shows the four leading causes of data loss in the cloud. Data loss in the cloud is a situation where data stored in cloud-based systems or services are destroyed or inaccessible by system failure or mishandling in storage, transmission, or processing. The leading causes of cloud data loss include accidental deletion (human errors), cyberattacks (insiders or malware), service outages, and data corruption.

- *Accidental deletion:* This involves accidentally deleting files, directories, or entire databases by authorized users with sufficient privileges.
- *Cyberattacks* include malicious activities and insider and malware (ransomware) attacks, which can result in data loss in the cloud. Malicious users and insiders may gain unauthorized access to cloud accounts or exploit vulnerabilities to delete, encrypt, or compromise data. The insiders intentionally delete or alter data.
- *Service outages:* Outages or disruption of cloud services in the cloud may cause data loss.
- *Data corruption:* Data corruption may occur during transmission, storage, or processing in the cloud environment due to hardware failures, software bugs, or improper data handling practices, leading to data loss in the cloud.

A healthcare organization can mitigate the risk of data loss by deploying suitable data loss preventive measures such as regular data backups and security practices. Service level agreements (SLAs) with cloud service providers (CSPs) should include guarantees for data availability, backup and recovery processes, and response times in case of data loss incidents.

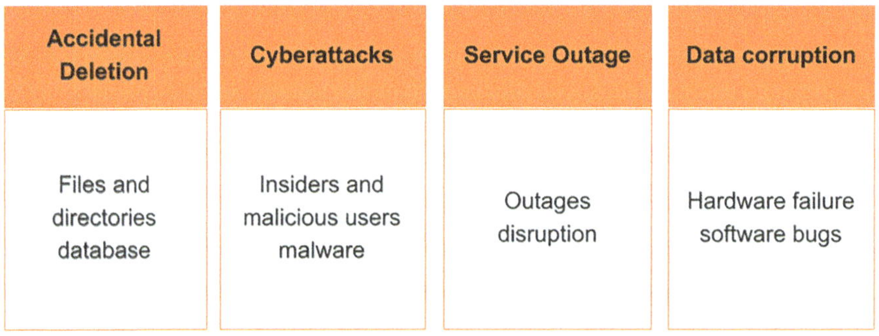

Accidental Deletion	Cyberattacks	Service Outage	Data corruption
Files and directories database	Insiders and malicious users malware	Outages disruption	Hardware failure software bugs

Fig. 4.3 Four fundamental causes of data loss in the cloud

4.4.7 Data Discovery and Classification

Data discovery and classification are essential processes in data management that involve identifying, categorizing, and understanding the data assets within an organization. Data discovery is locating and understanding data assets within an organization. Figure 4.4 shows the common discovery steps. It involves identifying the data sources, assessing their content and structure, and gaining insights into the overall data landscape.

- *Identify data sources:* The familiar sources include databases, data warehouses, file systems, cloud repositories, third-party systems, and other systems or applications that store or generate data.
- *Assess and analyze data:* It dives deeper into each data source to understand the content and structure of the data. Perform the analysis of data schemas, tables, attributes, and models to gain insights into the data structure and relationships.
- *Identify sensitive data:* It finds sensitive data in discovered data sources. Sensitive data include personally identifiable information (PII), financial data, health records, or any other data subject to privacy or compliance regulations.
- *Document findings:* It is essential to document your findings and insights from the data discovery process. This includes creating reports or data dictionaries summarizing the discovered data sources and their characteristics.

Data classification allows an organization to categorize information assets and define their sensitivity and confidentiality. It helps to identify the appropriate level of security protection and control requirements for the data. Data classification is a prerequisite to establishing guidelines and system requirements for the secure data life cycle, which includes generation, collection, access, storage, transmission, archiving, and disposal of data. Security objectives (confidentiality, integrity, and availability) will determine the classification level. A loss of confidentiality, integrity, and availability is the unauthorized disclosure, modification or destruction, and disruption of access to or use of information, respectively. Figure 4.5 shows the

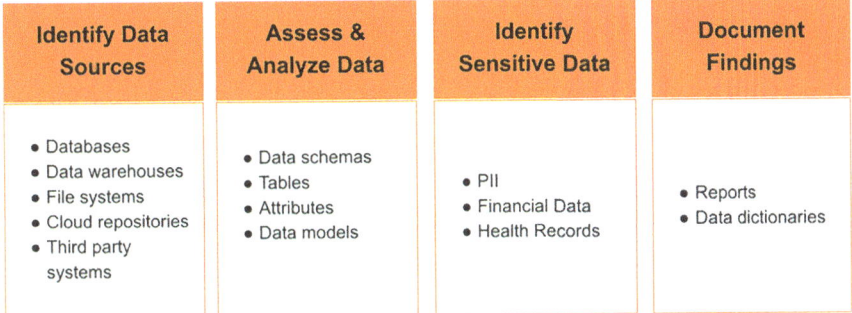

Fig. 4.4 Data discovery steps

Fig. 4.5 An impact and
damage pyramid

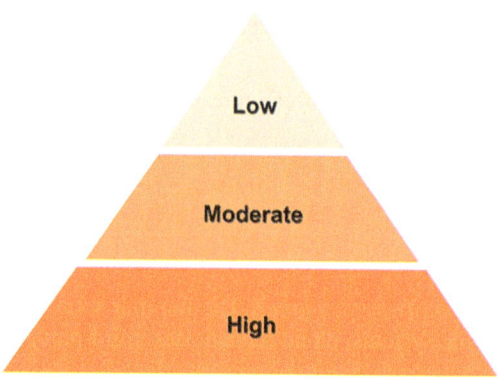

relationship of different impacts and their damages with a pyramid. There are three
levels of potential impact on organizations or individuals (Photopoulos, 2008b):

- *Low impact:* A limited adverse effect on the organization due to losing confidentiality, integrity, or availability. Low impact slightly degrades or does not affect
the organization's ability to perform its primary functions, causing minor financial loss and minimal harm to individuals. If the potential impact is low or limited, the healthcare provider will determine whether corrective actions are
required or decide to accept the risk.
- *Moderate impact:* A moderate adverse effect on organizational operations, organizational assets, or individuals. Moderate impact significantly degrades the
organization's ability to perform its primary functions, causes significant financial loss, and causes moderate harm to individuals, which does not involve the
loss of personally identifiable information. If the potential impact is moderate,
corrective actions are needed, and a plan must be developed to incorporate these
actions within a reasonable period.
- *High impact:* A severe or catastrophic adverse effect on organizational operations, assets, or individuals. The high impact severely or completely degrades the
organization's ability to perform its primary functions, causes significant damage to organization assets and reputations, and causes substantial financial loss
and severe harm to individuals, including the loss of personally identifiable
information and exposure to fraud and identity theft. If the potential impact is
high, there is a strong need for corrective measures in place as soon as possible.

Various data classification schemes have been developed and can be used depending on the need and nature of the organization. Three expected classification levels
are confidential, internal, and public. Figure 4.6 shows the data classification hierar-
chy. Similarly, Fig. 4.7 presents data examples for the three classes.

Confidential data: Confidential data are sensitive information whose unauthorized disclosure could have a severe adverse impact on the organization (e.g., substantial financial, legal, and reputation loss). Confidential data are highly protected
and accessible only to authorized individuals or groups within the organization.
This data category often includes personally identifiable information, financial

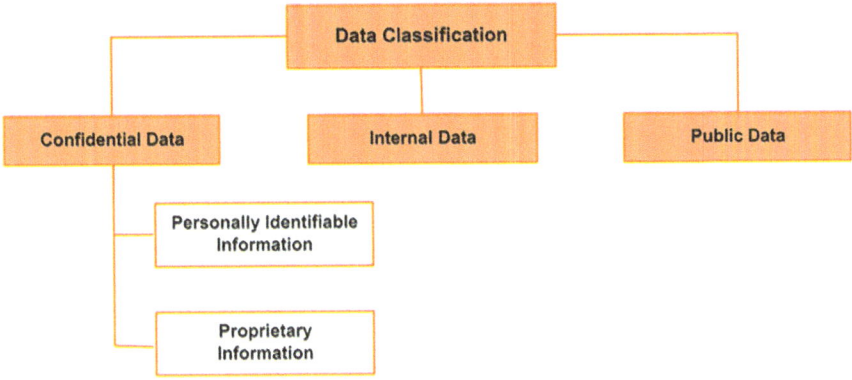

Fig. 4.6 Data classification

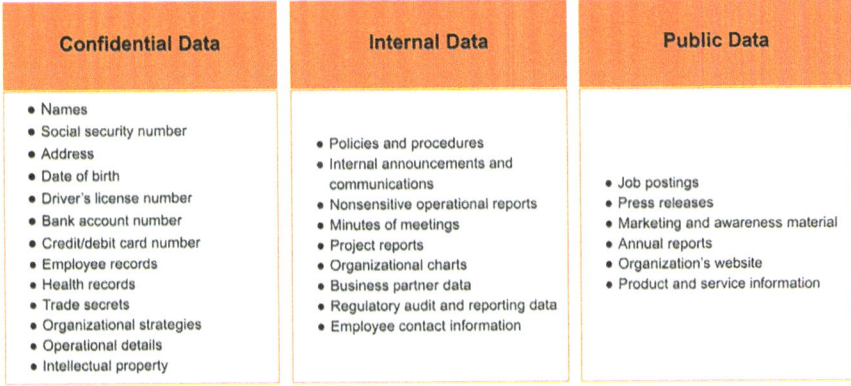

Fig. 4.7 Example of data classification

information, healthcare information, trade secrets, or any data that, if disclosed or accessed by unauthorized individuals, could cause harm to individuals or the organization. The confidential class of data classification can be divided into two further classes:

1. *Personally identifiable information (PII):* It includes a name, social security number (or any other identifier number), address, date of birth, driver's license number, bank account number, credit/debit card number, etc.
2. *Proprietary information:* It is confidential non-public information related to or associated with the organization's products, business, or activities, including financial data or statements, research and development, existing and future product designs and specifications, marketing plans or techniques, trade secrets, copyrights, and patents, etc.

   - *Internal data:* Internal data consist of information intended for internal use within the organization. These data are not sensitive to disclosure within the organization but are not intended for external distribution. Internal data include business plans, internal reports, operational data, or non-public information that does not fall under the susceptible category of confidential data.

- *Public data:* Public data are freely accessible and intended for public use. They are not sensitive in context or content, require no special protection, and can be freely disseminated without potential harm. Examples of public data include press releases, marketing materials, job postings, and any data that is not confidential or sensitive.

4.5 Data Protection and Privacy

4.5.1 Definition and Importance of Data Protection

Data protection in healthcare refers to the practices and methods taken to protect healthcare data from unauthorized access, loss, corruption, or misuse throughout its lifecycle. The data lifecycle refers to the stages through which data passes from its initial creation to its eventual deletion or archival. Data protection encompasses the technical, management, and legal procedures and practices implemented to ensure security goals such as confidentiality, integrity, and data availability. Healthcare data protection aims to mitigate risks and protect the data against potential security attacks.

4.5.2 Principles of Data Protection and Regulations

Data protection principles refer to a set of rules and guidelines that govern the secure handling, processing, and storage of data. In healthcare, data protection principles and regulations define rules and policies to ensure the privacy and security of healthcare information. Patient information, such as medical records, diagnoses, treatment plans, and personal identifiers, must be protected against unauthorized access or disclosure. Access controls, encryption, secure storage, and audit trails should be in place to maintain data integrity and prevent breaches. Healthcare providers can maintain patient trust, protect sensitive data, and contribute to healthcare information security and privacy by applying data protection principles and regulations.

Healthcare providers should be aware of the data protection regulations and their applications to their jurisdiction. The Health Insurance Portability and Accountability Act (HIPAA, 1996) and the General Data Protection Regulation (GDPR, 2016) set guidelines for the protection and privacy of patient data in the USA and the European Union, respectively.

The Personal Information Protection and Electronic Documents Act (PIPEDA, 2019) is a data protection act that defines the governing rules for data collection, usage, and disclosure by private sector organizations in Canada.

4.5.3 Definition and Importance of Data Privacy

Data privacy refers to individuals' right to control the collection, use, and disclosure of their personal information. It is essential because it provides a mechanism to protect patient's personal data and medical information from unauthorized access and ensures their confidentiality and privacy rights. A healthcare provider can ensure data privacy by implementing appropriate measures such as data encryption, access controls, data minimization, consent management, and privacy impact assessments.

Ensuring data privacy, healthcare organizations can build trust, comply with legal requirements, mitigate risks, and maintain positive relationships with their patients and other stakeholders whose data they use.

4.5.4 Data Protection vs Data Privacy

Data privacy concerns the regulations and policies governing personal information use when collected, used, or shared with any entity. On the other hand, data protection is the mechanism that includes tools and procedures to enforce the policy and regulation, including the prevention of unauthorized access or misuse of personal information. Data privacy involves obtaining consent, providing transparency in data handling practices, and respecting legal and ethical obligations regarding personal data use. In contrast, data protection consists of safeguarding data against unauthorized access, loss, corruption, or misuse throughout its lifecycle. Therefore, data privacy primarily focuses on the individual's rights and preferences regarding using their data. In contrast, data protection encompasses security measures to safeguard all data types.

Both data privacy and data protection are crucial for ensuring compliance with laws and regulations, maintaining trust with individual patients, and mitigating the risks of cyberattacks on healthcare systems.

4.5.5 Data Protection Technologies and Practices

Data protection technologies and practices are a set of security control and measurement tools designed to protect data from unauthorized access, loss, corruption, and misuse. They are essential in protecting sensitive patient data and ensuring compliance with healthcare privacy regulations. Access controls and authentications, data encryption, data loss prevention, data backup and disaster recovery, secure messaging and communication, regulatory compliances, incident response planning, etc., are critical data protection technologies and practices.

By implementing these data protection technologies and practices, a healthcare provider can establish a robust security mechanism to protect patients' sensitive data and mitigate risks associated with data breaches and other potential cyberattacks.

4.5.5.1   Data Discovery

Data discovery is finding and understanding an organization's data assets. It involves identifying data sources and assessing their content and structure. Data discovery helps healthcare organizations gain insights into their data, assess data quality, identify risks, and ensure compliance with data privacy and security regulations.

4.5.5.2   Data Loss Prevention (DLP)

Data Loss Prevention (DLP) monitors and controls data flows to prevent unauthorized data disclosure or loss. DLP can identify and prevent sensitive data from being transmitted outside the organization or enforce policies on data handling and sharing.

4.5.5.3   Storage with Built-in Data Protection

It is a built-in data protection mechanism in storage systems that includes integrated security mechanisms to protect data from various cybersecurity threats and ensure its integrity, availability, and confidentiality. This system offers inherent data protection capabilities, reducing the need for additional external measures. The common built-in protection mechanisms in storage systems are as follows:

- *Redundant array of independent disks (RAID):* RAID is a technology that combines multiple physical disks into a single logical unit to provide increased performance, fault tolerance, and data redundancy. Different RAID levels (e.g., RAID 1, RAID 5, RAID 6) offer various levels of data protection by mirroring or stripping data across multiple drives, allowing for data recovery in case of drive failures.
- *Snapshot and backup capabilities:* It is a backup system with a storage system. The snapshot mechanism captures copies of data in a specific time interval, enabling quick recovery from accidental data loss or corruption. Backup capabilities allow regular data backups to separate storage media and protect against data loss from hardware failures, malware attacks, or disasters.

- *Data integrity checking:* It ensures data integrity using checksums or hash functions. These techniques generate unique values for data blocks and verify their integrity during each operation.
- *Erasure coding:* A coding technique that enables data to be divided into fragments and distributed across storage devices. This allows data recovery even if some storage devices or fragments become unavailable. It offers high data availability and fault tolerance, reducing the risk of data loss.
- *Encryption:* It protects data at rest by encrypting it before storing it on the storage system. It ensures the confidentiality or privacy of the stored data.
- *Data replication and mirroring:* Data replication and mirroring mechanisms maintain copies of data across multiple physical devices or geographical locations. This provides high availability of data.

4.5.5.4   Backup and Replication

The primary purpose of backup and replication is to prevent catastrophic data loss due to unforeseen events such as natural disasters, hardware failures, or malicious software attacks, including ransomware attacks. So, I think that's not working well because we're not moving fast enough, or we're not moving in that direction as quickly as some people want. The backup system usually saves data at regular intervals, safely keeps it offsite, and is used to restore the original data if an incident happens. Data replication is creating copies of data, synchronizing, and distributing it across a network of servers and data centers. It increases the system's availability and makes a faster recovery process.

4.5.5.5   Firewalls

A firewall is a dedicated computer (device) that interfaces with computers outside a network and has special security precautions built into it to protect sensitive data on computers within the network. It provides perimeter defense. A firewall serves outside the network, especially Internet connection and dial-in lines. A firewall imposes network service restrictions; only authorized traffic, as defined by the local security policy, can pass through it. There are four types of firewalls:

- *Packet filtering firewalls (PFF):* PFFs are the simplest form of firewalls. They examine each IP packet and permit or deny it according to predefined rules. They apply rules to each incoming and outgoing IP packet and then forward or discard it. This firewall is typically configured to filter packets going in both directions.
- *Stateful packet filtering firewalls (SPFF):* SPFF looks at each packet and applies rules or tests, but the regulations or tests applied to each packet may be modified depending on packets that have already been processed or in the case of an application relay it will maintain state. It keeps track of client-server sessions and

checks each packet to see whether it belongs to one session. These firewalls can detect bogus packets that are out of context.

- *Circuit-level gateway firewalls: A circuit-level firewall doesn't simply allow or disallow packets but also determines whether the connection between ends is valid according to* predefined rules. A typical use of circuit-level gateways is when the system administrator trusts the internal users.
- *Proxy firewalls (PF):* PF is the most secure form of firewall, which looks through the packet contents and filters messages at the application layer to protect network resources. It is also known as an application gateway firewall, as it limits the applications a network can support, increasing security levels. The network protocol packets.

4.5.5.6   Authentication and Authorization

Authentication is verifying the identity of a user or entity attempting to access a system, application, service, or resource. It ensures the user is who they claim to be before granting access. After successful authentication, authorization determines what actions or resources a user or entity can access. It defines the permissions and privileges granted to authenticated users based on their roles and responsibilities. A healthcare organization can implement authentication and authorization mechanisms to control user access to their software system, applications, services, or data.

4.5.5.7   Encryption

Data encryption converts plaintext into ciphertext using an encryption algorithm and a secret cryptographic key. Encryption aims to secure and protect data from unauthorized access during transmission or storage. It provides confidentiality and integrity to sensitive data, including healthcare and finance.

4.5.5.8   Endpoint Protection

Endpoint protection is a cybersecurity approach to prevent, detect, and respond to the various security threats that target endpoint devices within a network. Endpoint devices typically include desktop computers, laptops, smartphones, tablets, servers, and any other electronic device that connects to a network. The endpoint protection method can have a multi-layered defense strategy that combines various security measures to safeguard data and systems from different types of cyberattacks. The standard endpoint protections are as follows:

- *Antivirus and antimalware:* These endpoint protection mechanisms include traditional antivirus and antimalware capabilities that help detect and remove known malware, viruses, and other malicious software from devices.

- *Firewall:* A firewall monitors and controls incoming and outgoing network traffic on endpoint devices. It helps prevent unauthorized access to the devices and protects them against network-based attacks.
- *Endpoint protection platform (EPP):* This platform integrates security solutions that leverage personal firewall, port and device control, and antimalware capabilities to provide endpoint protection across an organization.
- *Endpoint detection and response (EDR):* It is a security solution that detects threats, investigates the entire lifecycle of the danger, and provides insights into what happened, how it got in, where it has been, what it's doing now, and what to do about it. EDR helps eliminate the threat before it can spread across the organization. EDR improves malware detection over antivirus capabilities.
- *Extended detection and response (XDR):* XDR solution uses EDR capabilities to extend protection endpoints by monitoring the data combined from different sources such as network traffic, user logs, cloud workloads, servers, email, and more. It takes a more holistic and integrated approach to threat detection, analysis, and response across multiple security layers and data sources within an organization's environment. It uses the latest technologies to provide higher visibility and collects and correlates threat information while employing analytics and automation to help detect current and future cyberattacks.

4.5.5.9   Data Erasure

Data erasure methods permanently remove all data from a storage device. It is also known as data clearing, wiping, or sanitization. Using proper data erasure methods is necessary to ensure the privacy and security of the healthcare system.

4.5.5.10   Disaster Recovery

Disaster recovery (DR) consists of computing technologies and best practices designed to prevent or minimize data loss and business disruption resulting from catastrophic events such as cyberattacks, natural disasters, equipment failures, civil emergencies, and criminal or military attacks. DR for healthcare cyberattacks is critical to ensuring patient safety, data security, and continuity of healthcare services in the face of cybersecurity incidents. A healthcare organization should prepare a well-defined incident response plan that outlines the steps to be taken in the event of a cyberattack. This plan should involve clear roles and responsibilities for staff, procedures for isolating affected systems, and communication methods for notifying patients, regulatory authorities, and law enforcement agencies.

4.6   How to Protect Healthcare Data

4.6.1   Educate Healthcare Staff

Staff members, including those in the healthcare sector, are among the biggest cybersecurity threats to any organization. A simple human error or negligence can result in expensive consequences and attacks. Cybersecurity awareness training for the healthcare staff can help to reduce cybersecurity incidents. Healthcare organizations can conduct regular training sessions to educate their staff, including seminars, workshops, and online learning. A simulated phishing exercise can help to test employees. A well-designed end-user security education contributes to thwarting phishing threats (Arachchilage & Love, 2014). The following five standard methods can be used to raise security awareness:

- Conventional delivery method
- Instructor-led delivery method
- Online delivery method
- Game-based delivery method
- Simulation-based delivery method

4.6.2   Restrict Access to Data and Applications

Healthcare data can be protected by restricting access to specific applications and users. Access restrictions ensure that only authorized users have access to personally identifiable information (PII), medical data, and other confidential information from getting into the mishap internally or externally. Multi-factor authentication (MFA) is used to authenticate the users. It requires two or more elements of proof of identity. For example, password and fingerprint (biometric) information is known only to the user, such as a password or PIN, something that only the authorized user would possess, such as a card or key, or something unique to the authorized user, such as biometrics including facial recognition, fingerprints, etc.

Identity and access management (IAM) is a security management platform that enables an organization to manage user access control based on groups or roles. It simplifies data access control management deployment in healthcare organizations with streamlined compliance and regulations such as GDPR (GDPR, 2016) or HIPPA (HIPAA, 1996). IAM verifies the user, software, or hardware by validating their credentials against a database, granting only the necessary access. IAM also supports audits and reports that allow organizations to identify and monitor blockages, errors, and suspicious user behavior and take or suggest appropriate action.

4.6.3   Implement Data Usage Controls

It is a protective data control method that monitors and detects malicious data activity; if it is found, it flags and blocks the data access immediately. Healthcare organizations can use data controls to block specific actions involving sensitive information and other medical records, such as uploading or copying the data to external devices by unauthorized users or suspicious users. Implementing data usage control tools protects data from real-time unauthorized access or data breaches.

4.6.4   Log and Monitor Use

Logging and monitoring user activity is an effective security measure for any organization, including the healthcare industry. It helps identify security incidents, track user behavior, and detect potential threats or suspicious activities. The logging mechanisms are used to record relevant activities in healthcare IT infrastructure. This includes access attempts, file modifications, login attempts, system changes, and any other events that may be significant for security analysis. Real-time monitoring can help to alert security personnel promptly about detecting suspicious activities or potential security attacks.

4.6.5   Encrypt Data at Rest and in Transit

Encrypting data at rest and during transmission is crucial to maintaining the confidentiality and integrity of sensitive healthcare data. Encryption of data at rest, often utilizing the Advanced Encryption Standard (AES) algorithm, protects information on storage devices. Encryption in transit safeguards data when sent over networks using protocols like HTTPS and SSL/TLS.

Virtual private networks (VPNs) offer secure encrypted links over public networks. VPNs connect computers over insecure networks like the Internet, establishing an encrypted channel. They primarily provide a protected communication path between a device and a distant network, especially over distant geographical locations, though distance isn't a necessity.

4.6.6   Secure Mobile Devices

Smartphones and tablets are commonly used to access patient data and medical applications. The four potential cyber threats to intelligent mobile devices are security threats from mobile devices, network connectivity, web application services, and mobile apps installed on the devices. Securing mobile devices is crucial in the healthcare industry, where doctors, patients, and other staff use smartphones and tablets to access health records and medical applications.

Security measures such as encryption, strong authentication, and management tools can help keep mobile devices secure. Device-level encryption protects data stored on the device. Robust authentication methods or multi-factor authentication (MFA) can prevent unauthorized access to mobile devices. Mobile device management tools can help enforce security policies, deploy updates, and wipe the devices in case of loss and theft.

A healthcare organization can reduce the risk of cyberattacks and protect sensitive patient information by deploying mobile device security measures and ensuring compliance with healthcare data protection regulations such as HIPAA (HIPAA, 1996).

4.6.7   Mitigate Connected Device Risks

Using the Internet of Things (IoT) and other connected devices increases the risk of cyberattacks on organizations, including the healthcare industry. In healthcare systems, mitigating the risks associated with connected devices is crucial to ensure the security and privacy of data and prevent potential cyberattacks. Implementing the following practices can help to reduce the risks associated with the connected devices:

• Use a separate network for the IoT-connected devices.
• Continuously monitor IoT device networks to identify sudden activity changes.
• Always turn off non-essential services on devices before using them or remove non-essential services entirely before use.
• Use multi-factor authentication mechanisms.
• Keep all connected devices up to date.

4.6.8   Conduct Regular Risk Assessments

Conducting regular risk assessments of healthcare organizations can proactively identify and address potential security risks. It can help enhance their security and protect patient data from cyberattacks. Risk assessments help to identify potential security vulnerabilities, evaluate the impact of threats, and prioritize security measures to protect healthcare data.

4.6.9   Backup Data to a Secure, Offsite Location

Backup data to a secure, offsite location protects valuable data from various security threats, for example, hardware failure, data corruption, cyberattacks, natural disasters, and physical damage. It ensures data availability and business continuity in the event of a disaster. Offsite data backups are essential in data protection and disaster recovery strategies against potential data loss risks. It helps to mitigate the impact of ransomware attacks.

4.6.10   Carefully Evaluate the Security and Compliance Posture of Business Associates

Carefully assessing all potential business associates is one of healthcare organizations' most crucial security measures. It ensures the protection of patient data and adheres to applicable regulations. Identify all the business associates with whom a healthcare organization shares protected health information (PHI). Business associates are third-party entities that handle PHI on behalf of healthcare providers. Conducting their security risk assessments helps to identify potential security vulnerabilities and risks related to PHI and confirm their adherence to privacy and security rules (HIPAA, 1996).

4.7   Chapter Summary

This chapter presents data and information security, including healthcare information and security protection methods. Data and information in healthcare, such as electronic health records, administrative data, claims data, and clinical trial data, including patient or disease registries and health surveys, are described. Information security methods—authentication and authorization, encryption, data masking, hardware-based security, backups, and recovery techniques—are discussed. Common data threats and vulnerabilities are discussed, with best practices to reduce them. Data protection and privacy regulations, including the industry's best practices, are presented.

After understanding all the fundamental concepts, the following questions are addressed in this chapter:

- What are the data types and various sources of information in the healthcare industry?
- What security measures can be applied to healthcare data protection?
- What are data threats and vulnerabilities in healthcare data?
- What are the data protection principles and best practices in healthcare systems?

- What are the types of authentication mechanisms used in healthcare systems?
- What is authorization? What are the approaches for access control?
- Which access control mechanism is commonly used in healthcare data access control?
- What are the regulations for protecting healthcare data?
- What are the methods of cybersecurity training for healthcare professionals?
- What are hardware-based security methods?

References

Arachchilage, N. A., & Love, S. (2014). Security awareness of computer users: A phishing threat avoidance perspective. *Computers in Human Behavior, 38*, 304–312. https://doi.org/10.1016/j. chb.2014.05.046

Arafin, M. T., & Qu, G. (2021). Hardware-based authentication applications. In B. Halak (Ed.), *Authentication of embedded devices: Technologies, protocols and emerging applications* (pp. 145–181). Springer International Publishing. https://doi.org/10.1007/978-3-030-60769-2_6

Bahache, A. N., Chikouche, N., & Mezrag, F. (2022). Authentication schemes for healthcare applications using wireless medical sensor networks: A survey. *SN Computer Science., 3*, 382. https://doi.org/10.1007/s42979-022-01300-z

Cooper, M. J., & Schaffer, K. B. (2019, March). *Security requirements for cryptographic modules, Federal Inf. Process. Stds. (NIST FIPS)*. National Institute of Standards and Technology (NIST). National Institute of Standards and Technology (NIST). https://doi.org/10.6028/NIST. FIPS.140-3.

Costa, D. (2017, March). *CERT definition of 'Insider Threat'–updated*. Carnegie Mellon University, software engineering Institute's insights (blog). Retrieved 7 16, 2023, from https://insights.sei. cmu.edu/blog/cert-definition-of-insider-threat-updated/

Costan, V., Lebedev, I., & Devadas, S. (2017). Secure processors part I: Background, taxonomy for secure enclaves, and Intel SGX architecture. *Foundations and Trends® in Electronic Design Automation, 11*, 1–248. https://doi.org/10.1561/1000000051

Ferraiolo, D. (2003). Role-based access control. *Art.*

Fotache, M., Munteanu, A., Strîmbei, C., & Hrubaru, I. (2023). Framework for the assessment of data masking performance penalties in SQL database servers. Case study: Oracle. *IEEE Access, 11*, 18520–18541. https://doi.org/10.1109/ACCESS.2023.3247486

GDPR. (2016). General data protection regulation. *Official Journal of the European Union.*

Häyrinen, K. (2008). Definition, structure, content, use, and impacts of electronic health records: A research literature review. *International Journal of Medical Informatics, 77*(5), 291–304. https://doi.org/10.1016/j.ijmedinf.2007.09.001

HIPAA. (1996, August 21). *H.R.3103-104th congress (1995–1996): Health insurance portability and accountability act of 1996*. https://www.congress.gov/bill/104th-congress/house-bill/3103

Library, H. S. (2023). Data resources in the health sciences. *Data resources in the health sciences*. Retrieved Jun 27, 2023, from https://guides.lib.uw.edu/hsl/data

Mavrovouniotis, S. A. (2014). Hardware security modules. In K. A. Markantonakis (Ed.), *Secure smart embedded devices, platforms and applications* (pp. 383–405). Springer. https://doi. org/10.1007/978-1-4614-7915-4_17

Nelson, S. (2011). Introduction to backup and recovery. In S. Nelson (Ed.), *Pro data backup and recovery* (pp. 1–16). Apress. https://doi.org/10.1007/978-1-4302-2663-5_1

OWASP. (2023). *SQL injection, The OWASP foundation*. SQL injection. Retrieved July 12, 2023, from https://owasp.org/www-community/attacks/SQL_Injection

Photopoulos, C. (2008a). Chapter 1–introduction. In C. Photopoulos (Ed.), *Managing catastrophic loss of sensitive data* (pp. 1–14). Syngress. https://doi.org/10.1016/B978-1-59749-239-3.00001-8

Photopoulos, C. (2008b). Chapter 2–data classification. In I. C. Photopoulos (Ed.), *Managing catastrophic loss of sensitive data* (pp. 15–45). Syngress. https://doi.org/10.1016/B978-1-59749-239-3.00002-X

PIPEDA. (2019, May). *Office of the privacy commissioner of Canada.* (Office of the privacy commissioner of Canada) The personal information protection and electronic documents act (PIPEDA). Retrieved July 10, 2023, from https://www.priv.gc.ca/en/privacy-topics/privacy-laws-in-canada/the-personal-information-protection-and-electronic-documents-act-pipeda

Shar, L. K., & Tan, H. B. (2013). Defeating SQL injection. *Computer, 46*(3), 69–77. https://doi.org/10.1109/MC.2012.283

Stallings, W. (2011). *Network security essentials: Applications and standards* (4th ed.). Pearson Education.

Syafitri, W., Shukur, Z., Mokhtar, U. A., Sulaiman, R., & Ibrahim, M. A. (2022). Social engineering attacks prevention: A systematic literature review. *IEEE Access, 10*, 39325–39343. https://doi.org/10.1109/ACCESS.2022.3162594

TCG. (2019, November). *Trusted platform module (TPM), Trusted platform module library specification, family "2.0", Level 00, Revision 01.59.* Trusted Platform Module (TPM). Retrieved from https://trustedcomputinggroup.org/work-groups/trusted-platform-module/

Wang, F., & Preininger, A. (2019). AI in health: State of the art, challenges, and future directions. *Yearbook of Medical Informatics, 28*(1), 016–026. https://doi.org/10.1055/s-0039-1677908

WannaCry. (2017, May 15). *The WannaCry ransomware attack was temporarily halted. But it's not over yet.* VOX technology. Retrieved July 5, 2023, from https://www.vox.com/new-money/2017/5/15/15641196/wannacry-ransomware-windows-xp

WHO. (2023). *International clinical trials registry platform (ICTRP).* World health organization. Retrieved Jun 27, 2023, from https://www.who.int/clinical-trials-registry-platform

.

Chapter 5
Personal Security

5.1 Introduction

A cybersecurity strategy is crucial in today's dynamic healthcare environment to protect patient data, privacy, and the integrity of the healthcare system. As medical processes become increasingly digitized, healthcare professionals are becoming more vulnerable to cyberattacks, from data breaches to ransomware attacks. To meet these challenges, it is imperative to address personal security, especially that of patients, doctors, and staff (Fig. 5.1).

Cyberattacks can disrupt healthcare services and compromise sensitive medical information, endangering patient safety. Moreover, cyberattacks targeting doctors can disrupt care delivery, compromising patients' and doctors' safety. Additionally, the human element remains one of the most significant cybersecurity threats, making healthcare staff cybersecurity crucial (Jalali et al., 2019; Nifakos et al., 2021; Alanazi, 2023). Comprehensive training programs are necessary to equip healthcare professionals with the skills to effectively recognize and mitigate cyber risks (Hijji & Alam, 2022; Niki et al., 2022).

This chapter emphasizes the significance of developing a cybersecurity awareness and resilience culture to ensure personal safety and organizational integrity in today's digital healthcare systems. It also outlines the importance of awareness training programs in equipping healthcare professionals with the skills to effectively recognize and mitigate cyber risks.

D. P. Sharma et al., *Understanding Cybersecurity Management in Healthcare*,
Progress in IS, https://doi.org/10.1007/978-3-031-68034-2_5

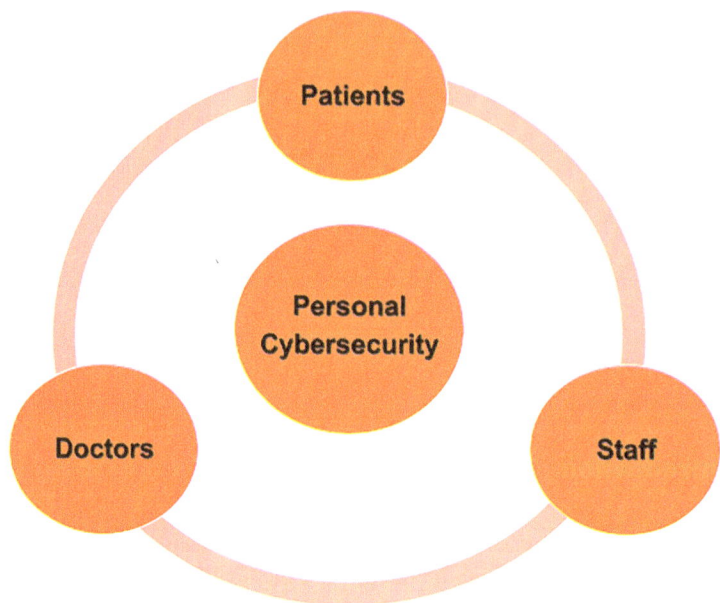

Fig. 5.1 Personal cybersecurity in healthcare

5.2 Patient Cybersecurity

As healthcare digitizes, cybersecurity becomes increasingly important to protect patient privacy and data. While these advancements offer improved care, they make healthcare a prime target for cyberattacks. Breaches in patient confidentiality and disruptions in care delivery pose significant risks to patient safety. Protecting patient data and maintaining trust in healthcare institutions require ongoing vigilance, collaboration, and innovation to effectively address evolving cyber risks and threats.

5.2.1 The Importance of Cybersecurity in Protecting Patient

As mentioned earlier, healthcare is undergoing a profound digital transformation, marked by the widespread adoption of EHRs, interconnected medical devices, and digital healthcare (Rodrigues et al., 2013; Jalali et al., 2019). While these innovations promise improved patient care, the healthcare sector has become an attractive target for cyberattacks by digitizing patient data and medical processes. These attacks, ranging from data breaches to ransomware incidents, pose significant threats to patient confidentiality, data integrity, and timely care delivery.

Cybersecurity breaches can directly and indirectly affect patient safety. Unauthorized access to medical records can result in misdiagnoses or improper treatments, endangering patient well-being. Also, disruptions caused by cyberattacks can delay the timely delivery of critical care, particularly in emergencies (Jalali et al., 2019). Protecting patient data, ensuring the integrity of medical processes, and preserving trust in healthcare institutions are all integral components of this multifaceted endeavor. It is an area that demands continuous research, collaboration, and innovation to address the constantly evolving cyber threats and uphold the highest standards of patient care and safety.

5.2.2 How Do Cyberattacks Threaten Patient Safety?

Cyberattacks pose an ongoing and significant threat to patient safety in healthcare. These attacks disrupt critical healthcare services, compromise patient data, introduce vulnerabilities in medical devices, and can lead to direct patient harm, including delayed treatments, medication errors, or breaches of personal health information, negatively impacting patient health and well-being (Seh et al., 2020; Niki et al., 2022; Yeo & Banfield, 2022).

Cyberattacks often cause delays in accessing EHRs and essential systems, affecting the timeliness and accuracy of patient diagnosis and treatment (Niki et al., 2022). This may result in patients facing life-threatening conditions in emergencies. Compromised patient data, including sensitive medical records and personal information, raises concerns about patient privacy and can result in identity theft and fraud (Yeo & Banfield, 2022). When cybersecurity incidents occur within healthcare organizations, patients can lose trust in the security of their personal health information and the competence of the healthcare system, preventing them from seeking necessary medical care (Wasserman & Wasserman, 2022). Therefore, addressing cyber threats and enhancing cybersecurity in a digitalized healthcare system is crucial to protecting patient safety.

5.2.3 How Do Cyberattacks Threaten Patient Privacy?

Cyberattacks can compromise patient confidentiality and impact healthcare privacy in various ways, such as unauthorized access to EHRs and online health data. Breaches of these records can put patients' sensitive health data at risk, including medical histories, treatment plans, and other confidential information. Cyberattacks in healthcare can also lead to identity theft, which may result in financial losses for individuals and emotional distress when patient data is stolen (Smith, 2016). Security breaches can undermine patient trust in online healthcare platforms, potentially discouraging individuals from using online healthcare services (Hall & McGraw, 2014). Additionally, the legal and regulatory consequences of healthcare organizations or providers failing to protect patient privacy adequately may include fines, legal action, and reputational damage (Tariq & Hackert, 2023). On the other hand, the psychological impact on patients cannot be underestimated. A breach of personal health information can cause significant anxiety and stress (Kilovaty, 2021).

Online healthcare services must implement a robust cybersecurity strategy to protect patient privacy. Encrypting patient data is essential for protecting it from unauthorized access (Kruse et al., 2017). Therefore, it is to protect patient data and maintain the security of online healthcare platforms to ensure patient trust and privacy, especially when using remote healthcare services.

5.3 Doctors' Cybersecurity

As healthcare transitions into the digital age, cybersecurity is also a vital concern for doctors. Effective cybersecurity programs become essential as they provide care and handle sensitive patient data online. These programs protect patient information, ensure compliance with regulations, and mitigate the risks of cyberattacks. However, doctors often face challenges maintaining cybersecurity due to their focus on clinical training. Cybersecurity breaches disrupt healthcare services and threaten doctors' privacy and professional integrity. With cybercriminals targeting their information, breaches can lead to financial losses, reputational damage, and identity theft. Thus, doctors' cybersecurity is crucial for preserving patient privacy, data integrity, and quality healthcare delivery.

5.3.1 The Importance of Cybersecurity in Protecting Doctors

Doctors should consider several critical considerations regarding cybersecurity. Vital cybersecurity programs in healthcare facilities enhance awareness and provide information security training to healthcare professionals (Alhuwail et al., 2021). As more patients access healthcare services online, doctors find themselves uniquely positioned to discuss and provide relevant and valuable online resources. These resources include videos, interactive social media channels, and websites (Tan & Goonawardene, 2017).

Compared with nurses and administrators, doctors demonstrate the lowest cybersecurity scores. This is possibly due to doctors focusing primarily on clinical training and development (Alhuwail et al., 2021). Clinical training is often perceived as providing more immediate benefits and being more relevant to doctors' jobs. However, cybersecurity programs must be concise, practical, and able to highlight the importance and urgency of the issue. This requires creating an environment that protects organizational data, such as sensitive patient information, and aligning healthcare data security programs with national policies and regulations (Sher et al., 2017; Alhuwail et al., 2021). In digitized healthcare systems, cybersecurity is essential for doctors, ensuring patient privacy and data integrity while maintaining quality healthcare.

5.3.2   How Do Cyberattacks Threaten Doctors' Safety?

As mentioned above, cyberattacks pose a dual threat to doctors, jeopardizing various aspects of their professional lives and patient care. Therefore, safeguarding healthcare cybersecurity is essential to protect doctors, their patients, and the integrity of the healthcare system. Cyberattacks can disrupt healthcare services by targeting hospital information systems, particularly EHR systems and medical devices (Martin et al., 2017; Javaid et al., 2023). To diagnose patients and prescribe treatments, doctors rely heavily on these systems. Any system disruption due to cyberattacks can impede doctors' ability to deliver timely and accurate care, potentially compromising patient safety. Moreover, cybercriminal hacking or ransomware attacks targeting healthcare facilities can lead to misdiagnoses, patient harm, and service disruptions. Doctors critically depend on precise records for informed decision-making. Thus, such incidents can cause care delays and increase stress levels (Owens, 2020; Alanazi, 2023).

5.3.3   How Do Cyberattacks Threaten Doctors' Privacy?

With cyberattacks, doctors face challenges in keeping patient confidentiality and protecting their privacy and professional integrity. Cyberattacks can result in doctors' financial and professional information being stolen. They may suffer economic losses and reputational damage from identity theft and illegal activities using this information. A compromised credential can also be used for unauthorized access to healthcare systems, leading to further cyber threats (Jiang & Bai, 2019; Looi et al., 2024). On the other hand, doctors are trusted with sensitive health information, such as medical histories, test results, and treatment plans. Cyberattacks such as data breaches can compromise the confidentiality of this information, violating patient privacy laws and regulations, resulting in legal consequences and damage to their professional reputation if they are associated with a patient data breach (Alanazi, 2023).

5.4   Staff Cybersecurity

With cyberattacks rising, healthcare professionals must be equipped to recognize and respond effectively to potential cybersecurity threats. However, many staff members lack the knowledge and tools to address cybersecurity challenges adequately. Investing in comprehensive cybersecurity training programs can help ensure staff remain vigilant and capable of protecting patient data and organizational integrity (Niki et al., 2022).

5.4.1 The Importance of Cybersecurity in Protecting Staff

The human element is one of the most significant risks in cybersecurity; thus, having a well-trained, knowledgeable staff is crucial. Healthcare staff are increasingly at the forefront of cyber threats but often lack adequate awareness and training to respond (Niki et al., 2022). This gap underscores the critical need for cybersecurity education among healthcare professionals. Investing in training ensures that staff are aware, responsible, and capable of protecting their organization from potential harm. Hence, cybersecurity training for healthcare staff is vital to teach them how to recognize phishing emails and report suspicious activities.

5.4.2 How Do Cyberattacks Threaten Staff Safety?

Given the trust patients place in the healthcare system, cybersecurity in healthcare is more than just a duty (Niki et al., 2022). The rise in cyberattacks targeting healthcare institutions highlights the significant disruptions such incidents can cause. While healthcare staff may have previously viewed cyberattacks, they often find themselves unprepared and lacking the necessary tools to address these cybersecurity challenges effectively (Boddy et al., 2017; Ghafur et al., 2019). Regular and brief training sessions keep staff informed and proactive against new evolving threats (Rajamäki et al., 2018; Javaid et al., 2023). Ensuring the safety of healthcare staff requires a comprehensive approach to cybersecurity education.

5.4.3 How Do Cyberattacks Threaten Staff Privacy?

Cybersecurity within the healthcare industry lags significantly behind other sectors. Especially home-based staff lack digital literacy, making them easy targets for cyberattacks (Furnell & Shah, 2020; Kim et al., 2020; Sardi et al., 2020). We mentioned that human error stands as the leading cause of most security incidents, such as cyberattacks due to opening a phishing email, even within organizations with robust cybersecurity measures. Research indicates a significant correlation between such errors and heavy workloads, a common occurrence among healthcare staff (Evans et al., 2019; Jalali et al., 2020). Healthcare organizations need to promote a culture of cybersecurity awareness and resilience to protect their staff's privacy.

5.4.4 System Security for Staff

System security for healthcare staff encompasses a range of embedded features and functions designed to implement robust security controls and address vulnerabilities effectively, such as utilizing models and concepts to establish security frameworks, conducting model-based evaluations to assess system security, and deploying security capabilities to protect against potential threats (Borky & Bradley, 2019). Healthcare organizations must proactively identify and address vulnerabilities, employ strategies to mitigate risks, select trusted components to enhance system security, and consider necessary mechanisms to establish and maintain the required level of system security over time, ensuring ongoing protection against potential threats (He et al., 2021).

On the other hand, healthcare organizations must engage in ongoing activities to enforce policies and procedures, detect and prevent or mitigate attacks, and maintain robust system security strategies. This includes operations security to safeguard critical resources, implementing measures for incident response to address security breaches promptly, and establishing protocols for attack prevention and response. Managing software vulnerabilities is essential to mitigate potential risks, along with effective change and configuration management to maintain system integrity (Borky & Bradley, 2019; Jalali et al., 2019). These procedures must be in place to preserve system security resilience and robustness, ensuring healthcare systems' continued functionality and security in the face of potential disruptions or attacks.

5.4.5 Security Awareness for Staff

Cybersecurity awareness is crucial to keeping healthcare staff updated on the latest cyberattacks and threats and protecting their organizations from financial, personal, and reputational damage (Hijji & Alam, 2022).

5.4.5.1 Security Awareness Training for Staff

Effective cybersecurity training programs for healthcare staff should provide basic training on cybersecurity fundamentals, covering threat awareness, risk management, data protection principles, and relevant best practices tailored to healthcare environments (Arain et al., 2019). Additionally, interactive security awareness training modules are essential to educating staff on phishing awareness, password security, social engineering techniques, and safe computing practices, empowering them to recognize and mitigate common cyber threats (Kruse et al., 2017). Customized role-based training ensures that staff understand their specific responsibilities and how to apply cybersecurity principles in their daily tasks. Compliance training is also crucial, ensuring that staff are knowledgeable about regulatory requirements such as HIPAA and GDPR (Taitsman et al., 2013; Yuan & Li, 2019). Simulated phishing exercises increase staff awareness and preparedness, while incident response training equips them with the necessary skills to detect, manage, and respond to cybersecurity incidents and breaches (Daengsi et al., 2022). Together, these elements form a comprehensive cybersecurity training program to enhance staff awareness and resilience against evolving cybersecurity threats in the healthcare sector.

5.4.5.2   Why Is it Important to Educate Staff on Cybersecurity?

By educating staff on cybersecurity, healthcare settings can safeguard sensitive patient data against cyberattacks and maintain patient privacy (Daengsi et al., 2021, 2022). Comprehensive training helps mitigate cyber risks arising from human error, reducing the likelihood of staff falling victim to phishing attacks or other cyber threats (Alhuwail et al., 2021; Hijji & Alam, 2022). It ensures compliance with regulatory requirements, avoiding costly penalties associated with non-compliance (Jaïdi et al., 2016). Additionally, well-trained staff are vital in maintaining operational continuity by effectively responding to cyber incidents and minimizing disruptions to healthcare operations and patient care (Addis & Kutar, 2018). Lastly, cybersecurity education empowers staff to actively defend against cyber threats and contribute to overall organizational cybersecurity measures (Borky & Bradley, 2019).

5.5   Chapter Summary

This chapter delves into the critical topic of personal security in healthcare, emphasizing the importance of patient, doctor, and staff cybersecurity. With the increasing threat of cyberattacks, robust measures are essential to safeguard patient data, privacy, and organizational integrity. Through vigilance, collaboration, and comprehensive training, healthcare professionals can improve their defenses against evolving cyber threats, ensuring the security of patient care in a digitalized healthcare system. In the next chapter, we look at how various components of healthcare infrastructure can be protected against cyberattacks.

After understanding all the fundamental concepts, the following questions are addressed in this chapter:

- How do cyberattacks impact patient safety, privacy, and the integrity of the healthcare system?
- What are the specific risks associated with cyberattacks targeting patients, doctors, and healthcare staff?
- How can healthcare organizations align cybersecurity programs with regulatory requirements to protect patient data?

- What measures can healthcare organizations take to foster a culture of cybersecurity awareness and resilience among their staff?
- How can healthcare organizations effectively mitigate cyber risks through comprehensive training programs?
- What are the key components of a robust cybersecurity strategy for healthcare organizations?
- How do healthcare professionals contribute to maintaining cybersecurity within their organizations?

References

Addis, M. C., and Kutar, M. (2018). *The general data protection regulation (GDPR), emerging technologies and UK organisations: Awareness, implementation and readiness.* Accessed Mar 14, 2024, from https://aisel.aisnet.org/ukais2018/29/

Alanazi, A. T. (2023). Clinicians' perspectives on healthcare cybersecurity and cyber threats. *Cureus, 15*, e47026. https://doi.org/10.7759/cureus.47026

Alhuwail, D., Al-Jafar, E., Abdulsalam, Y., & AlDuaij, S. (2021). Information security awareness and behaviors of health care professionals at public health care facilities. *Applied Clinical Informatics, 12*, 924–932. https://doi.org/10.1055/s-0041-1735527

Arain, M. A., Tarraf, R., & Ahmad, A. (2019). Assessing staff awareness and effectiveness of educational training on IT security and privacy in a large healthcare organization. *Journal of Multidisciplinary Healthcare, 12*, 73–81. https://doi.org/10.2147/JMDH.S183275

Boddy, A., Hurst, W., Mackay, M., & Rhalibi, A. E. (2017). A study into data analysis and visualization to increase the cyber-resilience of healthcare infrastructures. In *Proceedings of the 1st International Conference on Internet of Things and Machine Learning IML '17. (New York, NY, USA: Association for Computing Machinery)* (pp. 1–7). https://doi.org/10.1145/3109761.3109793

Borky, J. M., & Bradley, T. H. (2019). Protecting information with cybersecurity. In *Effective model-based systems engineering* https://doi.org/10.1007/978-3-319-95669-5_10.

Daengsi, T., Pornpongtechavanich, P., & Wuttidittachotti, P. (2022). Cybersecurity awareness enhancement: A study of the effects of age and gender of Thai employees associated with phishing attacks. *Education and Information Technologies, 27*, 4729–4752. https://doi.org/10.1007/s10639-021-10806-7

Daengsi, T., Wuttidittachotti, P., Pornpongtechavanich, P., & Utakrit, N. (2021). A comparative study of cybersecurity awareness on phishing among employees from different departments in an organization. In *2021, the 2nd International Conference on smart computing and electronic Enterprise (ICSCEE) (IEEE)* (pp. 102–106). https://doi.org/10.1109/ICSCEE50312.2021.9498208

Evans, M., He, Y., Maglaras, L., & Janicke, H. (2019). HEART-IS: A novel technique for evaluating human error-related information security incidents. *Computer Security, 80*, 74–89. https://doi.org/10.1016/j.cose.2018.09.002

Furnell, S., and Shah, J. N. (2020). Home working and cyber security–an outbreak of unpreparedness? Computer Fraud & Security 2020, 6–12. Available at: https://www.sciencedirect.com/science/article/pii/S1361372320300841?casa_token=Xz4IIZF-saBcAAAAA:gcmkhKWKzoyTcxAOZfXlcidDn9Vq95huqI3dG4Z9hXerZAPr7H5nf17lIGhA0ZnBPEeqplphps6a

Ghafur, S., Grass, E., Jennings, N. R., & Darzi, A. (2019). The challenges of cybersecurity in health care: The UK National Health Service as a case study. *Lancet Digit Health, 1*, e10–e12. https://doi.org/10.1016/S2589-7500(19)30005-6

Hall, J. L., & McGraw, D. (2014). Privacy and security risks must be identified and addressed for telehealth to succeed. *Health Affairs, 33*, 216–221. https://doi.org/10.1377/hlthaff.2013.0997

He, Y., Aliyu, A., Evans, M., & Luo, C. (2021). Health care cybersecurity challenges and solutions under the climate of COVID-19: Scoping review. *Journal of Medical Internet Research, 23*, e21747. https://doi.org/10.2196/21747

Hijji, M., & Alam, G. (2022). Cybersecurity awareness and training (CAT) framework for remote working employees. *Sensors, 22*. https://doi.org/10.3390/s22228663

Jaïdi, F., Labbene-Ayachi, F., & Bouhoula, A. (2016). Advanced techniques for deploying reliable and efficient access control: Application to E-healthcare. *Journal of Medical Systems, 40*, 262. https://doi.org/10.1007/s10916-016-0630-2

Jalali, M. S., Bruckes, M., Westmattelmann, D., & Schewe, G. (2020). Why employees (still) click on phishing links: Investigation in hospitals. *Journal of Medical Internet Research, 22*, e16775. https://doi.org/10.2196/16775

Jalali, M. S., Razak, S., Gordon, W., Perakslis, E., & Madnick, S. (2019). Health care and cybersecurity: Bibliometric analysis of the literature. *Journal of Medical Internet Research, 21*, e12644. https://doi.org/10.2196/12644

Javaid, M., Haleem, A., Singh, R. P., & Suman, R. (2023). Towards insight cybersecurity for healthcare domains: A comprehensive review of recent practices and trends. *Cyber Security and Applications, 1*, 100016. https://doi.org/10.1016/j.csa.2023.100016

Jiang, J. X., & Bai, G. (2019). Evaluation of causes of protected health information breaches. *JAMA Internal Medicine, 179*, 265–267. https://doi.org/10.1001/jamainternmed.2018.5295

Kilovaty, I. (2021). *Psychological data breach harms. https://papers.ssrn.com›sol3›papers*. https://doi.org/10.2139/ssrn.3785734.

Kim, D.-W., Choi, J.-Y., & Han, K.-H. (2020). Risk management-based security evaluation model for telemedicine systems. *BMC Medical Informatics and Decision Making, 20*, 106. https://doi.org/10.1186/s12911-020-01145-7

Kruse, C. S., Smith, B., Vanderlinden, H., & Nealand, A. (2017). Security techniques for the electronic health records. *Journal of Medical Systems, 41*, 127. https://doi.org/10.1007/s10916-017-0778-4

Looi, J. C. L., Looi, R. C. H., Maguire, P. A., Kisely, S., Bastiampillai, T., & Allison, S. (2024). Psychiatric electronic health records in the era of data breaches—What are the ramifications for patients, psychiatrists, and healthcare systems? Australas. *Psychiatry, 32*, 121–124. https://doi.org/10.1177/10398562241230816

Martin, G., Martin, P., Hankin, C., Darzi, A., & Kinross, J. (2017). Cybersecurity and healthcare: How safe are we? *BMJ, 358*, j3179. https://doi.org/10.1136/bmj.j3179

Nifakos, S., Chandramouli, K., Nikolaou, C. K., Papachristou, P., Koch, S., Panaousis, E., et al. (2021). Influence of human factors on cyber security within healthcare Organisations: A systematic review. *Sensors, 21*. https://doi.org/10.3390/s21155119

Niki, O., Brien Saira, G., Arvind, S., & Mike, D. (2022). Cyber-attacks are a permanent and substantial threat to health systems. *Education must reflect that. Digit Health, 8*, 20552076221104665. https://doi.org/10.1177/20552076221104665

Owens, B. (2020). How hospitals can protect themselves from cyber-attacks. *CMAJ, 192*, E101–E102. https://doi.org/10.1503/cmaj.1095841

Rajamäki, J., Nevmerzhitskaya, J., & Virág, C. (2018). *Cybersecurity education and training in hospitals: Proactive resilience educational framework (Prosilience EF)*. In 2018 IEEE Global Engineering Education Conference (EDUCON) (IEEE), 2042–2046. https://doi.org/10.1109/EDUCON.2018.8363488.

Rodrigues, J. J. P. C., de la Torre, I., Fernández, G., & López-Coronado, M. (2013). Analysis of the security and privacy requirements of cloud-based electronic health records systems. *Journal of Medical Internet Research, 15*, e186. https://doi.org/10.2196/jmir.2494

Sardi, A., Rizzi, A., Sorano, E., & Guerrieri, A. (2020). Cyber risk in health facilities: A systematic literature review. *Sustainability: Science, Practice and Policy, 12*, 7002. https://doi.org/10.3390/su12177002

Seh, A. H., Zarour, M., Alenezi, M., Sarkar, A. K., Agrawal, A., Kumar, R., et al. (2020). Healthcare data breaches: Insights and implications. *Healthcare (Basel), 8.* https://doi.org/10.3390/healthcare8020133

Sher, M.-L., Talley, P. C., Cheng, T.-J., & Kuo, K.-M. (2017). How can hospitals better protect the privacy of electronic medical records? Perspectives from staff members of health information management departments. *Health Information Management, 46,* 87–95. https://doi.org/10.1177/1833358316671264

Smith, T. T. (2016). *Examining data privacy breaches in healthcare.* Walden University. Accessed Sep 5, 2023, from https://scholarworks.waldenu.edu/dissertations/2623/

Taitsman, J. K., Grimm, C. M., & Agrawal, S. (2013). It is protecting patient privacy and data security. *The New England Journal of Medicine, 368,* 977–979. https://doi.org/10.1056/NEJMp1215258

Tan, S. S.-L., & Goonawardene, N. (2017). Internet health information seeking and the patient-physician relationship: A systematic review. *Journal of Medical Internet Research, 19,* e9. https://doi.org/10.2196/jmir.5729

Tariq, R. A., & Hackert, P. B. (2023). *Patient confidentiality.* StatPearls Publishing. Accessed Sep 5, 2023, from https://www.ncbi.nlm.nih.gov/books/NBK519540/

Wasserman, L., & Wasserman, Y. (2022). Hospital cybersecurity risks and gaps: Review (for the non-cyber professional). *Front Digit Health, 4,* 862221. https://doi.org/10.3389/fdgth.2022.862221

Yeo, L. H., & Banfield, J. (2022). Human factors in electronic health records cybersecurity breach: An exploratory analysis. *Perspectives in Health Information Management, 19,* 1i. Available at: https://www.ncbi.nlm.nih.gov/pubmed/35692854

Yuan, B., & Li, J. (2019). The policy effect of the general data protection regulation (GDPR) on the digital public health sector in the European Union: An empirical investigation. *International Journal of Environmental Research and Public Health, 16.* https://doi.org/10.3390/ijerph16061070

Chapter 6
Healthcare System and Infra-Security

6.1 Introduction

The convergence of digitization and globalization has revolutionized various sectors, including healthcare, by enabling rapid expansion and efficient communication through the Internet and digital methods. Digital technologies such as blockchain, cloud computing, and artificial intelligence (AI) have empowered the healthcare sector to collect, analyze, and utilize extensive patient data. However, as mentioned in the previous chapters, integrating digital technologies in healthcare has raised concerns about security and privacy. Despite efforts to protect patient data, the healthcare sector faces challenges in maintaining data security, leading to frequent data breaches (Jalali et al., 2019). As healthcare continues its digital transformation, addressing security and privacy concerns remains crucial for the integrity and reliability of digital healthcare systems.

Information and data security, as well as personal security, were discussed in the two previous chapters. A key component of today's healthcare systems is infrastructure security, or infra-security, which ensures patient data's confidentiality, integrity, and availability and builds trust among stakeholders within the healthcare industry. Setting higher cybersecurity standards than current regulations is necessary to enhance cybersecurity capabilities and reduce vulnerabilities throughout the healthcare ecosystem (Jalali & Kaiser, 2018). This chapter explores implementing various infra-security measures by healthcare systems to protect healthcare infrastructure from cyberattacks. It also addresses how these measures enhance healthcare systems' integrity by ensuring resilience and reliability in an increasingly digital world.

D. P. Sharma et al., *Understanding Cybersecurity Management in Healthcare*, Progress in IS, https://doi.org/10.1007/978-3-031-68034-2_6

6.2   Healthcare Software Security

Many software programs are used in the healthcare industry to process health-related information, making healthcare software security crucial. These programs are employed by health-conscious individuals, health professionals, patients, and family caregivers to maintain, improve, or manage health at individual or community levels. Robust security measures are essential for these software systems to protect sensitive patient data and comply with regulatory requirements. By prioritizing healthcare software security, organizations demonstrate their commitment to safeguarding patient information and promoting trust in healthcare systems.

6.2.1   The Importance of Software Security in Healthcare

Critical software vulnerabilities pose significant risks to patient safety and data integrity in healthcare, including poor management of credentials, buffer out-of-bounds errors, and hard-coded credentials, leading to unintended actions, data corruption, and improper code execution. Implementing strong security measures, including encrypted passwords and robust authentication processes, is essential to mitigate these vulnerabilities (Mejía-Granda et al., 2024). For example, users should be required to enter a unique, strong password for the first time they log in rather than hard-coding default credentials. This approach enhances security across all programming languages and operating platforms, protecting sensitive data (Barrows & Clayton, 1996; Mejía-Granda et al., 2024). Implementing recommended measures and prioritizing software security in healthcare organizations helps safeguard patient safety, maintain the integrity of healthcare systems, and ensure trust.

6.2.2   Healthcare Software Security Frameworks

Healthcare software security frameworks provide comprehensive guidelines and standards for designing, implementing, and managing secure healthcare information systems. These frameworks can help healthcare organizations establish robust security measures to protect sensitive patient data and comply with regulatory requirements. The following are some notable healthcare software security frameworks:

• *Center for Internet Security (CIS) Controls* provides organizations with prioritized actions to improve cybersecurity. Healthcare organizations can effectively leverage these controls to address common security challenges and threats and mitigate cyberattacks against modern healthcare systems and networks (Cyber attacks: In the healthcare sector, 2017).

- *Health Information Trust Alliance Common Security Framework (HITRUST CFS)*, created by security industry experts, offers a comprehensive framework that incorporates various security controls and regulatory requirements, such as HIPAA, to assess and manage healthcare information security risks effectively (Bosworth et al., 2014; Schreider et al., 2017).
- *International Organization for Standardization (ISO) 27001* is a widely recognized standard for information security management systems (ISMS), which provides a framework to protect patient data, mitigate cyber threats, and comply with regulations like GDPR and HIPAA. Information security management systems (ISMS) based on ISO 27001 are widely recognized as providing a framework for protecting patient data, addressing cyber threats, and complying with regulations like GDPR and HIPAA (ISO 27001 for the medical industry | ISMS. Online, n.d.). Organizations can build trust, enhance their security posture, and improve patient outcomes by adopting ISO 27001 (ISO 27001 for the medical industry | ISMS.Online, n.d.).
- *The National Institute of Standards and Technology (NIST) Cybersecurity Framework* provides a risk-based approach to managing cybersecurity risk. It is widely adopted in the healthcare industry (NIST General Information, Created December 24, 2008, Updated March 9, 2022).
- *The Payment Card Industry Data Security Standard (PCI DSS) sets security requirements and best practices for protecting sensitive patient data within healthcare organizations' financial sectors* (Oluomachi et al., 2024).

Adopting and implementing these software security frameworks can demonstrate healthcare organizations' commitment to safeguarding patient data and privacy.

6.3 Infra-Security in Healthcare

As mentioned earlier, healthcare infrastructure is crucial in ensuring patient data confidentiality, integrity, and availability, cultivating trust among stakeholders, and thus safeguarding healthcare systems. Enhancing cybersecurity capabilities and reducing vulnerabilities requires improving patient care, boosting staff well-being, strengthening compliance and risk management practices, and promoting equity (Jalali & Kaiser, 2018).

6.3.1 What Is Infra-Security in Healthcare?

Healthcare infra-security refers to the protection of physical and cyber threats to the various components of the healthcare infrastructure to ensure its resilience in case of attack. In current policies, data privacy is more prominent than data security, so policymakers must take comprehensive measures to ensure data security (Jalali & Kaiser, 2018). A higher level of cybersecurity should be required for hospitals than currently. Implementing these measures should not only improve cybersecurity capabilities, but resource availability throughout the entire healthcare system should also be reduced. The healthcare industry must collectively reduce cybercrime and ensure a robust and secure healthcare environment (Luxon, 2015).

6.3.2   How Does Infra-Security Work in the Healthcare System?

Infrastructure is the backbone of the healthcare system. It comprises several elements: physical space, equipment, access, information technology (IT) systems, and staff. These components ensure that patient's dignity and privacy are respected at all stages of the healthcare system (Luxon, 2015).

A fundamental objective in the healthcare industry is to raise standards of care and promote well-being for all patients, fostering a positive, high-quality healthcare experience. Healthcare professionals' welfare can be prioritized through infra-security, improving patient outcomes (Luxon, 2015; Paul et al., 2023).

6.3.3   How Do Healthcare Systems Benefit from Infra-Security?

The need for infra-security in the healthcare system can be recognized by highlighting its benefits. Here are some examples:

- *Compliance and risk management:* Complying with healthcare security requirements is essential, but compliance alone does not guarantee complete security (Jalali & Kaiser, 2018). Compliance and risk management must be prioritized beyond regulatory requirements to improve infra-security and ensure cyber resilience in healthcare systems (Humaidi & Balakrishnan, 2018).
- *Efficiency and timeliness:* Implementing reliable infra-security measures while protecting patient privacy supports efficient and timely healthcare operations. A variety of innovative approaches, such as the implementation of lightweight online algorithms, filtering out noise from signals, and employing differential privacy techniques, allow healthcare systems to provide services more efficiently, reducing wait times and improving timely access to healthcare while maintaining authentication timeliness and accuracy (Huang et al., 2019; Zhou et al., 2019).
- *Equity and accessibility:* Biases in healthcare practices increase inequities, reducing trust and healthcare access. Infra-security initiatives help address disparities in the healthcare system by reaching underserved populations, promoting health equity, and providing appropriate care regardless of social or economic background (Sieck et al., 2021; Koehle et al., 2022).
- *Improved quality of care and patient experience:* Implementing robust infra-security measures protects patient data and mitigates the risk of data breaches,

resulting in improved patient care and satisfaction. Prioritizing secure data storage ensures accurate medical decisions, which increases patients' trust in healthcare providers (Shojaei et al., 2024).
- *Staff well-being:* Promoting staff well-being through infra-security measures creates a more supportive work environment, reduces burnout rates, and enhances job satisfaction, improving patient care (Darling-Hammond et al., 2020).
- *Sustainability:* Healthcare infrastructure security demands sustainability, just as all systems do. Innovative security measures can help address challenges such as remote deployments and prolonged exposure to security risks (Ahmed et al., 2016; Salam, 2020). The sustainability of healthcare systems is based on energy efficiency requirements that reduce environmental impact, security, and privacy considerations (Frustaci et al., 2018).

6.3.4   Types of Infra-Security in Healthcare

Numerous key components of healthcare infrastructure serve as robust defenses against cyber threats. Here, we discuss these key infra-security measures (Fig. 6.1) and how they help secure healthcare systems against modern threats.

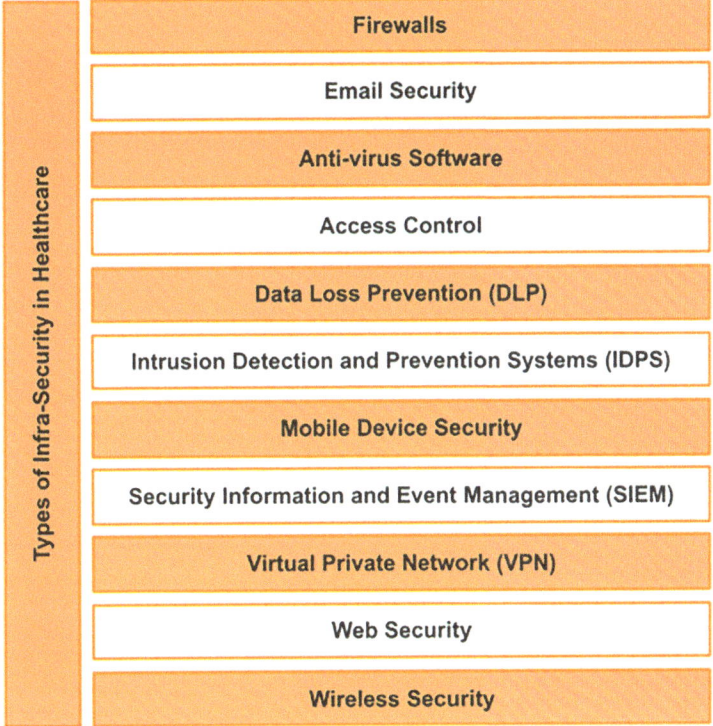

Fig. 6.1 Different types of infra-security in healthcare

6.3.4.1   Firewalls

Healthcare systems are vulnerable to reconnaissance attacks, in which attackers gather target information. As these systems are highly interconnected and information is shared constantly between hospitals, doctors, and patients, they require robust monitoring and cybersecurity protection (Somasundaram & Thirugnanam, 2021). Based on Open Systems Interconnection's (OSI) layer classification (Sobeslav et al., 2017) (Fig. 6.2), firewalls act as filters for Internal Protocol (IP) addresses, packet attributes, or connection states. They serve as the first line of defense against significant attacks in healthcare systems (Anwar et al., 2021). With the growth of intelligent healthcare environments, firewall rules must be more innovative and efficient. Effective firewall practices significantly decrease internal and external attack risks, balancing security and network performance. Based on good practices during creation or at an architectural level, structural advantages contribute to the optimal ratio of complex vulnerabilities. Here, we present various firewall types and generations to meet different requirements (Fig. 6.3). Table 6.1 compares these firewalls based on their pros and cons.

- *Traditional firewalls:* Traditional firewalls control the traffic that enters or exits from a network. Here are some examples:
  - *Packet filtering firewalls*, a primary firewall type at the network layer of the OSI model (level 3), use IP-based rules to allow or deny traffic. While effec-

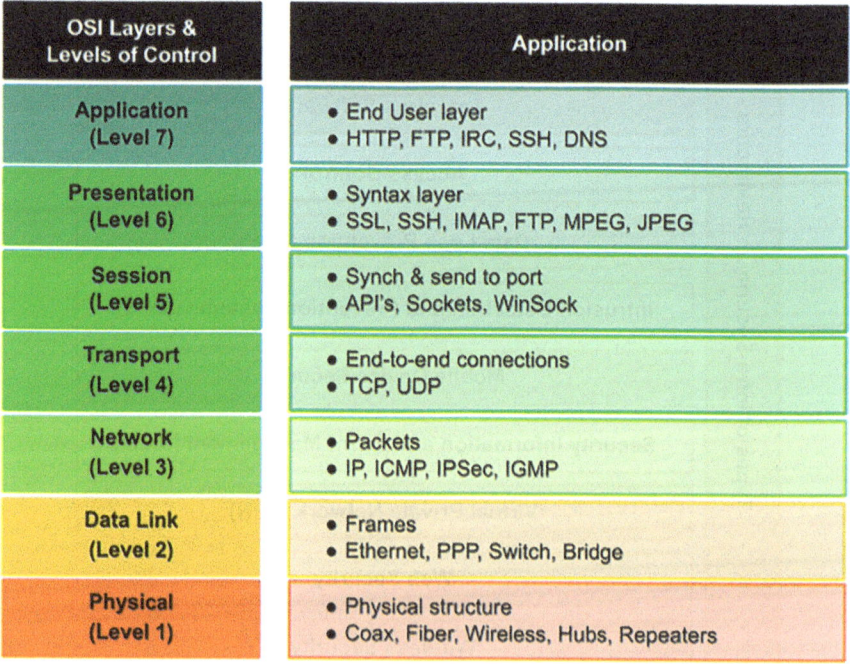

Fig. 6.2 OSI reference model, levels of control, and applications (adapted from Sobeslav et al., 2017)

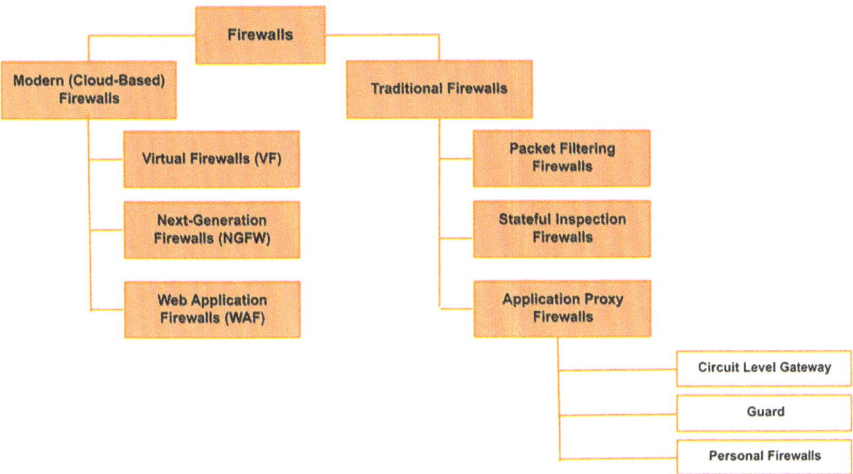

Fig. 6.3 Different categories of firewalls

tive in discarding unnecessary and potentially malicious traffic, its stateless nature poses limitations by not preserving traffic information, making it a potential target for attacks. Despite the simplicity, it's best suited for basic network rules, allowing specific hosts and denying insecure ones (Brownell, 2004; Anwar et al., 2021).

– *Stateful inspection firewalls*, functioning at the session layer of the OSI model (level 5), preserve and inspect packet information dynamically, allowing for customizable network settings and preventing attack risks. Despite efficient security, there's a trade-off with potential performance issues, highlighting the ongoing challenge of balancing security and network performance (Wadhwa & Pal, n.d.; Anwar et al., 2021).

– *Application proxy firewalls*, functioning at the application level of the OSI model (level 7), ensure security by acting as a gateway with a stateful mechanism, preventing direct packet transmission and enabling deep packet inspection. While effective for specific applications like e-commerce websites, periodic checks are necessary to address potential bottleneck risks and maintain optimal network performance (Zalenski, 2002; Anwar et al., 2021). Application proxy firewalls include the following three types:

> *Circuit-level gateways, functioning at the session layer of the OSI (level 5), offer robust protection and privacy in private networks commonly used for virtual private networks (VPNs). While suitable for specific applications, their* inability to filter individual packets may lead administrators to prefer stateful inspection firewalls for more precise control (Sharma & Parekh, 2017; Anwar et al., 2021).
> *Guard*, operating at the application level of the OSI model (level 7), is a sophisticated proxy firewall that prioritizes security over network performance. It employs advanced rules, including cryptographic measures that

Table 6.1 Pros and cons of different generations and types of firewalls

Generations	Firewalls	OSI Layer	Pros	Cons
Traditional Firewalls	Packet Filtering Firewalls	3	• Facilitate easy configuration • Exhibit efficient packet processing.	• Face challenges in protecting the entire network. • Risk potential attacks with misleading firewall configurations. • Lack the ability to filler at the application layer.
	Stateful Inspection Firewalls	5	• Manage multi-packets and maintains fewer open ports. • Efficiently handle threats and effectively blocks attacks, including DDoS attacks, with data packet memory capabilities.	• Requires a high level of configuration expertise. • Poses a risk of network issues if not regularly maintained. • Exhibits ineffectiveness in handling stateless protocols.
	Application Proxy Firewalls	7	• Employs a "proxy" network approach with a man-in-the-middle behavior. • Conducts deep packet inspection for thorough security analysis. • Translates addresses and collaborates with Network Address Translation (NAT) and IDS/IPS for a comprehensive firewall system.	• Requires advanced troubleshooting skills to avoid false positive patterns.
	Circuit Level Gateway	5	• Screens all virtual network extensions in tandem with Virtual Private Network (VPN). • Provides strong protection for private networks with good privacy rules.	• Lacks individual packet filtering capability. • Requires changes in network protocols, showing limited adaptability.
	Guard	7	• Acts like a proxy firewall with advanced rules. • Possesses cryptographic capabilities and manages data quality.	• Efficiently screens all virtual network extensions, especially when used in tandem with Virtual Private Network (VPN). • Offers strong protection for private networks with robust privacy rules.
	Personal Firewall	7	• Acts as a subnetwork defender. • Compatible with SaaS delivery models.	• Provides subnetwork defense for single or multiple hosts within the same network.

Modern (Cloud-Based) Firewalls	Virtual Firewalls (VF)	2	• Apply universally across cloud platforms. • Offer protection across a wide range of machines.	• Address implementation constraints in WAN networks using Wi-Fi devices/software-based technology. • Incur extra design charges to mitigate the risk of network exposure.
	Next-Generation Firewalls (NGF)	2-7	• Extend protection to OSI layer. • Ensure compatibility with Intrusion Detection System (IDS)/Intrusion Prevention System (IPS). • Leverage Access Control List capabilities. • Incorporate advanced threat intelligence.	• Demand excessive complexity and high investments. • Not intended for standard network environments, both cloud and non-cloud, due to certain functionalities.
	Web Application Firewalls (WAF)	2, 7	• Provide a highly specific solution against major malicious attacks at the application level with adaptive capabilities for the target layer. • Utilize encryption and SSL force mode to establish secure connections.	• Demand advanced troubleshooting skills to prevent false positive patterns.

may complicate decryption, making it suitable for systems focused solely on securing sensitive data (Anwar et al., 2021).

Personal firewalls, also functioning at the application level of the OSI model (level 7), serve as subnetwork defenders in workstations within the software-as-a-service (SaaS) cloud environments. Frequently integrated as proprietary-based software in cloud platforms, personal firewalls typically offer limited network customization capabilities (Ling-Fang, 2012).

- *Modern (cloud-based) firewalls:* These new types of firewalls are designed for cloud networks, including firewall as a service (FWaaS), typically applied to SaaS delivery models. By filtering traffic between virtual machines and network devices, they offer a cost-effective solution for intelligent healthcare environments (Anwar et al., 2021). The following are some examples:

  - *Virtual firewalls (VF):* As virtual environments are increasingly applied to enterprise network architecture, there has been a growing demand for virtual firewall devices, software that acts as a hypervisor in virtual machines (VMs) or kernel modules, rather than physical devices, which target network systems that are more oriented toward virtualization (Dezhabad & Sharifian, 2018).
  - *Next-generation firewalls (NGFW):* These firewalls gained popularity due to the rise of sophisticated applications and evolving malicious threats, addressing the adaptability limitations of traditional firewalls in recognizing diverse web activities. NGFW acts as an all-in-one security solution, enforcing network policies, implementing intrusion prevention systems, and operating autonomously across OSI layers 2 to 7, making it a robust firewall. Additional capabilities include website filtering, antivirus inspection, quality of service (QoS), and bandwidth analysis, but its complexity and high investment requirement may not be universally necessary for all organizations (Weidman, 2014).
  - *Web application firewalls (WAF):* WAF operates at the OSI model's application layer, ensuring security for web applications. In response to the growing significance of cloud networks, WAF has extended to cloud-based solutions, retaining its characteristics in an elastic, scalable, and pay-as-you-go model (IFIP Networking Conference, 2016). However, these advantages come with some risks that necessitate complex troubleshooting, and traditional firewall types, like stateful inspection firewalls, may still operate in cloud environments due to topology constraints rather than being specifically designed for targeted environments (Cheng & Day, 2014).

6.3.4.2   Email Security

Email protocols usually do not provide robust security and privacy protection, as most information is sent as clear text. Despite these vulnerabilities, email remains a predominant communication method. Email security is essential for confidentiality, integrity, and authenticity. Security gaps can be mitigated through safe practices, including identity verification, message encryption, separate transmission of decryption passwords, malware scanning, and logging in compliance with regulations (Ladouceur, 2014; Filkins et al., 2016). Here, we provide some recommendations for enhancing and maintaining email security (Filkins et al., 2016):

- Avoid clicking links, downloading files, or opening attachments from unknown senders; only open attachments when expected and from trusted sources.
- Be suspicious of emails requesting personal information, even if they seem to be from a trusted business, as phishing sites can mimic legitimate websites.
- Verify the true destination of links in emails to ensure they match the displayed information, as disparities may indicate a potential attack.
- Be cautious when receiving emails from unfamiliar senders, unsolicited offers, or responding to links asking for private information.
- Verify the legitimacy of emails by checking the sender's address, mainly if they use personal email domains.

6.3.4.3 Antivirus Software

Antivirus software is essential for healthcare network security, demanding regular updates to combat evolving cyber threats (Javaid et al., 2023). Like a firewall, its installation is critical for securing computers and sensitive medical information (Tervoort et al., 2020). Antivirus software requires automatic updates and reminders, facilitating timely maintenance. The healthcare industry is also urged to shift to advanced security solutions, replacing traditional antivirus software with advanced solutions (Javaid et al., 2023).

6.3.4.4 Access Control

Access control has a crucial role in ensuring security in healthcare infrastructures. It allows authorized access while preventing unauthorized entry. There are a variety of access control challenges in healthcare systems, from IoT-enabled hospitals to the security of patient information (Almalawi et al., 2023). The high speed of data generation is one of the factors that make IoT devices appealing to healthcare systems. The healthcare system could benefit from data encryption (Ali et al., 2022) or blockchain for storing and protecting data (Fan et al., 2020; Thilagam et al., 2022).

6.3.4.5 Data Loss Prevention (DLP)

Privacy, trust, and liability concerns arise from the potential exposure, leakage, and loss of private medical data. Data loss prevention (DLP) can help minimize inaccurate information dissemination and misuse of sensitive data that threaten the healthcare system (Al-Issa et al., 2019; Javaid et al., 2023), thereby increasing patient trust. It requires implementing measures, including encrypting data, classifying information, managing access control, maintaining physical security, establishing a comprehensive data breach plan, and conducting regular assessments, such as ethical hacking tests (Wolvaardt, 2022).

6.3.4.6   Intrusion Detection and Prevention Systems (IDPS)

Another essential infra-security measure in healthcare is intrusion detection and prevention systems (IDPS). These systems play a crucial role in early threat detection, protection against malware, compliance with security standards, and ensuring the confidentiality and integrity of patient data. Their deployment helps healthcare organizations maintain a robust security posture and instill trust in handling sensitive healthcare information (Scarfone & Mell, 2007).

Intrusion detection systems (IDS) monitor for unusual patterns or unauthorized activities and aim to determine potential attacks on a medical device. Thus, they allow immediate response by patients or practitioners, such as turning off the device (Scarfone & Mell, 2007; Tervoort et al., 2020). Detection techniques used by IDS are classified as follows by Mitchell and Chen (2014):

- *Knowledge-based:* IDS can only detect predefined signatures of known attacks.
- *Behavior-based:* IDS observes the device operation under normal behavior and triggers an alert if there is a sudden deviation from this baseline behavior. This technique has the advantage of detecting non-predefined attacks and is more sensitive to false positives than knowledge-based techniques.
- *Behavior-specification-based:* IDS relies on preconfigured behavior specifications to determine how a device should behave. Unlike behavior-based systems, they do not dynamically adapt their definition of normal behavior, which requires manual intervention for each device.

IDS responds to a security event by alerting a security operation center (SOC) and, in some cases, actively interfering with the system, transforming it into an intrusion prevention system (IPS) (Tervoort et al., 2020). IPS goes further than IDS by actively blocking threats in real time (Scarfone & Mell, 2007).

6.3.4.7   Mobile Device Security

A growing number of healthcare organizations are utilizing mobile devices to improve the usability of electronic systems, make them more accessible for practitioners, and remove the physical ties that connect them to a single location. There are, however, many significant security risks and concerns about information security, data protection, and patient safety (Kim et al., 2014; Hewitt et al., 2017; Kraushaar & Bohnet-Joschko, 2022). To increase the adoption of mobile device security mechanisms to prevent potential breaches and threats, healthcare professionals should be made aware of security issues, and appropriate organizational policies and practices must be implemented (Hewitt et al., 2017; Wani et al., 2020; Kraushaar & Bohnet-Joschko, 2022). Among the best practices are automating registration and deregistration of devices, installing secure configurations and updates remotely for bring your own devices (BYOD), managing the remote installation of enterprise applications (apps), such as antivirus and antimalware, and conducting network vulnerability scans, encrypting hospital data, securing remote connections through VPNs, tracking the location of devices, and remotely executing actions like wiping, locking, and securing devices, identifying and managing jailbroken/rooted devices and unapproved third-party apps, as well as allowlisting and blocklisting apps and devices (Wani et al., 2020; Kraushaar & Bohnet-Joschko, 2022). These functionalities collectively contribute to mobile device security in healthcare systems.

6.3.4.8 Security Information and Event Management (SIEM)

Like the other infrastructures, security information and event management (SIEM) systems play a critical role in securing healthcare infrastructures amidst evolving cybersecurity threats. As healthcare data become electronic, cloud-based, and distributed among numerous stakeholders, SIEMs provide invaluable capabilities to protect sensitive health information (González-Granadillo, et al., 2021a). The healthcare sector faces unique challenges, including the increasing digitization of diagnostics and health data. Modern security operations centers rely on such systems for collecting, storing, and correlating events (Miller et al., 2010; Bryant & Saiedian, 2020). SIEMs offer a centralized solution to monitor, detect, and respond to potential threats, ensuring the security of patient information (Cerullo et al., 2014; González-Granadillo, et al., 2021b). The use of SIEM technologies in healthcare involves monitoring absolute and relative signal strengths, comparing received signals against expected ones, and identifying anomalies in power grid infrastructures (Cerullo et al., 2014). The ability of SIEMs to collect and correlate data from various sources enables security administrators in healthcare to identify potential threats and define appropriate mitigation strategies. While healthcare infrastructure components have security features, the possibility provided by SIEMs through a unified dashboard is crucial for effectively protecting data (González-Granadillo, et al., 2021a). Thus, SIEM systems are indispensable for safeguarding healthcare infrastructures by providing real-time analysis, threat detection, and effective incident response. The ongoing development and investment in healthcare-specific SIEM solutions are crucial for adapting to the healthcare industry's dynamic nature of cybersecurity threats.

6.3.4.9 Virtual Private Network (VPN)

As remote work becomes more common in healthcare, the use of VPNs increases in accessing internal networks. However, these technologies come with security risks. VPNs have known vulnerabilities, making them targets for cybercriminals.

Healthcare systems are increasingly vulnerable to distributed denial-of-service (DDoS) attacks, and wireless connectivity complicates remote working (Offner et al., 2020). The health sector has implemented technical controls like network segmentation, multi-factor authentication, and intrusion detection systems to address cybersecurity challenges (Argaw et al., 2020). However, there's a need for more research, emphasizing innovative solutions such as the zero-trust principle and exploring technologies like blockchain for healthcare interoperability (He et al., 2021). The health sector lags in cybersecurity, necessitating the adaptation of general cybersecurity practices for healthcare.

6.3.4.10   Web Security

With healthcare increasingly relying on digital technologies for data management, telemedicine, and electronic health records (EHRs), web security is crucial to securing sensitive information. Web security encompasses a range of measures to prevent unauthorized access, data breaches, and cyberattacks targeting web-based systems (Paul et al., 2023). In the healthcare system, where patient privacy and confidentiality are paramount, web security becomes even more critical (Abouelmehdi et al., 2017). To mitigate the risk of data breaches, robust encryption protocols, access controls, and intrusion detection systems should be implemented (Kim et al., 2020). Integrating digital technologies such as cloud computing and mobile health (mHealth) applications necessitates robust web security measures to protect patient data against unauthorized access and cyber threats (Kim et al., 2020; Paul et al., 2023). However, despite efforts to enhance web security in healthcare, challenges persist. The healthcare sector faces unique cybersecurity risks due to the high value of medical data and the complex interconnectedness of healthcare systems (Coventry & Branley, 2018). Additionally, the rapid pace of digital transformation in healthcare exacerbates the challenge of ensuring web security while maintaining operational efficiency (Bereznoy, 2018).

To address these challenges, the healthcare industry must prioritize investment in web security infrastructure and employ a multi-layered approach to cybersecurity. This involves implementing technical controls and providing comprehensive training to healthcare staff to raise awareness of cybersecurity threats and best practices (Popov et al., 2022; Paul et al., 2023). By adopting a proactive strategy toward web security and integrating it as a fundamental component of healthcare infrastructure, organizations can mitigate the risk of data breaches and cyberattacks, safeguarding patient privacy and maintaining the trust of stakeholders (Abouelmehdi et al., 2017).

6.3.4.11   Wireless Security

Healthcare systems must ensure wireless security as IoT revolutionizes the sector (Dang et al., 2023). While these IoT devices offer benefits like real-time monitoring and personalized treatment, they also introduce security vulnerabilities (Li et al.,

2024). Practical measures such as encryption protocols (e.g., WPA2, WPA3), access control mechanisms (e.g., strong passwords, multi-factor authentication), and continuous monitoring are crucial to protect patient data and prevent unauthorized access (Alshammari, 2023). Anonymization techniques like de-identification and differential privacy also uphold patient privacy while allowing for meaningful data analysis (Şahin & Dogru, 2023; Vasa & Thakkar, 2023). Patients' control over their data and informed consent are essential for transparency and trust in healthcare systems. Collaboration among healthcare professionals, regulators, and researchers is vital to developing innovative solutions that address evolving security challenges in healthcare IoT environments (Alshammari, 2023).

6.4   Apps Security in Healthcare

Healthcare apps have revolutionized global health delivery by facilitating telemedicine and expanding health coverage to remote areas. However, they also pose significant privacy and security risks due to vulnerabilities and cyberattacks (Haleem et al., 2021). Despite the benefits of healthcare apps, concerns about privacy violations persist. Here, we describe some common vulnerabilities in healthcare apps, which can lead to data breaches, compromising patient confidentiality and system integrity. Managing these risks requires healthcare institutions to collaborate with developers so that data-sharing practices are transparent and users can make informed decisions about their privacy. Strong security measures, including two-factor authentication, systematic security models, and comprehensive data protection strategies, are imperative (Pool et al., 2024). Prioritizing transparency and user privacy can help keep sensitive health information protected from cyber threats, which can be achieved with healthcare apps.

6.4.1   Healthcare Apps and Data Privacy

Advanced telemedicine technologies and high-quality network services have revolutionized global health delivery. Over the past decade, healthcare apps have enhanced healthcare quality by allowing seamless medical information exchange across distant locations, reducing travel time for doctors and patients, and improving healthcare equity and accessibility (Haleem et al., 2021; Koehle et al., 2022). These apps have improved the efficiency of medical office staff by streamlining processes and expanding health coverage to rural areas where traditional healthcare is unavailable. Furthermore, for those facing financial or geographical barriers to quality healthcare, healthcare apps have emerged as valuable tools for providing preventive treatment, facilitating remote diagnosis and treatment planning, and, thus, supporting long-term health (Hajesmaeel-Gohari & Bahaadinbeigy, 2021).

6.4.2 Healthcare Apps Vulnerability and Attacks

While healthcare apps provide convenience and accessibility to medical services, they expose patient information to significant privacy and security risks due to vulnerabilities and cyberattacks. Some examples of the severity of healthcare data breaches include the theft of 78.8 million patient records from the American health insurance provider Anthem Blue Cross (Lord, 2018), the sale of Australian Medicare card information on the darknet (Elton-Pym, 2017), and another major data breach from an American healthcare provider affecting 8.9 million individuals, including personal and protected health information (Alder, 2023). Healthcare organizations are more vulnerable to data breaches than other sectors because multiple actors have access to personal health information (Gordon et al., 2017). Some of the most common vulnerabilities in healthcare apps are:

- *Client-side injection:* Client-side injection vulnerabilities in healthcare apps stem from inadequate data sanitization practices, leaving data susceptible to exploitation by attackers (Hassan et al., 2020). Injection attacks leverage poor sanitization of user input to execute unauthorized commands within the system, bypassing security measures (Majid et al., 2022). Unlike reflected and stored cross-site scripting (XSS) attacks (Nithya et al., 2015), which exploit server-side vulnerabilities, Document Object Model (DOM)-based XSS vulnerabilities arise from client-side script execution, posing challenges for detection and prevention (Rodríguez et al., 2020; Kaur et al., 2023). Tools like the Browser Exploitation Framework (BeEF) enable attackers to assess web browser security and exploit vulnerabilities present in client-side scripts (Pau et al., 2018). By establishing connections with victim browsers, attackers can compromise systems through various attack modules, underscoring the importance of robust data sanitization to mitigate these vulnerabilities in healthcare apps.
- *Improper or broken authentication:* As access to health information becomes increasingly facilitated by smart devices and patients seek care from multiple providers, ensuring the privacy and sharing of this data has become a prominent concern. The healthcare sector faces unique challenges related to authentication, interoperability, data sharing, medical record exchange, and mHealth considerations (McGhin et al., 2019). Poor implementation of authentication mechanisms in healthcare apps, utilizing transferred or used authentication keys, especially in complex authentication systems, can lead to unauthorized access to sensitive data, posing risks to patient confidentiality and system integrity, particularly in blockchain systems. Furthermore, many healthcare apps have unique requirements that still need to be addressed by existing blockchain experiments (Sahi et al., 2018; McGhin et al., 2019; Sasi et al., 2023).
- *Insecure client-server connection:* Using an unprotected connection is among healthcare apps' most common security issues. Most apps use HTTP to connect to remote servers over the Internet, which lacks security features. Public infrastructure increases the risk of redirection of observation, modification, and communication, compromising data integrity and confidentiality. Ensuring that

public servers are available is crucial, highlighting the importance of securing these connections (Müthing et al., 2019).

- *Insecure data storage:* Insufficient security solutions and incorrect encoding and file permissions may allow unauthorized access to sensitive data (Gejibo et al., 2012).

- *Insecure session handling:* The healthcare app uses cookies to store session information, just like other apps. However, attackers can use intercepted cookies to hijack sessions, potentially revealing user information that is unauthorized to them. Protecting cookies with a secure connection and implementing robust cookie schemes to mitigate these risks is essential. It is also important to avoid sending session cookies or authorization tokens over insecure connections to prevent unauthorized access. Because cookies are stored on users' devices until a session ends, their security is necessary, especially since some cookies are essential to the application's basic functions and cannot be turned off (Sivakorn et al., 2016; Müthing et al., 2017).

- *Poor binary protection:* Binary protection involves implementing security measures to safeguard the compiled form of a mobile application's source code. Healthcare apps lacking proper binary protection are vulnerable to cybercriminals who can reverse engineer the binary to access sensitive data like source code and algorithms. Insufficient binary protections leave apps susceptible to threats compromising confidentiality, integrity, and availability, underscoring the necessity for comprehensive security measures and highlighting the need for comprehensive security measures. To safeguard sensitive healthcare data and minimize cyberattack risks, robust binary protection measures are essential (Heiding et al., 2023).

- *Poor cryptography:* Since healthcare app data is stored publicly on the blockchain and is shared among all participants, encryption and access control are essential. Cryptographic systems involve encryption algorithms and keys to secure stored data. Current critical management practices face challenges. Using one key for all blocks is risky because compromising the key would expose all data, while assigning one key per block is impractical due to the high storage and recovery costs (Zhao et al., 2017). Cryptographic techniques such as digital signatures allow healthcare apps to prevent unauthorized users from accessing or intercepting confidential information. However, the limitations of IoT resources in healthcare can affect the resilience, efficiency, and effectiveness of cryptographic systems and lead to malware or other malicious attacks (Vithanwattana et al., 2016; Sasi et al., 2023).

- *Poor server-side control:* While mHealth servers generally exhibit improved security, some still have configuration problems. These issues could impact patient communication, display false information, or facilitate data transmission to malicious apps. Following developer recommendations can minimize or prevent common security issues in these apps (Müthing et al., 2019).s

- *Sensitive data exposure:* Most healthcare apps are developed with a focus on data analysis rather than data collection and storage. Therefore, data leakage, primarily through other apps installed on the device, is a common vulnerability in healthcare apps, which can expose private information to cybercriminals (Thantilage et al., 2023). Protecting patient data in healthcare apps requires robust security measures, such as two-factor authentication and systematic security models, including technical de-identification and restrictive data access, to mitigate security risks (Puppala et al., 2016).

6.4.3   Cybersecurity Risk of Healthcare Apps

While healthcare apps can serve as valuable tools to improve patient care and protect patient privacy and security by adopting robust cybersecurity measures, concerns about the privacy risks associated with these apps have been raised. Top-rated medicines-related mobile apps routinely share user data, but this practice is not transparent (Grundy et al., 2019). Several factors contribute to privacy violations in healthcare apps, such as password sharing and insecure connections (Parker et al., 2019; Pool et al., 2024). To address these risks, healthcare institutions must collaborate with business associates and conduct regular data audits to ensure compliance with regulations. Developers must disclose all data-sharing practices and allow users to choose what data to share and with whom (Grundy et al., 2019). Patients should also be informed of the potential privacy risks of apps before they are recommended, ensuring that privacy is a top priority in digital health (Pool et al., 2024). By promoting transparency and informed decision-making, healthcare apps can continue to improve patient care while protecting user privacy and security.

6.5   Chapter Summary

This chapter explored the critical importance of protecting healthcare infrastructure from cyberattacks by implementing infra-security measures. We discussed the role of different infra-security strategies in ensuring patient data confidentiality, integrity, and availability, promoting trust among stakeholders, and enhancing operational efficiency in the face of evolving cybersecurity challenges. In the following two chapters, we delve into the detection and prevention of cyberattacks in healthcare, exploring strategies and technologies to identify and mitigate cyber threats to safeguard patient data and maintain the integrity of healthcare systems.

After understanding all the fundamental concepts, the following questions are addressed in this chapter:

• What are some common vulnerabilities in healthcare apps that can lead to data breaches?
• How do client-side injection vulnerabilities pose a risk to healthcare app security, and what are some mitigation strategies?

- Why is improper authentication a concern in healthcare apps, and how can it lead to unauthorized access?
- What are the security implications of using insecure client-server connections in healthcare apps?
- How can inadequate data storage practices in healthcare apps compromise data security?
- What risks are associated with insecure session handling in healthcare apps, and how can they be mitigated?
- Why is binary protection important for healthcare apps, and what are the consequences of insufficient protection?
- How do current cryptographic practices impact the security of healthcare app data?
- What are some potential issues with server-side control in healthcare apps, and how can they be addressed?
- How can healthcare institutions promote transparency and user privacy in healthcare apps to mitigate privacy risks?

References

Abouelmehdi, K., Beni-Hssane, A., Khaloufi, H., & Saadi, M. (2017). Big data security and privacy in healthcare: A review. *Procedia Computer Science, 113*, 73–80. https://doi.org/10.1016/j.procs.2017.08.292

Ahmed, E., Yaqoob, I., Gani, A., Imran, M., & Guizani, M. (2016). Internet-of-things-based innovative environments: State of the art, taxonomy, and open research challenges. *IEEE Wireless Communications, 23*, 10–16. https://doi.org/10.1109/MWC.2016.7721736

Alder, S. (2023). Managed care of North America hacking incident impacts 8.9 million individuals. *HIPAA Journal.*

Ali, A., Pasha, M. F., Ali, J., Fang, O. H., Masud, M., Jurcut, A. D., et al. (2022). Deep learning based homomorphic secure search-able encryption for keyword search in Blockchain healthcare system: A novel approach to cryptography. *Sensors, 22.* https://doi.org/10.3390/s22020528

Al-Issa, Y., Ottom, M. A., & Tamrawi, A. (2019). eHealth cloud security challenges: A survey. *Journal of Healthcare Engineering, 2019*, 7516035. https://doi.org/10.1155/2019/7516035

Almalawi, A., Khan, A. I., Alsolami, F., Abushark, Y. B., & Alfakeeh, A. S. (2023). Managing security of healthcare data for a modern healthcare system. *Sensors, 23.* https://doi.org/10.3390/s23073612

Alshammari, H. H. (2023). The internet of things healthcare monitoring system is based on the MQTT protocol. *Alexandria Engineering Journal, 69*, 275–287. https://doi.org/10.1016/j.aej.2023.01.065

Anwar, R. W., Abdullah, T., & Pastore, F. (2021). Firewall best practices for securing smart healthcare environment: A review. *NATO Advanced Science Institutes Series E: Applied Sciences, 11*, 9183. https://doi.org/10.3390/app11199183

Argaw, S. T., Troncoso-Pastoriza, J. R., Lacey, D., Florin, M.-V., Calcavecchia, F., Anderson, D., et al. (2020). Cybersecurity of hospitals: Discussing the challenges and working towards mitigating the risks. *BMC Medical Informatics and Decision Making, 20*, 146. https://doi.org/10.1186/s12911-020-01161-7

Barrows, R. C., & Clayton, P. D. (1996). Confidentiality of electronic health data: Methods for protecting personally identifiable Information: January 1990 through march 1996: 448

selected citations. *Journal of the American Medical Informatics Association, 3*, 139. https://
doi.org/10.1136/JAMIA.1996.96236282

Bereznoy, A. (2018). Multinational business in the era of global digital REVOLUTION. *World
Economy and International Relations, 62*, 5. https://doi.org/10.20542/0131-2227-2018-62-9-5-17

Bosworth, S., Kabay, M. E., & Whyne, E. (2014). *Computer security handbook*. Wiley. Available
at: https://play.google.com/store/books/details?id=7OD7ngEACAAJ

Brownell, D. (2004). *Authenticated firewall tunneling framework*. US Patent. Accessed Dec 6, 2023,
from https://patentimages.storage.googleapis.com/6d/46/45/965971eb1777ac/US6754831.pdf

Bryant, B. D., & Saiedian, H. (2020). We are improving SIEM alert metadata aggregation with
a novel kill-chain-based classification model. *Computer Security, 94*, 101817. https://doi.
org/10.1016/j.cose.2020.101817

Cerullo, G., Formicola, V., Iamiglio, P., & Sgaglione, L. (2014). Critical infrastructure protection:
Having SIEM technology cope with network heterogeneity. *arXiv [cs.CR]*. Available at: http://
arxiv.org/abs/1404.7563

Cheng, S.-M., & Day, M.-Y. (2014, November 21–23). *Technologies and applications of artificial
intelligence: 19th International Conference, TAAI 2014 Proceedings*. Springer. Available at:
https://play.google.com/store/books/details?id=CCW7BQAAQBAJ

Coventry, L., & Branley, D. (2018). Cybersecurity in healthcare: A narrative review of trends, threats
and ways forward. *Maturitas, 113*, 48–52. https://doi.org/10.1016/j.maturitas.2018.04.008

Cyber attacks: In the healthcare sector. (2017). *Center for internet security*. Accessed Apr 23,
2024, from https://www.cisecurity.org/insights/blog/cyber-attacks-in-the-healthcare-sector

Dang, V. A., Vu Khanh, Q., Nguyen, V.-H., Nguyen, T., & Nguyen, D. C. (2023). Intelligent healthcare: Integration of emerging technologies and internet of things for humanity. *Sensors, 23*.
https://doi.org/10.3390/s23094200

Darling-Hammond, L., Flook, L., Cook-Harvey, C., Barron, B., & Osher, D. (2020). Implications
for educational practice of the science of learning and development. *Applied Developmental
Science, 24*, 97–140. https://doi.org/10.1080/10888691.2018.1537791

Dezhabad, N., & Sharifian, S. (2018). Learning-based dynamic, scalable load-balanced firewall
as a service in network function-virtualized cloud computing environments. *The Journal of
Supercomputing, 74*, 3329–3358. https://doi.org/10.1007/s11227-018-2387-5

Elton-Pym, J. (2017). *Medicare data breach is the tip of the iceberg in the world of Australian dark
web fraud*. Accessed Feb 24, 2019, from https://www.sbs.com.au/news/medicare

Fan, K., Pan, Q., Zhang, K., Bai, Y., Sun, S., Li, H., et al. (2020). A secure and verifiable data sharing scheme based on Blockchain in vehicular social networks. *IEEE Transactions on Vehicular
Technology, 69*, 5826–5835. https://doi.org/10.1109/TVT.2020.2968094

Filkins, B. L., Kim, J. Y., Roberts, B., Armstrong, W., Miller, M. A., Hultner, M. L., et al. (2016).
Privacy and security in the era of digital health: What should translational researchers know
and do about it? *American Journal of Translational Research, 8*, 1560–1580. Available at:
https://www.ncbi.nlm.nih.gov/pubmed/27186282

Frustaci, M., Pace, P., Aloi, G., & Fortino, G. (2018). Evaluating critical security issues of the IoT
world: Present and future challenges. *IEEE Internet of Things Journal, 5*, 2483–2495. https://
doi.org/10.1109/JIOT.2017.2767291

Gejibo, S., Mancini, F., Mughal, K. A., Valvik, R. A. B., & Klungsøyr, J. (2012). Secure data
storage for mobile data collection systems. In *Proceedings of the international conference
on Management of Emergent Digital EcoSystems MEDES '12* (pp. 131–144). Association for
Computing Machinery. https://doi.org/10.1145/2457276.2457300

González-Granadillo, G., Faiella, M., Medeiros, I., Azevedo, R., & González-Zarzosa, S. (2021a).
ETIP: An enriched threat intelligence platform for improving OSINT correlation, analysis,
visualization, and sharing capabilities. *Journal of Information Security and Applications, 58*,
102715. https://doi.org/10.1016/j.jisa.2020.102715

González-Granadillo, G., González-Zarzosa, S., & Diaz, R. (2021b). Security Information and
event management (SIEM): Analysis, trends, and usage in critical infrastructures. *Sensors, 21*.
https://doi.org/10.3390/s21144759

Gordon, W., Fairhall, A., & Landman, A. (2017). Threats to information security–public health implications. *The New England Journal of Medicine, 377*, 707–709. https://doi.org/10.1056/NEJMp1707212

Grundy, Q., Chiu, K., Held, F., Continella, A., Bero, L., & Holz, R. (2019). Data sharing practices of medicines related apps and the mobile ecosystem: Traffic, content, and network analysis. *BMJ, 364*, l920. https://doi.org/10.1136/bmj.l920

Hajesmaeel-Gohari, S., & Bahaadinbeigy, K. (2021). The most used questionnaires for evaluating telemedicine services. *BMC Medical Informatics and Decision Making, 21*, 36. https://doi.org/10.1186/s12911-021-01407-y

Haleem, A., Javaid, M., Singh, R. P., & Suman, R. (2021). Telemedicine for healthcare: Capabilities, features, barriers, and applications. *Sensors International, 2*, 100117. https://doi.org/10.1016/j.sintl.2021.100117

Hassan, R., Qamar, F., Hasan, M. K., Aman, A. H. M., & Ahmed, A. S. (2020). Internet of things and its applications: A comprehensive survey. *Symmetry, 12*, 1674. https://doi.org/10.3390/sym12101674

Heiding, F., Katsikeas, S., & Lagerström, R. (2023). Research communities in cyber security vulnerability assessments: A comprehensive literature review. *Computer Science Review, 48*, 100551. https://doi.org/10.1016/j.cosrev.2023.100551

Hewitt, B., Dolezel, D., & McLeod, A., Jr. (2017). Mobile device security: Perspectives of future healthcare workers. *Perspectives in Health Information Management, 14*, 1c. Available at: https://www.ncbi.nlm.nih.gov/pubmed/28566992

He, Y., Aliyu, A., Evans, M., & Luo, C. (2021). Health care cybersecurity challenges and solutions under the climate of COVID-19: Scoping review. *Journal of Medical Internet Research, 23*, e21747. https://doi.org/10.2196/21747

Huang, P., Guo, L., Li, M., & Fang, Y. (2019). Practical privacy-preserving ECG-based authentication for IoT-based healthcare. *IEEE Internet of Things Journal, 6*, 9200–9210. https://doi.org/10.1109/JIOT.2019.2929087

Humaidi, N., & Balakrishnan, V. (2018). The indirect effect of management support on users' compliance behavior towards information security policies. *Health Information Management, 47*, 17–27. https://doi.org/10.1177/1833358317700255

IFIP Networking Conference (2016). *2016 IFIP networking conference (IFIP networking) and workshops*. IEEE. Available at: https://play.google.com/store/books/details?id=fdQ-zwEACAAJ

ISO 27001 for the medical industry | ISMS.Online (n.d.). Accessed Apr 23, 2024, from https://www.isms.online/sectors/iso-27001-for-the-medical-industry/

Jalali, M. S., & Kaiser, J. P. (2018). Cybersecurity in hospitals: A systematic, organizational perspective. *Journal of Medical Internet Research, 20*, e10059. https://doi.org/10.2196/10059

Jalali, M. S., Razak, S., Gordon, W., Perakslis, E., & Madnick, S. (2019). Health care and cybersecurity: Bibliometric analysis of the literature. *Journal of Medical Internet Research, 21*, e12644. https://doi.org/10.2196/12644

Javaid, M., Haleem, A., Singh, R. P., & Suman, R. (2023). Towards insight cybersecurity for healthcare domains: A comprehensive review of recent practices and trends. *Cyber Security and Applications, 1*, 100016. https://doi.org/10.1016/j.csa.2023.100016

Kaur, J., Garg, U., & Bathla, G. (2023). Detection of cross-site scripting (XSS) attacks using machine learning techniques: A review. *Artificial Intelligence Review, 56*, 12725. https://doi.org/10.1007/s10462-023-10433-3

Kim, D.-W., Choi, J.-Y., & Han, K.-H. (2020). Medical device safety management using cybersecurity risk analysis. *IEEE Access, 8*, 115370–115382. https://doi.org/10.1109/ACCESS.2020.3003032

Kim, H.-S., Lee, K.-H., Kim, H., & Kim, J. H. (2014). Using mobile phones in healthcare management for older people. *Maturitas, 79*, 381–388. https://doi.org/10.1016/j.maturitas.2014.08.013

Koehle, H., Kronk, C., & Lee, Y. J. (2022). Digital health equity: Addressing power, usability, and trust to strengthen health systems. *Yearbook of Medical Informatics, 31*, 20–32. https://doi.org/10.1055/s-0042-1742512

Kraushaar, J., & Bohnet-Joschko, S. (2022). Smartphone use and security challenges in hospitals: A survey among resident physicians in Germany. *International Journal of Environmental Research and Public Health, 19.* https://doi.org/10.3390/ijerph192416546

Ladouceur, R. (2014). Family physicians and electronic communication. *Canadian Family Physician, 60,* 310. Available at: https://www.ncbi.nlm.nih.gov/pubmed/24733314

Li, C., Wang, J., Wang, S., & Zhang, Y. (2024). A review of IoT applications in healthcare. *Neurocomputing, 565,* 127017. https://doi.org/10.1016/j.neucom.2023.127017

Ling-Fang, H. (2012). The firewall technology study of network perimeter security. In *2012 IEEE Asia-Pacific services computing conference* (IEEE), 410–413. https://doi.org/10.1109/APSCC.2012.23.

Lord, N. (2018). Top 10 most significant healthcare data breaches of all time. *Data Insider, 25.*

Luxon, L. (2015). Infrastructure–the key to healthcare improvement. *Future Hospital Journal, 2,* 4–7. https://doi.org/10.7861/futurehosp.2-1-4

Majid, M., Habib, S., Javed, A. R., Rizwan, M., Srivastava, G., Gadekallu, T. R., et al. (2022). Applications of wireless sensor networks and internet of things frameworks in the industry Revolution 4.0: A systematic literature review. *Sensors, 22.* https://doi.org/10.3390/s22062087

McGhin, T., Choo, K.-K. R., Liu, C. Z., & He, D. (2019). Blockchain in healthcare applications: Research challenges and opportunities. *Journal of Network and Computer Applications, 135,* 62–75. https://doi.org/10.1016/j.jnca.2019.02.027

Mejía-Granda, C. M., Fernández-Alemán, J. L., Carrillo-de-Gea, J. M., & García-Berná, J. A. (2024). Security vulnerabilities in healthcare: An analysis of medical devices and software. *Medical & Biological Engineering & Computing, 62,* 257–273. https://doi.org/10.1007/s11517-023-02912-0

Miller, D. R., Harris, S., Harper, A., VanDyke, S., & Blask, C. (2010). *Security information and event management (SIEM) implementation.* McGraw Hill Professional.

Mitchell, R., & Chen, I.-R. (2014). A survey of intrusion detection techniques for cyber-physical systems. *ACM Computing Surveys, 46,* 1–29. https://doi.org/10.1145/2542049

Müthing, J., Brüngel, R., & Friedrich, C. M. (2019). Server-focused security assessment of Mobile health apps for popular Mobile platforms. *Journal of Medical Internet Research, 21,* e9818. https://doi.org/10.2196/jmir.9818

Müthing, J., Jäschke, T., & Friedrich, C. M. (2017). Client-focused security assessment of mHealth apps and recommended practices to prevent or mitigate transport security issues. *JMIR mHealth and uHealth, 5,* e147. https://doi.org/10.2196/mhealth.7791

NIST General Information (Created December 24, 2008, Updated March 9, 2022). *NIST.* Accessed Apr 20, 2024, from https://www.nist.gov/director/pao/nist-general-information

Nithya, V., Pandian, S., & Malarvizhi, C. (2015). A survey on detection and prevention of cross-site scripting attack. *International Journal of Security and Its Applications, 9,* 139–152. https://doi.org/10.14257/IJSIA.2015.9.3.14

Offner, K. L., Sitnikova, E., Joiner, K., & MacIntyre, C. R. (2020). Towards understanding cyber-security capability in Australian healthcare organizations: A systematic review of recent trends, threats, and mitigation. *Intelligence and National Security, 35,* 556–585. https://doi.org/10.1080/02684527.2020.1752459

Oluomachi, E., Ahmed, A., Ahmed, W., & Samson, E. (2024). Assessing the effectiveness of current cybersecurity regulations and policies in the US. *arXiv [cs.CR].* Available at: http://arxiv.org/abs/2404.11473

Parker, L., Halter, V., Karliychuk, T., & Grundy, Q. (2019). How private is your mental health app data? An empirical study of mental health app privacy policies and practices. *International Journal of Law and Psychiatry, 64,* 198–204. https://doi.org/10.1016/j.ijlp.2019.04.002

Pau, G., Chaudet, C., Zhao, D., & Collotta, M. (2018). Next generation wireless Technologies for the Internet of things. *Sensors, 18.* https://doi.org/10.3390/s18010221

Paul, M., Maglaras, L., Ferrag, M. A., & Almomani, I. (2023). Digitization of healthcare sector: A study on privacy and security concerns. *ICT Express, 9,* 571–588. https://doi.org/10.1016/j.icte.2023.02.007

Pool, J., Akhlaghpour, S., Fatehi, F., & Burton-Jones, A. (2024). A systematic analysis of failures in protecting personal health data: A scoping review. *International Journal of Information Management, 74*, 102719. https://doi.org/10.1016/j.ijinfomgt.2023.102719

Popov, V. V., Kudryavtseva, E. V., Kumar Katiyar, N., Shishkin, A., Stepanov, S. I., & Goel, S. (2022). Industry 4.0 and digitalisation in healthcare. *Materials, 15*, 2140. https://doi.org/10.3390/ma15062140

Puppala, M., He, T., Yu, X., Chen, S., Ogunti, R., & Wong, S. T. C. (2016). Data security and privacy management in healthcare applications and clinical data warehouse environment. In *2016 IEEE-EMBS international conference on biomedical and health informatics (BHI)* (pp. 5–8). (IEEE). https://doi.org/10.1109/BHI.2016.7455821

Rodríguez, G. E., Torres, J. G., Flores, P., & Benavides, D. E. (2020). Cross-site scripting (XSS) attacks and mitigation: A survey. *Computer Networks, 166*, 106960. https://doi.org/10.1016/j.comnet.2019.106960

Sahi, M. A., Abbas, H., Saleem, K., Yang, X., Derhab, A., Orgun, M. A., et al. (2018). Privacy preservation in e-healthcare environments: State of the art and future directions. *IEEE Access, 6*, 464–478. https://doi.org/10.1109/ACCESS.2017.2767561

Şahín, Y., & Dogru, I. (2023). *An enterprise data privacy governance model: Security-centric multi-model data anonymization.* Muhendis. Arast. Ve Gelistirme Derg. https://doi.org/10.29137/umagd.1272085

Salam, A. (2020). Internet of things for sustainability: Perspectives in privacy, cybersecurity, and future trends. In A. Salam (Ed.), *Internet of things for sustainable community development: Wireless communications, sensing, and systems* (pp. 299–327). Springer International Publishing. https://doi.org/10.1007/978-3-030-35291-2_10

Sasi, T., Lashkari, A. H., Lu, R., Xiong, P., & Iqbal, S. (2023). A comprehensive survey on IoT attacks: Taxonomy, detection mechanisms, and challenges. *Journal of Information and Intelligence.* https://doi.org/10.1016/j.jiixd.2023.12.001

Scarfone, K. A., & Mell, P. M. (2007). *Guide to intrusion detection and prevention systems.* DIANE Publishing Company, Available at: https://play.google.com/store/books/details?id=Pd-KGQAACAAJ.

Schreider, T., & SSCP, CISM, C|CISO, and ITIL Foundation. (2017). *Building effective cybersecurity programs: A security Manager's handbook.* Rothstein Publishing, Available at: https://play.google.com/store/books/details?id=R8E6DwAAQBAJ.

Sharma, R., & Parekh, C. (2017). Firewalls: A study and its classification. *IJARCS, 8*, 1979–1983. https://doi.org/10.26483/ijarcs.v8i5.3412

Shojaei, P., Vlahu-Gjorgievska, E., & Chow, Y.-W. (2024). Security and privacy of Technologies in Health Information Systems: A systematic literature review. *Computers, 13*, 41. https://doi.org/10.3390/computers13020041

Sieck, C. J., Sheon, A., Ancker, J. S., Castek, J., Callahan, B., & Siefer, A. (2021). Digital inclusion as a social determinant of health. *NPJ Digital Medicine, 4*, 52. https://doi.org/10.1038/s41746-021-00413-8

Sivakorn, S., Polakis, I., & Keromytis, A. D. (2016). The cracked cookie jar: HTTP cookie hijacking and the exposure of private Information. In *2016 IEEE symposium on security and privacy (SP)* (IEEE), 724–742. https://doi.org/10.1109/SP.2016.49.

Sobeslav, V., Balik, L., Hornig, O., Horalek, J., & Krejcar, O. (2017). Endpoint firewall for local security hardening in an academic research environment. *Journal of Intelligent Fuzzy Systems, 32*, 1475–1484. https://doi.org/10.3233/jifs-169143

Somasundaram, R., & Thirugnanam, M. (2021). Review of security challenges in healthcare internet of things. *Wireless Networks, 27*, 5503–5509. https://doi.org/10.1007/s11276-020-02340-0

Tervoort, T., De Oliveira, M. T., Pieters, W., Van Gelder, P., Olabarriaga, S. D., & Marquering, H. (2020). Solutions for mitigating cybersecurity risks caused by legacy software in medical devices: A scoping review. *IEEE Access, 8*, 84352–84361. https://doi.org/10.1109/ACCESS.2020.2984376

Thantilage, R. D., Le-Khac, N.-A., & Kechadi, M.-T. (2023). Healthcare data security and privacy in data warehouse architectures. *Informatics in Medicine Unlocked, 39*, 101270. https://doi.org/10.1016/j.imu.2023.101270

Thilagam, K., Beno, A., Lakshmi, M. V., Wilfred, C. B., George, S. M., Karthikeyan, M., et al. (2022). Secure IoT healthcare architecture with a deep learning-based access control system. *Journal of Nanomaterials, 2022*. https://doi.org/10.1155/2022/2638613

Vasa, J., & Thakkar, A. (2023). Deep learning: Differential privacy preservation in the era of big data. *Journal of Computer Information Systems, 63*, 608–631. https://doi.org/10.1080/08874417.2022.2089775

Vithanwattana, N., Mapp, G., & George, C. (2016). mHealth–investigating an Information security framework for mHealth data: Challenges and possible solutions. In *2016 12th international conference on intelligent environments (IE)* (pp. 258–261). (IEEE). https://doi.org/10.1109/IE.2016.59

Wadhwa, S., & Pal, K. (n.d.). *We provide security through VPNs by using tunneling and firewalls.* Accessed Dec 6, 2023, from https://citeseerx.ist.psu.edu/document?repid=rep1&type=pdf&doi=5faf53a501a66bcf0d7a18d347673c931f4bf0b8

Wani, T. A., Mendoza, A., & Gray, K. (2020). Hospital bring-your-own-device security challenges and solutions: Systematic review of Gray literature. *JMIR mHealth and uHealth, 8*, e18175. https://doi.org/10.2196/18175

Weidman, G. (2014). *Penetration testing: A hands-on introduction to hacking.* No Starch Press. Available at: https://play.google.com/store/books/details?id=T_LlAwAAQBAJ.

Wolvaardt, E. (2022). Data protection and privacy: An introduction. *Community Eye Health, 35*, 21. Available at: https://www.ncbi.nlm.nih.gov/pubmed/36035104

Zalenski, R. (2002). Firewall technologies. *IEEE Potentials, 21*, 24–29. https://doi.org/10.1109/45.985324

Zhao, H., Zhang, Y., Peng, Y., & Xu, R. (2017). Lightweight backup and efficient recovery scheme for health Blockchain keys. In *2017 IEEE 13th international symposium on autonomous decentralized system (ISADS)* (IEEE), 229–234. https://doi.org/10.1109/ISADS.2017.22.

Zhou, W., Jia, Y., Peng, A., Zhang, Y., & Liu, P. (2019). The effect of IoT new features on security and privacy: New threats, existing solutions, and challenges yet to be solved. *IEEE Internet of Things Journal, 6*, 1606–1616. https://doi.org/10.1109/JIOT.2018.2847733

Chapter 7
Detection and Prevention of Cyberattacks in Healthcare

7.1 Introduction

Detection and prevention of cyberattacks in healthcare are crucial to protect sensitive patient data and ensure the integrity and availability of healthcare systems and services. The healthcare industry is a prime target for cyberattacks. There are some reasons why the healthcare industry is the prime target (Bhosale, 2021).

- Private patient information is worth a lot of money to attackers.
- Medical devices are an easy entry point for attackers.
- Staff need to access data remotely, opening more opportunities for attack.
- Workers don't want to disrupt convenient working practices by introducing new technology.
- Healthcare staff aren't educated about online risks.
- The number of devices used in hospitals makes it hard to stay on top of security.
- Healthcare information needs to be open and shareable.
- Smaller healthcare organizations are also at risk.

Healthcare organizations can use advanced detection and prevention methods to identify and prevent cyberattacks. Numerous studies focus on identifying and understanding the risks associated with attacks on healthcare systems and services. Understanding cybersecurity in healthcare and applying best practices for detection and prevention is essential in minimizing financial loss, reputation, and, most importantly, patient safety risks (Ghafur et al., 2019). Vulnerabilities with medical devices and products are increasing day by day. A report shows 993 vulnerabilities within 966 medical products and devices, revealing a 59% increase from 2022. 64% of these vulnerabilities were found in software, while 16% have been weaponized (Health-ISAC, 2023). This chapter presents how to detect and prevent cyberattacks in the healthcare industry.

© The Author(s), under exclusive license to Springer Nature
Switzerland AG 2024
D. P. Sharma et al., *Understanding Cybersecurity Management in Healthcare*,
Progress in IS, https://doi.org/10.1007/978-3-031-68034-2_7

7.2   Cyberattack Phases in Healthcare

Advanced attackers used sophisticated, intelligent, and persistent attack tools and techniques (Cho, 2020). The key characteristics of these advanced attackers are as follows:

- *Persistent attackers:* These persistent, multi-stage attackers start attacking as outside attackers and continue to break into the system as inside attackers.
- *Adaptive attackers:* dynamically learn system and external environmental conditions.
- *Stealthy attackers:* do not always exhibit an identifiable attacking behavior.
- *Incentive-driven attackers:* rational and sensitive to incentives (e.g., attack success and attack cost).

In healthcare, advanced attackers can leverage more complex and nuanced attack strategies during cyberattacks. Modern advanced persistent threats or advanced attackers in computer-networked systems typically use seven phases of cyberattacks (Hutchins, 2011). The advanced attacker typically uses these seven attack phases to attack healthcare organizations. Each phase has its own set of objectives and tactics. These seven phases of cyberattacks with their goals and activities concerning the healthcare organization are presented in Fig. 7.1 and described below:

1. *Reconnaissance:* This phase involves researching, identifying, or selecting targets, often by crawling Internet websites to obtain target information, such as email addresses, social relationships, or information regarding technologies the target system uses. Attackers gather information about the target healthcare organization using various methods, such as social engineering, to collect information about the organization's systems, network architecture, and users.
2. *Weaponization:* Using an automated tool, this phase uses a remote access trojan coupled with an exploit to create a deliverable payload (e.g., Adobe Portable Document Format or Microsoft Office documents). It involves making the actual malicious payload or weapon that will be used to exploit vulnerabilities in the target healthcare system.
3. *Delivery:* In healthcare, this phase involves transmitting malicious content (weapons) or payload to the organization's targeted healthcare system. The gun is transmitted to a targeted healthcare system using delivery vectors for weaponized payload by APT actors (e.g., email attachments, websites, or USB removable media).

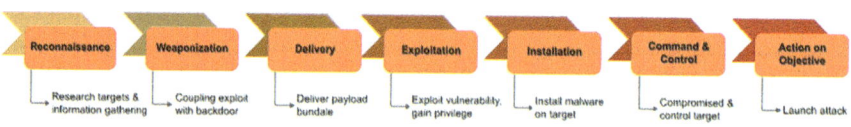

Fig. 7.1 Cyberattack phases

4. *Exploitation:* After the weapon/malicious code is delivered to a victim host, the intruders' code is triggered by exploitation, commonly targeting application or OS vulnerabilities. Successful exploitation leads to unauthorized access to sensitive patient data, disruption of healthcare services, or other serious consequences.

5. *Installation:* The attackers can stay inside the target environment (healthcare system) by installing a remote access trojan or backdoor on the target (or victim) system. This leads to unauthorized access, data exfiltration, or disruption of critical healthcare services.

6. *Command and control:* In this phase, attacked compromised hosts try to establish a communication channel by beaconing outbound to an Internet controller server. Upon establishing the communication channel, the attacker can take control of the compromised systems, exfiltrating data or issuing commands to execute specific actions.

7. *Actions on objectives:* After the previous six phases are successfully performed, attackers launch attacks to breach security goals (e.g., data integrity, availability, confidentiality) by carrying out specific actions to fulfill their goals.

Applying proactive and adaptive cybersecurity strategies can help protect sensitive patient data and maintain the integrity of healthcare services from the evolving nature of advanced cyberattacks on healthcare organizations.

7.3 Healthcare Facility Insider Threat

An insider threat in the healthcare sector is potentially a person within a healthcare organization or a contractor who has access to assets or inside information concerning the organization's security practices, data, and computer systems (HHS, 2022). There are several types of insider threats within an organization, all with different goals—for example, careless workers, malicious insiders, inside agents, disgruntled employees, and third parties. Most companies invest more money in insider threats with malicious intent. However, negligent insider threats are more common. Careless workers are unintentional insider threats that pose a significant risk to the health sector. An example is an employee leaving an unencrypted mobile device or laptop containing sensitive data unattended. The device(s) could be stolen, or data could be copied while the device is unattended. Malicious insiders have a grievance against a company and choose to act on it. The inside agent is a type of insider threat that works on behalf of an external group to compromise an organization's network and carry out a data breach or other attack. This is dangerous because it provides an outside group with the access and privileges of an insider. Disgruntled employees of healthcare organizations can be a significant threat because of their access to systems. They are considered emotional threat actors with an intent to cause harm to their healthcare organization. Insider threats are not just internal employees but can also take the form of third parties who provide elevated permissions on the healthcare systems CVSS (2023), CISA (2023) and EPSS (2023), Grance & Jansen (2011), HIPPA (2023), Ioannis Agrafiotis (2018), Luis et al. (2013), MedicalITG (2023).

The malicious insiders of the healthcare systems can perform the following potentially harmful activities (Ahmed, 2018):

- Gain access to patients' data through healthcare applications.
- Modify the healthcare applications to execute any malicious code.
- Manipulate data stored in healthcare database storage.
- Leak or delete the healthcare data storage backup.
- Perform collusion attacks.

7.4   Most Common Cyberattacks in Healthcare

7.4.1   Phishing

Phishing is a common cyberattack in healthcare systems that involves tricking individuals (patients, doctors, or staff) into revealing their sensitive information, such as login credentials or personal details. It misguides individuals or organizations into either revealing information or accomplishing an action harmful to their computer, called phishing. Phishing is more inclined toward a technique than an attack. Phishing uses emails that redirect individuals to reveal their details or stimulate the download of malicious software (Bhosale, 2021). In 2017, Kaleida Health, New York's largest provider, was attacked twice, compromising the health records of more than 3000 patients at a time (Vankamamidi & Naresh, 2020).

7.4.2   Man-in-the-Middle (MitM) Attacks

In this attack, an attacker intercepts and alters the communication between two parties (patients, doctors, healthcare providers, or other stakeholders), which can lead to the theft of sensitive patients and other related data or the injection of malicious code or content. An attacker can hijack sensitive patients or other medical information and take control of the transmitted data, for example, the theft of opioid prescriptions or the manipulation of pacemakers and other medical devices (Poremba, 2023). Attackers can explore Bluetooth and Wi-Fi channels to launch the MitM attack on hospital premises. For example, to launch the MitM attack in a Bluetooth channel, the attacker can create a proxy gateway between two mobile devices connected via Bluetooth. This allows the attacker to extract plaintext information from the network traffic and modify a packet in real time. In healthcare systems, devices often communicate using Bluetooth interfaces, and the Bluetooth discoverable option for these devices is usually turned on, making them vulnerable to this attack. The attacker, without the consent of the devices, can create a pair between two

Bluetooth-enabled devices and listen to or modify the confidential information exchanged between them. This way, the attacker can collect EMRs from patients' or doctors' malware-infected mobile devices (Hasan, 2016).

7.4.3   Attacks to Network Vulnerabilities

Bluetooth Low Energy (BLE), ZigBee, Wi-Fi, Radio Frequency (RF), and Ethernet are the communication network protocols used in healthcare communications. These networks could be vulnerable to targeted and sophisticated attacks due to improper configuration of protocol, use of obsolete proprietary protocol, and inefficient existing security solutions (Yaqoob, 2019). BLE is an appropriate approach for sensor-based medical devices due to low power consumption and is designed explicitly for connecting small sensor-based devices to portable stations. Security in BLE is present in three modes: no security, passkey, and numeric comparison, but it is still vulnerable to MITM and sniffing attacks. ZigBee is an important technology used by most sensor-based devices. It is an efficient technology that is extensively used in low-power settings. To connect the ZigBee network, each node should request the current network key using the preconfigured master key. However, such a standard is vulnerable to energy depletion attacks, DOS, replay attacks, and sniffing. Wi-Fi-, RF-, and Ethernet-connected medical devices pose different vulnerabilities and are prone to cyberattacks.

7.4.4   Ransomware Attacks

Ransomware attacks on healthcare encrypt healthcare data and demand payment for decryption. In May 2017, the WannaCry ransomware encrypted data and files on 230,000 computers in 150 countries and impaired the functionality of the National Health Service (NHS) in England (Smart, 2018). It blocked and prevented staff from accessing data and critical services Ghosh (2017).

7.4.5   Data Breaches

A data breach is an unauthorized disclosure or access to patient records, medical information, or other sensitive data stored within healthcare systems. The US Department of Health and Human Services defines a data breach as "the illegal use or disclosure of confidential health information that compromises the privacy or security of it under the privacy rule that poses a sufficient risk of financial, reputational, or another type of harm to the affected person" (Wikina, 2014). The different disclosure types that led to the data breaches are as follows (Seh, 2020):

- *Hacking incidents:* Hacking incidents comprise all cyberattacks used to gain unauthorized access to confidential data. Ransomware and malware are the main approaches used to expose protected healthcare information.
- *Unauthorized access (internal):* These include all types of attacks that lead to the exposure of confidential health data with the help of any internal source of an organization. This may be abuse of privileges, unauthenticated access/disclosure, etc.
- *Theft or loss:* This comprises all incidents that lead to the disclosure of protected healthcare information through theft or loss, such as the theft of hard disks, laptops, or any other portable device that contains protected healthcare data. This can also be because of catastrophic damage or the loss of these devices.
- *Improper disposal of unnecessary data:* Unnecessary but sensitive and confidential data should be appropriately disposed of so that it cannot later be retrieved. Improper disposal of this data can lead to the disclosure of protected health information. The inappropriate disposal attack type includes all breached incidents caused by the inappropriate disposal of unnecessary but sensitive and confidential health data.

7.4.6   DoS/DDoS Attacks

Distributed denial-of-service (DDoS) attacks on the healthcare sector disrupt the availability of critical healthcare services and compromise patient care. Distributed denial-of-service (DDoS) attacks on the healthcare sector disturb the availability of critical healthcare services and compromise patient care. This could affect access to electronic health records (EHR), telemedicine services, communication systems, and other essential services. For example, in 2014, a similar attack shut down the administration of Boston Children's Hospital, causing a lot of loss to the hospital (Bhosale, 2021; Iman Sharafaldin, 2019).

7.4.7   Network Attacks

Network attacks are malicious cyber activities or unauthorized actions in a network that aim to disrupt or destroy the normal functioning of a computer network, compromise the integrity of data, or gain unauthorized access to network resources. DoS/DDoS, phishing, packet sniffing, ARP spoofing/poisoning, etc., are common network attacks. A multi-layered security approach, including regular security audits and a continuous monitoring network, helps healthcare organizations protect against network attacks (Abdul et al. 2019; AWS 2023).

7.4.8 Wireless Attacks

Wireless attacks exploit the vulnerabilities of the wireless network connections (Wi-Fi, Bluetooth, etc.) to gain unauthorized access, intercept communications, or disrupt network services. Jamming attacks, bluejacking, Wi-Fi spoofing, etc., are common wireless attacks. Using strong encryption and keeping the software and firmware up to date helps protect a healthcare organization from wireless attacks (Suguna & Suhasini 2014).

7.4.9 Malware Attacks

Malware is "malicious software" designed to damage, exploit, or compromise computer systems, networks, or user devices (Bradfield, 2010). Malware is used to attack computer systems. Attacking using malware or malicious programs is also called software attacks. Viruses, worms, trojan horses, ransomware, etc., are typical examples of malware attacks. A healthcare organization can protect itself from malware attacks by using security measures such as antivirus and antimalware software.

7.4.10 Social Engineering Attacks

Social engineering attacks exploit human psychology and use various tactics to deceive or manipulate individuals into divulging sensitive information or performing actions that may lead to data breaches. Phishing (spear, vishing), baiting, pretexting, tailgating, etc., are common social engineering attacks in healthcare systems. Educating the staff on common phishing tactics and implementing strong authentication measures can help to reduce social engineering attacks in healthcare organizations. Several defense techniques, including machine learning (ML), can be used to prevent cyberattacks on healthcare services from social engineering attacks (Nguyen, 2022).

7.5 Detecting Cyberattacks in Healthcare

Detecting cyberattacks in healthcare involves implementing a defensive cybersecurity strategy with detection and network monitoring methods, including intrusion detection systems, network traffic monitoring, user and entity behavior analysis, vulnerability scanning, etc. IDS helps to indicate cyberattacks by monitoring network traffic and identifying unusual user behaviors. A hardware approach is also used to secure IoT-based healthcare monitoring systems (Tao, 2019). Mobile and IoT devices connected to healthcare applications have made it possible to remotely monitor patients' information and provide proper diagnostics whenever needed; however, it increases the attack surface and makes it hard to detect cyberattacks. Over the last decade, machine learning-based intrusion detection methods have been introduced to cybersecurity applications for hybrid network analysis, including misuse (intrusion) and anomaly detection. Misuse detection is used to detect known attacks using their signatures, while anomaly detection is used to identify any abnormal behavior in the network. Using ML to manage security issues in healthcare systems is the most promising technique for previously unseen zero-day attacks. It can identify attacks simply by monitoring data alteration or detecting changes in network traffic characteristics (Hady, 2020). Recently, a cognitive machine learning-assisted attack detection framework has been proposed to share healthcare data securely (Ahmad Ali AlZubi, 2021).

7.6 Preventing Cyberattacks in Healthcare

Preventive, detective, and corrective are three common security control mechanisms that are used in a healthcare organization to ensure confidentiality, integrity, and availability of patient's sensitive medical and personal data and/or services. The preventive methods for cyberattacks in the healthcare system involve a combination of strategies, tools, and practices designed to protect the systems, networks, and patient's data from unauthorized access, exploitation, and damage. Healthcare organizations can protect their system, services, and patient data by ensuring strong password policy, enabling multi-factor authentication, applying data encryptions, implementing firewalls, ensuring all medical and IT systems and applications are up to date with the latest security patches, etc. Preventing the cyberattack in healthcare involves a range of activities and measures to protect patient's sensitive personal and medical data and ensure the continuous operation of healthcare systems and services which has been shown in Fig. 7.2 (eHealthResearch 2023; Fernandes 2021; MicrosoftAzure 2023).

7.6.1 Implementing Security Awareness Training

Implementing security awareness training for staff and other healthcare system users improves the organization's overall cybersecurity posture. This includes training the healthcare staff on cybersecurity best practices and reporting suspicious activities (NIST 2012; NIST 2018a; NIST 2018b).

Fig. 7.2 Methods for preventing cyberattacks on healthcare

7.6.2   *Data Usage Control*

In the healthcare industry, data usage control refers to implementing control measures and policies to manage, monitor, and regulate patient data handling, access, and transmission. It ensures the confidentiality, integrity, and availability of sensitive healthcare-related information and prevents unauthorized access or data breaches. Access control mechanisms such as authentication and authorization are implemented to enforce data usage control and restrictions (GoogleCloud 2023).

7.6.3   Monitoring of Mobile and Connected Devices

Monitoring mobile and connected devices with the healthcare system ensures the security and privacy of sensitive patients and other data. Mobile device management (MDM) software can monitor mobile and connected devices used in healthcare systems. MDM software provides device enrollment, tracking, and location services. A healthcare organization can protect patient data and maintain a secure and compliant healthcare environment by implementing monitoring and management software tools.

7.6.4   Assessing and Implementing Security Controls

A healthcare organization can strengthen its security controls and better protect patient's data from potential cyberattacks by systematically assessing and implementing the security controls. It involves a comprehensive approach to safeguard sensitive patient data and ensure the organization's overall cybersecurity.

7.6.5   Creating a Cybersecurity Strategy

A cybersecurity strategy is a high-level plan for securing your organization's overall workspace, including computer servers, network communications, patient data, medical equipment, and services, from potential future cyberattacks. The outcome of implementing a cybersecurity strategy is to prevent, mitigate, and respond to cyberattacks.

7.6.6   Developing Cybersecurity Policies

A cybersecurity policy refers to directives designed to maintain cybersecurity (Bayuk, 2012). It codifies security goals to support constituents expected to modify their behavior in compliance with the policy to produce cybersecurity.

7.6.7   Conducting a Security Risk Assessment

A comprehensive risk assessment of a healthcare organization helps to identify and analyze potential vulnerabilities and implement effective security control measures to protect sensitive patient data and healthcare services. Risk assessment can help proactively identify and address the potential risk of cyberattacks that reduces the likelihood and impact of cyberattacks.

7.6.8   Conducting Employee Phishing Campaigns

Phishing campaigns are a proactive and effective strategy to enhance the cybersecurity posture of healthcare organizations. Conducting employee phishing campaigns involves simulating phishing attacks on employees to assess their susceptibility, educate them about phishing threats, and reduce the risk of actual phishing attacks. It educates employees about phishing attacks and tactics.

7.6.9   Installing Spam Filters and Antimalware Software

Spam filters and antimalware software are tools used to protect an organization's software systems and networks from various security threats, including malicious emails, phishing, and malware attacks. Install spam filters and antimalware software to prevent and mitigate cyberattacks on healthcare organizations.

7.7   Cyberattacks Response Procedures and Recovery Plans

NIST's official Computer Security Incident Handling Guide gives you comprehensive procedures for handling cyberattacks (Paul Cichonski, 2012). An incident response team is responsible for responding to cybersecurity incidents, such as data breaches, cyberattacks, and system failure. NIST's incident handling guide can be used to develop effective cyberattack response procedures and recovery plans for healthcare organizations to minimize the impact of incidents, protect patient data, and ensure the continuity of critical and emergency health services. NIST's guide introduced the cyber incident handling lifecycle with the four phases shown in Fig. 7.3 (Odun-Ayo 2017; Ranchal et al. 2020; S3 2023; Scarfone 2023; Schou & Hernandez 2015).

- *Preparation phase*: In this phase, the incident response team prepares for incidents, including compiling a list of IT assets such as networks, servers, and endpoints, identifying their importance, and identifying which ones are critical or hold patients' sensitive data.
- *Detection and analysis phase:* The detection phase involves collecting data from IT systems and medical equipment, security tools, publicly available information, and people inside and outside the organization, as well as identifying precursors and indicators. The analysis involves identifying a baseline or everyday

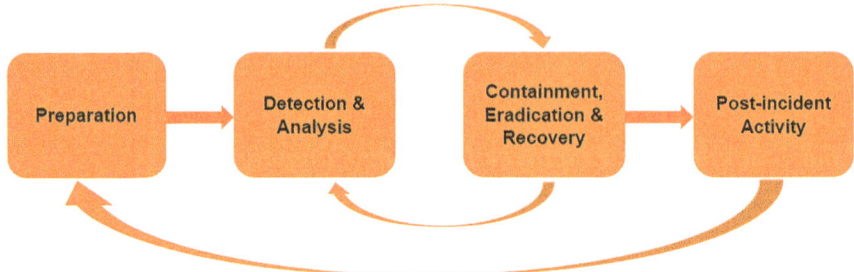

Fig. 7.3 NIST's incident response lifecycle (Paul Cichonski, 2012)

activity for the affected systems, correlating related events, and seeing if and how they deviate from normal behavior.

- *Containment eradication and recovery:* The main goal of the containment phase is to stop the attack before it overwhelms resources or causes damage. In the eradication and recovery phase, after the incident has been successfully contained, you should act to remove all elements of the incident from the environment. This might include identifying all affected hosts, removing malware, and closing or resetting passwords for breached user accounts. Once the threat is eradicated, restore systems and recover normal operations as quickly as possible, taking steps to ensure the same assets are not attacked again.
- *Post-incident activity:* Post-incident analysis is used to assess the effectiveness of the response and identify areas for improvement in the incident response plan.

Developing effective cyberattack response procedures and recovery plans can enhance healthcare organizations' resilience to cyberattacks and respond effectively to incidents when they occur (Woodward 2015; Zare 2018).

7.8 Chapter Summary

This chapter delves into the fundamental rationale behind the detection and prevention of cyberattacks in healthcare, emphasizing cyberattack kill-chain phases, cyberattacks, and detection and prevention strategies. It includes why the healthcare industry is becoming a prime target, how advanced attackers attack healthcare systems, what types of cyberattacks are possible in healthcare, and how to stay safe. It presents detection methods and discusses various prevention strategies.

After understanding the detection and prevention of cyberattack methods in healthcare, the following questions are addressed in this chapter:

- Why is the healthcare industry a prime target for cyberattacks?
- What are the characteristics of advanced attackers? Explain the typical cyberattack phases in the healthcare industry.

- Who are insider threats? What are the potential harmful activities by malicious insiders in the healthcare systems?
- What are the most common cyberattacks in the healthcare industry?
- What is data breach? What are the different disclosure types that led to the data breaches?
- What is a social engineering attack? How can you reduce social engineering attacks in healthcare organizations?
- What are the different methods that can be used to prevent cyberattacks in the healthcare system?
- What is cyberattack incident handling in healthcare? Explain NIST's cyberattacks response phases.

References

Abdul, R., Fathi, A., Meer, J. K., Salim, H., Shujing, C., Chen, S., & Xingchen, J. (2019). Survey: Cybersecurity vulnerabilities, attacks and solutions in the medical domain. *IEEE Access, 7*, 168774–168797. https://doi.org/10.1109/ACCESS.2019.2950849

Ahmad Ali AlZubi, M. A.-M. (2021). Cyber-attack detection in healthcare using cyber-physical systems and machine learning techniques. *Soft Computing, 25*, 12319–12332. https://doi.org/10.1007/s00500-021-05926-8

Ahmed, A. A. (2018). Malicious insiders attack in IoT based multi-cloud e-healthcare environment: a systematic literature review. *Multimedia Tools and Applications, 77*, 21947–21965.

AWS. (2023). *What is cloud storage?* Amazon Web Services (AWS). https://aws.amazon.com/what-is/cloud-storage/

Bayuk, J. L. (2012). *Cyber security policy guidebook.*

Bhosale, K. S. (2021). A study of cyber attacks: In the healthcare sector. In *2021 Sixth Junior Conference on Lighting (Lighting)* (pp. 1–6). IEEE. https://doi.org/10.1109/Lighting49406.2021.9598947

Bradfield, S. K. (2010). A general definition of malware. *Journal in Computer Virology*, 105–114. https://doi.org/10.1007/s11416-009-0137-1

Cho, J.-H. (2020). Toward proactive, adaptive defense: A survey on moving target defense. *IEEE Communications Surveys & Tutorials, 22*, 709–745.

CISA. (2023). M*itigation guide: Healthcare and public Health (HPH) sector.* Cybersecurity and Infrastructure Security Agency (CISA). Retrieved Nov 22, 2023, from https://www.cisa.gov/sites/default/files/2023-11/HPH-Sector-Mitigation-Guide-TLP-CLEAR_508c.pdf

CVSS. (2023). V*ulnerability metrics: Common vulnerability scoring system (CVSS).* National Vulnerability Database (NVD). https://nvd.nist.gov/vuln-metrics/cvss

eHealthResearch. (2023). D*efinition of likelihood, consequence, and risk levels.* National Center for e-Health Research: https://ehealthresearch.no/files/documents/Appendix-Definitions.pdf

EPSS. (2023). *Exploit Prediction Scoring System (EPSS).* Forum of incident response and security teams. https://www.first.org/epss/

Fernandes, L. (2021). Data security and privacy in times of pandemic. *Proceedings of the Digital Privacy and Security Conference.*

Ghafur, S., Grass, E., Jennings, N. R., & Darzi, A. (2019). The challenges of cybersecurity in health care: The UK National Health Service as a case study. *The Lancet Digital Health., 1*, e10. https://doi.org/10.1016/S2589-7500(19)30005-6

Ghosh, A. A. (2017). WannaCry: List of major companies and networks hit by ransomware around the globe. *International Business Times, 16.*

GoogleCloud. (2023). *Google cloud storage*. Storage. https://cloud.google.com/?hl=en

Grance, T., & Jansen, W. (2011). *Guidelines on security and privacy in public cloud computing*. Computer security division, National Institute of Standards and Technology, U.S. Department of Commerce. NIST Special Publication 800–144. From https://nvlpubs.nist.gov/nistpubs/Legacy/SP/nistspecialpublication800-144.pdf

Hady, A. A. (2020). Intrusion detection system for healthcare systems using medical and network data: A comparison study. *IEEE Access, 8*, 106576–106584. https://doi.org/10.1109/ACCESS.2020.3000421

Hasan, R. A. (2016). How secure is the healthcare network from insider attacks? An audit guideline for vulnerability analysis. In *IEEE 40th Annual Computer Software and Applications Conference (COMPSAC)* (pp. 417–422). IEEE. https://doi.org/10.1109/COMPSAC.2016.129

Health-ISAC. (2023). *Exploitable vulnerabilities that expose healthcare facilities surged nearly 60% since 2022, New Research Report Finds*. https://h-isac.org/2023-state-of-cybersecurity-for-medical-devices-and-healthcare-systems/

HHS. (2022). *Insider threats in healthcare*. U. S. Department of Health and Human Services. https://www.hhs.gov/sites/default/files/insider-threats-in-healthcare.pdf.

HIPPA. (2023). *Health information privacy*. U.S. Department of Health and Human Services (HHS). https://www.hhs.gov/hipaa/index.html

Hutchins, E. M. (2011). Intelligence-driven computer network defense informed by analysis of adversary campaigns and intrusion kill chains. *Leading Issues in Information Warfare & Security Research, 80*.

Iman Sharafaldin, A. H. (2019). We are developing a realistic distributed denial of service (DDoS) attack dataset and taxonomy. In *IEEE 53rd International Carnahan Conference on Security Technology*. IEEE.

Ioannis Agrafiotis, J. R. (2018). A taxonomy of cyber-harms: Defining cyber-attacks impacts and understanding how they propagate. *Journal of Cybersecurity, 4*(1). https://doi.org/10.1093/cybsec/tyy006

Luis, J., Fernández-Alemán, I. C., & Toval, A. P. (2013). Security and privacy in electronic health records: A systematic literature review. *Journal of Biomedical Informatics, 46*, 541–562.

MedicalITG. (2023). *Data backup and disaster recovery strategies for healthcare organizations*. Medical Information Technology Group: https://medicalitg.com/data-backup-and-disaster-recovery-strategies-for-healthcare-organizations/

MicrosoftAzure. (2023). *Microsoft Azure*. Azure. https://azure.microsoft.com/en-us/

Nguyen, C. A. (2022). Social engineering attacks in healthcare systems: A survey. In K. M. Choo (Ed.), *Lecture notes in networks and systems*. Springer International Publishing. https://doi.org/10.1007/978-3-030-84614-5_11

NIST. (2012). *Guide for conducting risk assessments NIST SP 800-30 rev.1*. National Institute of Standards and Technology (NIST), Computer Security Division Information Technology Laboratory. NIST. https://doi.org/10.6028/NIST.SP.800-30r1.

NIST. (2018a). *Cybersecurity framework V1.1*. NIST. NIST Cybersecurity Framework. https://www.nist.gov/cyberframework/framework

NIST. (2018b). *Risk management framework for information systems and organizations: A system life cycle approach for security and privacy*. NIST. NIST SP 800-37 rev. 2. https://doi.org/10.6028/NIST.SP.800-37r2.

Odun-Ayo, I. A. (2017). An overview of data storage in cloud computing. In *2017 International Conference on Next Generation Computing and Information Systems (ICNGCIS)* (pp. 29–34). IEEE. https://doi.org/10.1109/ICNGCIS.2017.9

Paul Cichonski, A. T. (2012). *Computer security incident handling guide, NIST SP 800-61 rev. 2*. NIST. https://doi.org/10.6028/NIST.SP.800-61r2.

Poremba, S. (2023). *Verizon*. How to prevent man-in-the-middle attacks in healthcare. Retrieved Nov 18, 2023, from https://www.verizon.com/business/resources/articles/s/how-to-prevent-man-in-the-middle-attacks-in-healthcare/

Ranchal, R., Bastide, P., Wang, X., Gkoulalas-Divanis, A., Mehra, M., Bakthavachalam, S. A., & Mohindra, A. (2020). Disrupting healthcare silos: Addressing data volume, velocity and variety with a cloud-native healthcare data ingestion service. *IEEE Journal of Biomedical and Health Informatics, 24*(11), 3182–3188. https://doi.org/10.1109/JBHI.2020.3001518

S3. (2023). *Amazon S3*. Amazon: https://aws.amazon.com/s3/

Scarfone, K. (2023). *TechTarget*. How to develop a cybersecurity strategy: Step-by-step guide. Retrieved Sep 12, 2023, from https://www.techtarget.com/searchsecurity/tip/How-to-develop-a-cybersecurity-strategy-Step-by-step-guide

Schou, C., & Hernandez, S. (2015). *Strategies, information assurance handbook: Effective computer security and risk management*. McGraw-Hill Education.

Seh, A. H. (2020). Healthcare data breaches: Insights and implications. *Healthcare, 8*. https://doi.org/10.3390/healthcare8020133

Smart, W. (2018). *Lessons learned review of the WannaCry ransomware cyber-attack* (pp. 10–1038). Department of Health and Social Care.

Suguna, S., & Suhasini, A. (2014). Overview of data backup and disaster recovery in the cloud. In *International Conference on Information Communication and Embedded Systems (ICICES2014)* (pp. 1–7). IEEE. https://doi.org/10.1109/ICICES.2014.7033804

Tao, H. A. (2019). Secured data collection with hardware-based ciphers for IoT-based healthcare. *IEEE Internet of Things Journal, 6*, 410. https://doi.org/10.1109/JIOT.2018.2854714

Vankamamidi, S., & Naresh, S. S. (2020). Internet of things in healthcare: Architecture applications challenges and solution. *Computer Systems Science and Engineering, 6*, 411–421.

Wikina, S. B. (2014). What caused the breach? An examination of the use of information technology and health data breaches. *Perspectives in Health Information Management, 11*.

Woodward, P. A. (2015). Cybersecurity vulnerabilities in medical devices: a complex environment and multifaceted problem. *Medical Devices: Evidence and Research*, 305–316. https://doi.org/10.2147/MDER.S50048

Yaqoob, T. (2019). Security vulnerabilities, attacks, countermeasures, and regulations of networked medical devices—A review. *IEEE Communications Surveys & Tutorials, 21*(4), 3723–3768. https://doi.org/10.1109/COMST.2019.2914094

Zare, H. M. (2018). Cybersecurity vulnerabilities assessment (a systematic review approach). In *Information Technology-New Generations: 15th International Conference on Information Technology*. Springer International Publishing.

Chapter 8
Cybersecurity Risk Analysis, Assessment, and Mitigation

8.1 Introduction

Cybersecurity risk analysis identifies, assesses, and prioritizes potential cyber threats, vulnerabilities, risks, and their impact on information confidentiality, integrity, and availability. The main goal of cybersecurity risk analysis is to develop strategies for managing and mitigating those risks effectively. A healthcare organization can better protect patient data, ensure the integrity of medical services, and contribute to overall patient safety by adopting a proactive and comprehensive approach to cybersecurity risk analysis, assessment, and mitigation strategies. This chapter presents an organizational approach for analyzing cybersecurity risks, assessment, and mitigation strategies in the healthcare industry (Bradfield 2010; Cho 2020; Fernandes 2021; Ghafur et al. 2019).

8.2 Vulnerability and Threat

Vulnerability is a weakness in an information system, system security procedures, internal controls, or implementation that a threat source could exploit (Hutchins 2011; Iman Sharafaldin 2019; Bhosale 2021). Software (operating systems or application programs) can have vulnerabilities. NIST defines vulnerability as "a flaw or weakness in system security procedures, design, implementation, or internal controls that could be exercised (accidentally triggered or intentionally exploited) and result in a security breach or a violation of the system's security policy" (NIST, Guide for Conducting Risk Assessments NIST SP 800–30 Rev.1, 2012). Vulnerabilities can be grouped into two general categories: technical and non-technical.

- *Non-technical* vulnerabilities include ineffective or non-existent policies, procedures, standards, or guidelines.

D. P. Sharma et al., *Understanding Cybersecurity Management in Healthcare*, Progress in IS, https://doi.org/10.1007/978-3-031-68034-2_8

- *Technical* vulnerabilities include holes, flaws, or weaknesses in developing information systems or incorrectly implemented and configured information systems. (NIST 2012; NIST 2018a; NIST 2018b)

A threat is any circumstance or event that has the potential to adversely impact organizational operations (including mission, functions, image, or reputation), organizational assets, individuals, or organizations through an information system through unauthorized access, destruction, disclosure, or modification of information, and denial of service (NIST, Guide for Conducting Risk Assessments NIST SP 800–30 Rev.1, 2012). The intent and method are targeted at intentionally exploiting a vulnerability or a situation and method that may accidentally exploit a vulnerability. Several types of threats may occur within an information system or operating environment. Threats may be grouped into general categories such as natural, human, and environmental. Examples of common threats in each of these general categories include:

- *Natural threats* such as floods, earthquakes, fires, and landslides.
- *Human threats* are enabled or caused by humans, including intentional or unintentional, for example, network or host-based attacks, malicious software uploads, unauthorized access to healthcare information, inadvertent data entry or deletion, and inaccurate data entry actions.
- *Environmental threats* are external factors such as power failures, pollution, chemicals, and liquid leakage.

8.2.1 Definition of Cybersecurity Vulnerability

A cybersecurity vulnerability is a flaw in a computer system, local network, communication network, software application, or any other information technology infrastructure (network and hardware) attackers could exploit to compromise the confidentiality, integrity, or availability of data or services. Cybersecurity vulnerabilities can come from various sources, including software programming errors, misconfigurations, usage of outdated software, insecure network connectivity, and software or system design flaws. Penetration testing, program code reviews, security audits, and regular and timely software updates can help to identify and mitigate the risk of exploitation and enhance the overall security posture of systems (Vankamamidi & Naresh 2020; Wikina 2014).

Analysis of the vulnerabilities of an organization includes the physical and infrastructure of an organization, software, networks, policies, and information system vulnerabilities. The most common vulnerabilities are buffer overflow, operating environment, resource exhaustion, race conditions, standardization of canonical form, violation of trust, injection attacks, cross-site scripting, non-secure cryptography storage, and failure to restrict URL access (Zare, 2018). A web service is quite common in interfacing medical devices, providing a graphical interface to configure or interact with a device. The weakness of using such an interface is that web services commonly contain vulnerabilities readily exploitable by attackers. Database servers support the structured query language (SQL) if the servers are not configured correctly to sanitize input data, which is highly vulnerable to SQL injection attacks. An SQL injection is a severe attack, as it degrades all three of the goals of information security (confidentiality, integrity, and availability). The attacker can delete all information in the database, rendering it unavailable. They can read all the info, breach confidentiality, and inject false data, which is a loss of data integrity. Application software used in IoT devices can also have vulnerabilities. In addition, the usage of medical devices can make the healthcare system more vulnerable (Woodward, 2015):

- Attackers can have vital medical device information, such as certification agencies' publication of device verification information, such as spectrum and radio frequency transmission data, published in device manuals.
- Using legacy operating systems and software and lack of timely software updates and patches.
- Lack of basic security features with medical devices.
- Using unencrypted web services to access healthcare systems.
- Use of compromised medical devices in another department of the healthcare organization network.
- Lack of awareness of cybersecurity issues and poor security practices in device development and certification.
- Limited power and resources of medical devices mean that encryption can slow down medical devices and reduce the usable battery life.

8.2.2 Types of Cybersecurity Vulnerabilities in Healthcare

Various cybersecurity vulnerabilities can lead to significant risks to the confidentiality, integrity, and availability of healthcare information, critical services, and infrastructure in the healthcare industry (Health-ISAC 2023; HHS 2022). Cyberattacks in the healthcare sector have resulted in significant losses since medical information is essential to human health. Each of the components of the healthcare system (databases, computers, IoT devices, and network connectivity) can have a vulnerability (Abdul et al., 2019). The various types of cybersecurity vulnerabilities in the healthcare system and their association are shown in Fig. 8.1 and described below.

- *Information storage:* It causes vulnerability in the medical domain when storing data in the database. The information storage is quantified and can be used to explore the patient's information. Since the information storage process is not entirely safe due to the ensured storage of information on the cloud, it breaks patient privacy and security. The attacker can crack the password and access the patient's sensitive information. In addition, the weaker authentication methods for medical devices, particularly sensor nodes, are paramount security concerns.
- *IoT connection:* IoT connection can pose many vulnerabilities because the medical staff and patients use IoT devices to access healthcare data and services. For

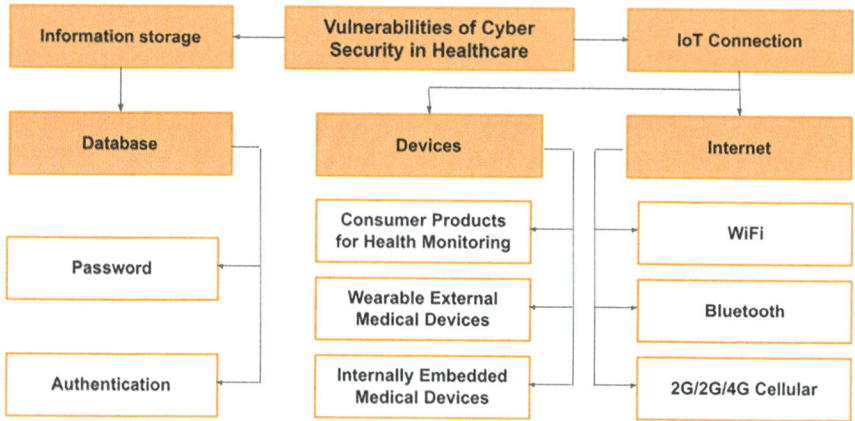

Fig. 8.1 Types of cybersecurity vulnerabilities in healthcare systems (Abdul et al., 2019)

example, IoT connection security depends on carriers such as Wi-Fi, Bluetooth, cellular technology, and the Internet, which can have many security flaws. The exchange of delicate and sensitive medical information is shared in IoT networks, as information exchange should be based on stable connections, but practically, it is impossible. As a result, data leakage and loss of such significant information occur.

In the healthcare system, vulnerabilities, whether accidentally triggered or intentionally exploited, could potentially result in a cybersecurity attack incident, for example, unauthorized access to the healthcare system or disclosure of healthcare information (Luis et al. 2013; Nguyen 2022). CISA identified and reported the top common vulnerabilities exposed in the healthcare and public health (HPH) sector in 2022, which are as follows (CISA, 2023):

- Web application vulnerability
- Encryption weaknesses
- Unsupported software
- Unsupported Windows operating systems (OS)
- Known exploited vulnerabilities (KEVs)
- Vulnerable services

Figure 8.2 shows the top vulnerabilities exposed volume by the HPH sector in 2022. The web application vulnerabilities and encryption weaknesses mainly occurred in comparison to others, such as unsupported software, unsupported Windows operating systems (OS), known exploited vulnerabilities (KEVs), and vulnerable services. Exposure to these vulnerabilities results from cyberattacks on healthcare systems, such as ransomware, data breaches, and denial of service. These can compromise the availability of healthcare services, patient privacy (confidentiality), and integrity of critical healthcare functions, services, and data.

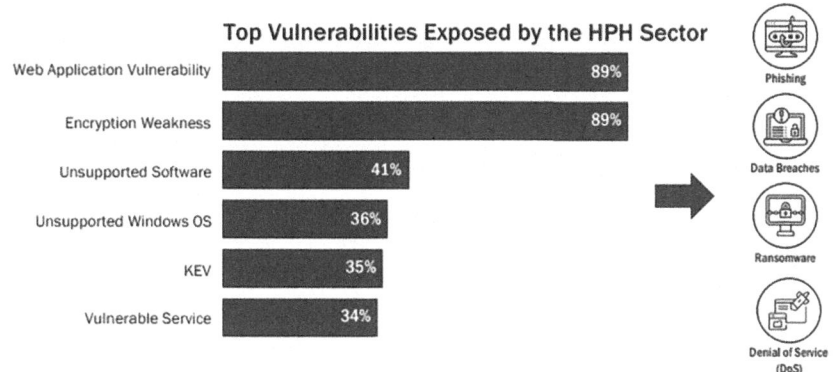

Fig. 8.2 Key vulnerabilities and threats to healthcare and public health (CISA, 2023)

8.2.3 Healthcare Cybersecurity Vulnerabilities Assessment

A vulnerability assessment is a systematic examination of an information system or product to determine the adequacy of security measures, identify security deficiencies, provide data to predict the effectiveness of proposed security measures, and confirm adequacy after implementation. A vulnerability scanner conducts credentialed and uncredentialed scans of network-accessible systems, identifies open ports and services running on those scanned systems, and looks for any known vulnerabilities when configured correctly. Once vulnerabilities are identified across your environment, evaluate and prioritize appropriately dealing with the risks according to your organization's risk strategy and policy (CISA, 2023). Assets of the healthcare organization, such as medical devices, server computers, operating systems, network connections, software, and services, can be assessed for vulnerability assessment. For prioritization, you can use the following steps and methods:

- Map your assets to business-critical functions by prioritizing assets that are most critical for ongoing operations or which, if affected, could impact your organization's business.
- Use threat intelligence information by prioritizing vulnerabilities actively exploited by threat actors. To assist, leverage CISA's KEV Catalog and other threat intelligence feeds.
- Leverage prioritization methodologies, ratings, and scores by using the Common Vulnerability Scoring System (CVSS) (CVSS, 2023) to assess the technical severity of vulnerabilities. Similarly, Exploit Prediction Scoring System (EPSS) (EPSS, 2023) can measure the likelihood of exploitation and help decide which vulnerabilities to prioritize.

8.3   Risk Analysis

Risk analysis is an ongoing process that should provide the organization with a detailed understanding of the risks to the confidentiality, integrity, and availability of healthcare services. A risk is the likelihood of a given threat triggering or exploiting a particular vulnerability and the resulting impact on the organization. This means that risk is not a single factor or event. Still, it is a combination of factors or events (threats and vulnerabilities) that, if they occur, may harm the organization—an effect of uncertainty on or within information and technology. Cybersecurity risks relate to the loss of confidentiality, integrity, or availability of information, data, or information (or control) systems and reflect the potential adverse impacts on organizational operations (i.e., mission, functions, image, or reputation) and assets, individuals, other organizations, and the Nation (NIST, Guide for Conducting Risk Assessments NIST SP 800–30 Rev.1, 2012). Cybersecurity risk is calculated by considering the identified security threats, the likelihood of exploitation of vulnerabilities, and information value, and these factors are related as follows:

Cybersecurity risk = Threat x Vulnerability x Information Value

In the healthcare system context, threats can be insiders who already have access to the healthcare system or outsider attackers who attempt to gain unauthorized access to patient records or disrupt medical services. The attackers attempt to gain access to a healthcare system, databases, or services to steal patients' and other sensitive data on or disrupt medical services. Vulnerabilities include outdated software, insecure network connections and configurations, or inadequate access controls deployment, for example, an unpatched and outdated medical imaging software system with known security vulnerabilities that a malware attack could exploit. Information value refers to how medical software systems handle essential or sensitive data. For example, patient records, medical histories, and treatment plans are susceptible and valued information (Ahmad Ali AlZubi 2021; Ahmed 2018; Bayuk 2012).

In healthcare, cybersecurity risk analysis involves identifying, assessing, and managing potential risks to the confidentiality, integrity, and availability of patient information and healthcare services. Healthcare organization risk can be analyzed and evaluated using NIST's cyber risk assessment framework (NIST, Risk Management Framework for Information Systems and Organizations: A System Life Cycle Approach for Security and Privacy, 2018a, 2018b). According to NIST, cyber risk assessments are used to identify, estimate, and prioritize risk to organizational operations, organizational assets, individuals, other organizations, and the Nation, resulting from the operation and use of information systems. The NIST's cybersecurity risk assessment process is concerned with answering the following questions:

- What are our organization's most crucial information technology assets?
- What are the potential cybersecurity threats (attacks) that mainly impact the business?

- What is the level (high/medium/low) of the potential impact of each identified threat?
- What are the vulnerabilities of the systems?
- What is the impact (high/medium/low) if those vulnerabilities are exploited?
- What is the likelihood (probability) of exploitation?

8.3.1   Sources of Risk

There are various sources of cybersecurity attack risks in the healthcare system. Here are some familiar sources of cybersecurity risks in healthcare:

- *Outdated software is a critical source of risk:* Older software used in healthcare systems may have unpatched vulnerabilities, which can lead to cyber threats.
- *Insider threats:* Employees, contractors, or other insiders may pose a risk by intentionally or unintentionally causing security incidents.
- *Supply chain vulnerabilities:* Healthcare organizations may be at risk when third-party vendors or suppliers have security weaknesses or vulnerabilities.
- *Unsecured IoT devices:* Wearable medical devices and other Internet of Things (IoT) devices used in healthcare can introduce security threats.

8.3.2   Consequences of Risk

Cybersecurity risks can have serious consequences or impacts on any organization, including healthcare. They can impact patient safety, data privacy, reputation, and the overall operations of healthcare systems. Figure 8.3 shows five risk consequences that harm organizations (Ioannis Agrafiotis, 2018):

- Physical or digital consequences cause physical or digital assets such as software, data, hardware, services, network, and network infrastructure. Some of the expected physical/digital consequences are as follows:
  - *Assets damaged or unavailable*—an asset that has been physically or digitally affected to the point where it is not available to fulfill its intended purpose.
  - *Destroyed*—an asset has been physically or digitally ruined or destroyed.
  - *Theft*—an asset has been physically or digitally stolen.
  - *Compromised*—an asset has been physically or digitally affected or compromised.
  - *Infected*—an asset has been physically or digitally contaminated.
  - *Exposed or leaked*—an asset has been physically or digitally disclosed.
  - *Corrupted*—an asset has been physically or digitally debased or its integrity affected.

Fig. 8.3 Risk consequences

- – *Reduced performance*—an asset's ability to function is lowered or inconsistent.
- – *Identity theft*—The theft of personal identity information (e.g., patients' records and doctor's records)
- Economic or financial consequences cause a financial loss, including disruption of the operations, reduced profit and growth, loss of finances or capital, compensation payments, and extortion payments.
- Psychological consequences are the harms caused to individuals and their mental well-being. These consequences mainly disrupt people (shareholders) and other organization stakeholders. They cause confusion, discomfort, frustration, shame, etc.
- Reputational consequences damage public perception and adversely affect how the public regards the organization. It also reduces corporate goodwill, damaging customer relationships, relationships with suppliers, and many more.
- Social and societal consequences are harms that may result in a social context or society more broadly. They can negatively change public perception—an adverse change in how society regards the organization.

The consequences can be described in four levels based on their impact on the organization. The four levels of implications and their definition are presented in

Table 8.1 (eHealthResearch, 2023). These consequences are described for the patient (user) and the service or healthcare organizations (service providers).

8.3.3 Risk Likelihood

Likelihood is the probability that a risk will occur. A cybersecurity risk likelihood is the probability that a given threat can exploit a given vulnerability. It is determined based on threats and vulnerabilities' discoverability, exploitability, and reproducibility. The likelihood levels can be described as frequency values or how easy it is for an attacker to exploit a threat. Risk likelihood can be divided into the following four levels, and each level's definition is presented in Table 8.2 (eHealthResearch, 2023; Yaqoob 2019; Tao 2019):

The risk value for each threat is calculated as the product of the consequence and likelihood, and it can be divided into three different levels: low, medium, and high (eHealthResearch, 2023). These three levels are defined in Table 8.3.

An organization should assign risk levels for all threat and vulnerability combinations identified during the risk analysis. For example, it might analyze the values assigned to the likelihood of threat occurrence and the resulting impact of threat occurrence. The risk level determination might be performed by assigning a risk

Table 8.1 Four levels of consequence

Levels	Consequences
Low	• **For the patient:** There will be no significant impact on health, negligible economic loss that can be restored/recovered, or a slight reduction in reputation • **For a healthcare organization**: No violation of law; or negligible/shallow economic loss which can be restored or recovered; or slight reduction of reputation in the short run
Moderate	• **For the patient:** There is no direct impact on health or a minor temporary impact; an economic loss that can be restored; or a slight reputation reduction caused by revealing less severe information (e.g., blood pressure level) • **For a healthcare organization**: Offense is a less severe violation of law that results in a warning or a command; economic loss can be restored; or a reduction of reputation that may influence trust and respect
Severe	• **For the patient:** Reduced health; a sizeable economic loss that cannot be restored; or severe loss of reputation caused by revealing sensitive and offending information • **For a healthcare organization**: Violating the law results in a minor penalty or fine, a sizeable economic loss that cannot be restored, or a severe loss of reputation that will influence trust and respect for a long time
Catastrophic	• **For the patient:** Death or permanent reduction of health; considerable economic loss which cannot be restored; or severe loss of reputation which permanently influences life, health, and economy • **For a healthcare organization:** Serious violation of law, which results in penalty or fine; considerable economic loss, which cannot be restored; or severe loss of reputation, which is devastating for trust and respect

Table 8.2 Levels of risk likelihood

Likelihood	Frequency	Ease of misuse and motivation
Very high	It occurs more often than every tenth connection, i.e., more frequently than 10% of the time/cases	It can be done without any knowledge about the system, without any additional equipment being used, or it can be performed by wrong or careless usage
High	Quite often. Occurs between 1% and 10% of the time/cases	It can be done with minor knowledge about the system or without any additional equipment being used, or it can be performed by wrong or careless usage
Moderate	May happen. Occurs between 0.1% and 1% of the time/cases	Average knowledge about the system is sufficient, or commonly available equipment can be used or performed deliberately
Low	Rarely. Occurs less than 0.1% of the time/cases	Detailed knowledge about the system or special equipment is needed, or it can only be performed deliberately and with the help of internal personnel

Table 8.3 Risk levels

Risk level	Definition
Low	This is an acceptable risk where the service can be used with the identified threats, but the threats must be observed to discover changes that could increase the risk level
Medium	The risk can be acceptable for this service. Still, for each threat, the development of the risk must be monitored regularly, with the following consideration: whether necessary measures have to be implemented
High	This is not an acceptable risk. With this risk, we cannot use the service before implementing risk-reducing treatment

level based on the average of the assigned likelihood and impact levels. The risk analysis process should be ongoing (NIST, Risk Management Framework for Information Systems and Organizations: A System Life Cycle Approach for Security and Privacy, 2018a, 2018b).

8.4   Designing and Implementing a Mitigation Strategy

Designing and implementing a mitigation strategy involves selecting the risk mitigation strategies, identifying and assessing potential risks and vulnerabilities, prioritizing risks, and developing the mitigation measures. Risks should be prioritized based on their severity and possible impact on your organization.

8.4.1 Types of Risk Response Strategies

Risk avoidance, acceptance, transfer, and mitigation are the most common risk response strategies. Figure 8.4 shows the four different types of risk response strategies.

- *Risk avoidance* strategy involves avoiding activities or situations that could result in risks. It prevents or eliminates exposure to potential hazards.
- *Risk acceptance strategy:* A risk acceptance strategy allows businesses or individuals to focus on their core competencies and strategic goals rather than potential risks. An organization acknowledges the risks but decides not to take any specific action, either because the potential impact is low or because mitigation measures are impractical or too costly. Acceptance involves taking no action to fix the effect of an exploited vulnerability.
- *Risk transfer strategy:* This strategy involves shifting or sharing the impact of a risk to another party. It affects one party assuming the liabilities of another party. This often occurs through insurance or outsourcing. For example, purchasing insurance is a typical example of transferring risk from an individual or organization to an insurance company.

Fig. 8.4 Risk response strategies

• *Risk mitigation* strategy involves using different methods to assess or measure risks, reducing the impact and likelihood of identified risks.

8.4.2   Steps of Risk Mitigation

Cybersecurity risk mitigation involves minimizing the impact and likelihood of potential cyberattacks and vulnerabilities. Figure 8.5 shows the five risk mitigation steps such as identify, access, treat, monitor, and report. Each step is discussed as follows:

• *Identify:* In this step, we identify the potential risks that could affect your organization. In the context of healthcare organizations, the possible risks related to patient safety, data security, and compliance with regulations are identified.
• *Assess:* It assesses the likelihood and impact of the identified risks. Prioritize the risks based on the implications for healthcare services, patient data, and overall healthcare operations.
• *Treat:* Risk treatment is an action to mitigate or manage the risk. Different strategies (e.g., avoidance, acceptance, reduction, and transfer) can be used in treating and managing the risk. Mitigation measures are taken into action (implemented) to reduce the risk.

Fig. 8.5 Risk mitigation steps

- *Monitor:* It is a risk monitoring step where we continuously monitor the effectiveness of the implemented mitigation measures. It includes a regular review of the risk landscape to identify new risks. It determines whether the treatment actions adopted worked correctly and accurately.
- *Report:* In this step, a risk report is prepared and submitted to the organization's senior management. A risk report summarizes potential risks, including the latest status of treatment actions and indications of trends in risk incidence.

8.4.3 Risk Management and the Cybersecurity Framework

NIST developed a cybersecurity framework (NIST CSF) that can be used to manage an organization's cybersecurity risks. It is a risk-based framework that has the following five functions (NIST, Cybersecurity Framework V1.1, 2018a, 2018b). Figure 8.6 shows the five functions of NIST's cybersecurity framework. The five functions of NIST CSF are:

- *Identify:* Develop an organizational understanding to manage cybersecurity risk to systems, assets, data, and capabilities. The activities involved in this function are as follows:

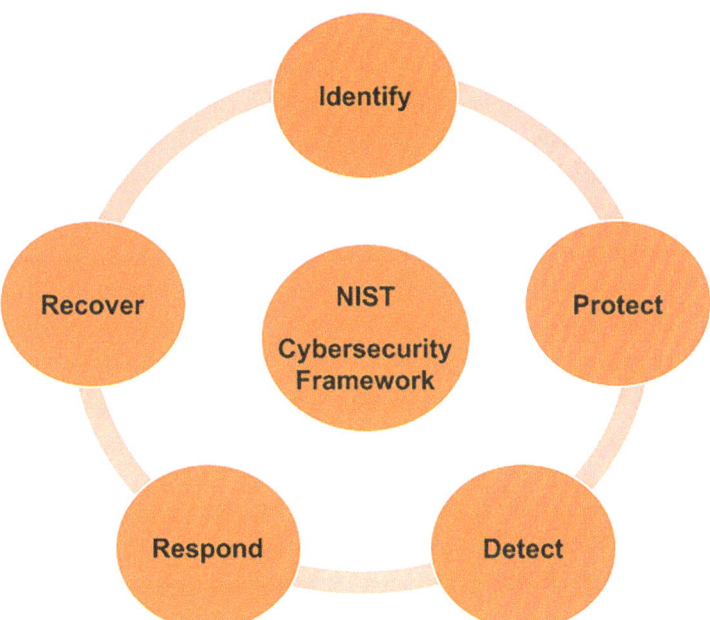

Fig. 8.6 NIST's cybersecurity risk assessment framework (NIST, Cybersecurity Framework V1.1, 2018a, 2018b)

  - Identify critical enterprise processes and assets

- Document information flow
- Maintain hardware and software inventory
- Establish cybersecurity policies that include roles and responsibilities
- Identify threats, vulnerabilities, and risks to assets

• *Protect:* Develop and implement the appropriate safeguard to ensure delivery of services. The protection function includes:

- Managing access to assets and information
- Protecting sensitive data
- Conducting regular backups
- Protecting devices
- Managing device vulnerabilities
- Training the users

• *Detect:* Develop and implement the appropriate activities to identify the occurrence of a cybersecurity event. The everyday activities in this detect function are:
• Test and update detection processes
• Maintain and monitor logs
• Know the expected data flows for your organization
• Understand the impact of cybersecurity events
• *Respond:* Develop and implement the appropriate activities to take action regarding a detected cybersecurity event. The everyday activities of this function are:
• Ensure response plans are tested
• Ensure response plans are updated
• Coordinate with internal and external stakeholders
• *Recover:* Develop and implement the appropriate activities to maintain resilience plans and restore any capabilities or services impaired due to a cybersecurity event. The everyday activities of this function are:
• Communicate with internal and external stakeholders
• Ensure recovery plans are updated
• Manage public relations and company reputation

8.5   Backing up and Recovery Plan

8.5.1   What Is Data Backup?

Data backup creates copies of data separately from the source for restoration or recovery. The primary purpose of data backup is to protect against data loss caused by various factors such as hardware failure, software problems, cyberattacks, human errors, or natural disasters. Choosing the correct method or technology is crucial to ensure that service recovery is smooth, simple, and cost-effective (Schou & Hernandez, 2015). And can consider the following factors to determine the right solution for the organization:

- *Criticality of data backing up all data can be costly:* An organization should consider the criticality of data for backup. A selected range should be determined by evaluating the allowable downtime for specific services. The organization must prioritize mission-critical information because this information can cause severe financial and reputation damage. When defining requirements for backup, do not ignore less critical services; in these cases, consider a less expensive, perhaps slower, backup approach.
- *Data size:* An organization should consider the volume of data to be backed up. This requirement should include the total data growth projection for 3 to 5 years. These requirements will ensure that the implemented solutions remain adequate.
- *Databases:* Databases are more crucial and require special attention since they may require high data volume equipment. Selecting the correct backup for such services is critical; maintaining integrity requires a highly accurate database backup system. Insufficient data backup capacity may cause the loss of precious information. Determine whether the database requires online backup solutions, which provide real-time backup, especially for mission-critical information.
- *Operating systems:* Determining the operating system is essential because some backup solutions may support multiple platforms, but some do not. Defining operating systems helps an organization choose a solution that caters to specific needs.
- *Timeframe:* An organization should determine the allowable timeframe to perform backups. Some organizations that provide 24/7/365 services will have a low tolerance for performance impact. During the backup process, an organization should anticipate a certain level of service degradation. Services that are not tolerant of degradation use different backup methods, and such services can consider high availability (HA) redundancy solutions and perform offline backup.

A backup infrastructure is a system designed to manage data backup that ensures the data's availability and recoverability. There is a wide range of backup infrastructure, from inexpensive to expensive solutions. Budget is a significant constraint in choosing a solution. Some of the standard backup infrastructure approaches are as follows:

- *Local area network-based tape backup:* This classic approach is set up by attaching tape media to the central backup and allowing backups via a LAN.
- *Network-attached storage (NAS)-based backup:* A collection of hard drives is attached to the network. It uses the LAN as the transmission medium; however, unlike LAN-based tape backup, NAS generally provides faster read and write speeds than tape media.
- *Storage area network (SAN)-based backup:* SANs can provide high data storage with a full range of data transmission capabilities. SAN is like NAS in network connectivity; however, SAN-based backup uses Fibre Channel and high-throughput technologies to transmit data from servers, which is appropriate for high-volume servers such as databases and file storage systems.
- *Cloud-based backup:* Cloud backup providers offer a variety of methods to back up information, including application programming interfaces and private

VLANs for fast WAN transmissions. Cloud providers may charge by the month for data storage and bandwidth consumed for backups and restoration. Cloud-based backup can be a data backup strategy for healthcare organizations that must keep their data available to end-users (patients, physicians, suppliers, etc.) during any cyber incident. The organizations need to have the reactionary capability to switch over to their recovery solution as quickly as possible. When a healthcare system is hit by cyberattacks (e.g., ransomware attacks, DDoS) or any incidents, the data are affected and become unavailable (Ghosh 2017; Grance & Jansen 2011; Hady 2020; Hasan 2016).

8.5.2   Importance of Data Backup and Recovery in Healthcare

Healthcare organizations rely heavily on digital data for patient information, including treatment, diagnoses, personal information, and other administrative processes. However, this dependence on digital data and technology also risks data loss and system failures. To mitigate these risks, healthcare organizations must implement robust data backup and disaster recovery strategies (MedicalITG, 2023). Data backup and recovery ensures healthcare data and critical services are protected and fully recoverable in the event of a cyberattack, system failure, or natural disaster. It is crucial to comply with HIPAA regulations (HIPPA, 2023), including patient data protection, business continuity, legal and compliance obligations, and cost savings.

- *Patient data protection:* Healthcare organizations handle sensitive patient information, including medical records, personal details, financial data, and other healthcare information. Data backup and disaster recovery ensure this information's confidentiality, integrity, and availability, protecting patients' privacy and complying with regulatory requirements such as HIPAA (HIPPA, 2023).
- *Prevention from ransomware attacks:* Healthcare organizations are often targeted by various cyberattacks, including ransomware attacks, in which malicious actors encrypt data and demand payment for its release. Regularly updated and secure backups help recover and restore data without paying a ransom.
- *Business continuity:* Cyberattacks and other incidents disrupt healthcare services. System downtime can have severe consequences for healthcare organizations, including delayed patient care, revenue loss, and damage to reputation. Implementing robust backup and recovery solutions minimizes downtime and allows organizations to recover quickly from system failures or data breaches.
- *Legal and compliance obligations:* Healthcare organizations have legal and regulatory obligations to safeguard patient data. Data backup and disaster recovery strategies help organizations meet these obligations and mitigate the risk of penalties or legal consequences resulting from data breaches or non-compliance.
- *Cost savings:* Data backup and disaster recovery also reduce the cost of recovering data in case of system failure, cyberattacks, or other disruptions. With a reliable and proper backup solution, organizations can quickly restore operations and avoid losses associated with downtime or data breaches.

8.5.3   Backup and Data Recovery Strategies

The data backup and recovery strategies define how organizations copy data, choose storage, and create robust backup and recovery methods that minimize the impact of data loss and support business continuity.

- *Copies of data:* An organization can deploy full, incremental, or differential backup solutions. Three standard backup solutions are as follows:

  - *Full backup:* It involves copying the entire system regardless of whether it is a file, system, or database.
  - *Incremental backup:* It involves copying only current changes to the system.
  - *Differential backup:* A cumulative backup copies files with all changes from the last full backup.
  - *Mirror backup:* It is stored in a non-compressed format that mirrors all the data and files and can be accessed like the original data.

- *Different types of storage (different devices):* An organization can use different backup storage media types to store data in different ways. This depends on the medium and protocols, including object, block, or file-based storage. Some standard backup storage media are:

  - *Optical disc Blu-ray/CD-RW/DVD-RW:* These optical disc devices are used for the backup media and are suitable for simple data backup.
  - *Hard drives:* Allocating additional hard drives for backup purposes can be considered another method of backup strategy. These external drives include hard disk drives (HDDs) and SSDs.
  - *Redundant mirror:* Hard drives can be configured to mirror one another.
  - *Tape media:* Tape media is a highly used backup method. Tape storage involves physical tapes that store digital data.
  - *Virtual tape library (VTL):* A VTL is a device comprised of a disk or array of disks that mimic a tape library. Virtual NAS, disk arrays, and the like can be used in backup situations.
  - *Data center:* A data center is a physical location or site offering one or more storage types.

- *Offsite backup (cloud-based data storage):* Offsite backup involves storing backup copies of data in a location physically separate from the on-premises network infrastructure (primary location). This separation ensures that data remain accessible even if the on-premises infrastructure experiences physical damage, system failure, cyberattacks, or other disasters. Cloud-based data storage services are utilized to store information. Cloud computing makes massive storage available for data and databases, and storing data on the cloud is one of its core activities. Cloud storage utilizes infrastructure spread across several geographical locations and uses the Internet, virtualization, encryption, and other technologies to ensure data security (Odun-Ayo, 2017). Cloud storage is a cloud computing model that enables data and files to be stored online through a cloud computing provider (CSP) that you access through the public Internet or a dedicated private network connection (AWS, 2023). Google Cloud storage (GoogleCloud, 2023), Microsoft Azure (MicrosoftAzure, 2023), Amazon's S3 (S3, 2023), etc., are the popular cloud storage CSP (Scarfone 2023; Seh 2020; Smart 2018).

8.5.4 Cloud-Based Data Recovery

Cloud-based data recovery involves recovering lost, deleted, or corrupted data from backup copies stored in cloud-based systems. These methods utilize cloud computing resources and ensure the availability and accessibility of data in case of cyberattacks (e.g., ransomware), data loss, or disasters. Cloud disaster recovery (CDR) is a strategy for storing and maintaining copies of data in a cloud-based environment as a security measure (e.g., data loss or services). It is a common disaster that disrupts healthcare system operations.

- *Natural disasters:* These are failures/disasters caused by earthquakes, floods, and hurricanes that can cause severe damage to physical infrastructure, including data centers, leading to data loss and service unavailability.
- *Cyberattacks:* These are due to cyberattack incidents (e.g., ransomware or DDoS) that disrupt healthcare operations/services and compromise sensitive data/services.
- *Hardware failures are* caused by aging infrastructure or manufacturing defects, which can lead to unexpected downtime and data loss.
- *Software* failures are due to software bugs or errors that lead to data corruption, loss, or unavailability.
- *Human errors* are accidental deletions or data modifications that can cause significant operational disruptions.
- *Network* failures can prevent access to critical applications, services, and data, impeding business operations (Paul Cichonski 2012; Poremba 2023).

A key concept in a disaster recovery plan (DRP) is the physical separation of the primary data sites and backup storage sites. When a process/transaction is switched from the failed primary to the backup site, it is called failover, and returning to the primary site is called failback. Switching is made to address the primary switch's causes, termed a failback. The following backup situations can be used based on how switching is linked at the primary site. (Suguna & Suhasini, 2014):

- *Cold standby* requires hardware, operating system, and application installation. This recovery can take multiple days.
- *Hot standby*: A second data center must provide availability within seconds or minutes. A hot site can take over processing while the leading site is down. A complete copy of the primary process may sometimes exist in the backup, with no need to install either the OS or the application.

- *Warm standby:* A trade-off between a hot and a cold site. The terms "hot" and "warm" are sometimes defined differently.

For the recovery, it is essential to consider two key measures: recovery time (RTO) and recovery point objective (RPO). These two measures are described below:

- *RTO:* It is a duration in which business functions are unavailable and must be repaired (includes time before a disaster is declared and time to perform tasks). RTO depends on the tasks needed to restore the transaction handling capabilities on the backup server.
- *RPO:* It is the duration between two successive backups and, thus, the maximum amount of data that can be lost when restoration is successful. Historically, the maximum value has been 24 h. If the backup is a synchronous mirrored system, RPO is effectively zero.

Recently, a cloud-native Healthcare Data Ingestion (HDI) service was proposed that provides organizations with a standard, interoperable, secure, compliant solution to acquire, store, consolidate, and use healthcare data in the cloud (Ranchal et al., 2020). It offers backup and disaster recovery to support failover and system recovery target times for data availability during disasters.

8.6   Chapter Summary

This chapter delves into cybersecurity risk analysis, assessment, and mitigation strategies in healthcare, emphasizing vulnerabilities, threats, risks, impact, risk consequences, risk levels, and cybersecurity framework with core five functions that can be used to manage the cybersecurity risk in the healthcare organization. It includes protecting healthcare data, including risk response strategies, risk mitigation steps, data backup, and recovery plans.

After understanding cybersecurity risk analysis, assessment, and mitigation methods/strategies in the healthcare industry, the following questions are addressed in this chapter:

- What do you mean by vulnerabilities and threats?
- What are the sources of cybersecurity vulnerabilities in healthcare systems?
- How does the usage of IoT devices and other medical devices make the healthcare system more vulnerable?
- What are the cybersecurity vulnerabilities and threats in healthcare systems? Explain their types.
- What is vulnerability assessment? How do you prioritize the assets for vulnerability assessment in healthcare organizations?
- What is risk analysis and what are the factors related to cybersecurity risks?
- How does NIST's risk analysis framework help in risk assessment in healthcare organizations?
- What are different sources of risks in healthcare?

- What are the risk consequences? What are four levels of risk consequences?
- What are risk mitigation strategies in the healthcare industry?
- What is data backup? Why is data backup and recovery important in healthcare?
- What is a disaster recovery plan (DRP)? What are two key measures in data recovery?
- What are the methods of data backup and data recovery strategies that are commonly used in the healthcare system?
- How is a cloud-based data recovery strategy used in healthcare data backup and recovery?

References

Abdul, R., Fathi, A., Meer, J. K., Salim, H., Shujing, C., Chen, S., & Xingchen, J. (2019). Survey: Cybersecurity Vulnerabilities, Attacks and Solutions in the Medical Domain. *IEEE Access, 7*, 168774–168797. https://doi.org/10.1109/ACCESS.2019.2950849

Ahmad Ali AlZubi, M. A.-M. (2021). Cyber-attack detection in healthcare using cyber-physical systems and machine learning techniques. *Soft Computing*, 12319–12332. https://doi.org/10.1007/s00500-021-05926-8

Ahmed, A. A. (2018). Malicious insiders attack in IoT based multi-cloud e-healthcare environment: A systematic literature review. *Multimedia Tools and Applications, 77*, 21947–21965.

AWS. (2023). *What is cloud storage?* Amazon Web Services (AWS). https://aws.amazon.com/what-is/cloud-storage/

Bayuk, J. L. (2012). *Cyber security policy guidebook.*

Bhosale, K. S. (2021). *A study of cyber attacks: In the healthcare sector. 2021 Sixth Junior Conference on Lighting (Lighting)* (pp. 1–6). IEEE. https://doi.org/10.1109/Lighting49406.2021.9598947

Bradfield, S. K. (2010). A general definition of malware. *Journal in Computer Virology*, 105–114. https://doi.org/10.1007/s11416-009-0137-1

Cho, J.-H. (2020). Toward proactive, adaptive defense: A survey on moving target defense. *IEEE Communications Surveys & Tutorials*, 709–745.

CISA. (2023). *Mitigation guide: Healthcare and public health (HPH) Sector.* Cybersecurity and Infrastructure Security Agency (CISA). Retrieved Nov 22, 2023, from https://www.cisa.gov/sites/default/files/2023-11/HPH-Sector-Mitigation-Guide-TLP-CLEAR_508c.pdf

CVSS. (2023). *Vulnerability metrics: Common vulnerability scoring system (CVSS).* National Vulnerability Database (NVD). https://nvd.nist.gov/vuln-metrics/cvss

eHealthResearch. (2023). *Definition of likelihood, consequence, and risk levels.* National Center for e-Health Research. https://ehealthresearch.no/files/documents/Appendix-Definitions.pdf

EPSS. (2023). *Exploit prediction scoring system (EPSS).* Forum of Incident Response and Security Teams. https://www.first.org/epss/

Fernandes, L. (2021). Data security and privacy in times of pandemic. *Proceedings of the Privacy and Security Conference.*

Ghafur, S., Grass, E., Jennings, N. R., & Darzi, A. (2019). The challenges of cybersecurity in health care: the UK National Health Service as a case study. *The Lancet Digital Health.* https://doi.org/10.1016/S2589-7500(19)30005-6

Ghosh, A. A. (2017). WannaCry: List of major companies and networks hit by ransomware around the globe. *International Business Times, 16.*

GoogleCloud. (2023). *Google cloud storage.* Storage. https://cloud.google.com/?hl=en

Grance, T., & Jansen, W. (2011). *Guidelines on security and privacy in public cloud computing.* Computer Security Division, National Institute of Standards and Technology, U.S. Department of Commerce. NIST Special Publication 800-144. https://nvlpubs.nist.gov/nistpubs/Legacy/SP/nistspecialpublication800-144.pdf

Hady, A. A. (2020). Intrusion detection system for healthcare systems using medical and network data: A comparison study. *IEEE Access, 8*, 106576–106584. https://doi.org/10.1109/ACCESS.2020.3000421

Hasan, R. A. (2016). How secure is the healthcare network from insider attacks? An audit guideline for vulnerability analysis. In *IEEE 40th Annual Computer Software and Applications Conference (COMPSAC)* (pp. 417–422). IEEE. https://doi.org/10.1109/COMPSAC.2016.129

Health-ISAC. (2023). *Exploitable vulnerabilities that expose healthcare facilities surged nearly 60% SINCE 2022, new research report finds.* https://h-isac.org/2023-state-of-cybersecurity-for-medical-devices-and-healthcare-systems/

HHS. (2022). *Insider threats in healthcare.* From U. S. Department of Health and Human Services. https://www.hhs.gov/sites/default/files/insider-threats-in-healthcare.pdf

HIPPA. (2023). *Health information privacy.* From the U.S. Department of Health and Human Services (HHS). https://www.hhs.gov/hipaa/index.html

Hutchins, E. M. (2011). Intelligence-driven computer network defense informed by analysis of adversary campaigns and intrusion kill chains. *Leading Issues in Information Warfare & Security Research, 80.*

Iman Sharafaldin, A. H. (2019). We are developing a realistic distributed denial of service (DDoS) attack dataset and taxonomy. In *IEEE 53rd International Carnahan Conference on Security Technology.* IEEE.

Ioannis Agrafiotis, J. R. (2018). A taxonomy of cyber-harms: Defining cyber-attacks impacts and understanding how they propagate. *Journal of Cybersecurity, 4*(1). https://doi.org/10.1093/cybsec/tyy006

Luis, J., Fernández-Alemán, I. C., & Toval, A. P. (2013). Security and privacy in electronic health records: A systematic literature review. *Journal of Biomedical Informatics, 46*, 541–562.

MedicalITG. (2023). *Data backup and disaster recovery strategies for healthcare organizations.* From medical information technology group. https://medicalitg.com/data-backup-and-disaster-recovery-strategies-for-healthcare-organizations/

Microsoft. (2023). *Microsoft azure.* Azure: https://azure.microsoft.com/en-us/

Nguyen, C. (2022). Social engineering attacks in healthcare systems: A survey. In K. M. Choo (Ed.), *Lecture notes in networks and systems.* Springer International Publishing. https://doi.org/10.1007/978-3-030-84614-5_11

NIST. (2012). *Guide for conducting risk assessments NIST SP 800-30 Rev.1.* National Institute of Standards and Technology (NIST), Computer Security Division Information Technology Laboratory. NIST. https://doi.org/10.6028/NIST.SP.800-30r1

NIST. (2018a). *Cybersecurity framework V1.1.* NIST. NIST Framework. https://www.nist.gov/cyberframework/framework

NIST. (2018b). *Risk management framework for information systems and organizations: A system life cycle approach for security and privacy.* NIST. NIST SP 800-37 Rev. 2. https://doi.org/10.6028/NIST.SP.800-37r2

Odun-Ayo, I. (2017). An overview of data storage in cloud computing. In *2017 International Conference on Next Generation Computing and Information Systems (ICNGCIS)* (pp. 29–34). IEEE. https://doi.org/10.1109/ICNGCIS.2017.9

Paul Cichonski, A. T. (2012). *Computer security incident handling guide, NIST SP 800-61 Rev. 2.* NIST. https://doi.org/10.6028/NIST.SP.800-61r2

Poremba, S. (2023). *Verizon.* How to prevent man-in-the-middle attacks in healthcare. Retrieved Nov 18, 2023, from https://www.verizon.com/business/resources/articles/s/how-to-prevent-man-in-the-middle-attacks-in-healthcare/

Ranchal, R., Bastide, P., Wang, X., Gkoulalas-Divanis, A., Mehra, M., Bakthavachalam, S. A., & Mohindra, A. (2020). Disrupting healthcare silos: Addressing data volume, velocity and variety with a cloud-native healthcare data ingestion service. *IEEE Journal of Biomedical and Health Informatics, 24*(11), 3182–3188. https://doi.org/10.1109/JBHI.2020.3001518

S3. (2023). *Amazon S3*. Amazon: https://aws.amazon.com/s3/

Scarfone, K. (2023). *TechTarget*. How to develop a cybersecurity strategy: Step-by-step guide. Retrieved Sep 12, 2023, from https://www.techtarget.com/searchsecurity/tip/How-to-develop-a-cybersecurity-strategy-Step-by-step-guide

Schou, C., & Hernandez, S. (2015). *Strategies, information assurance handbook: Effective computer security and risk management*. McGraw-Hill Education.

Seh, A. H. (2020). Healthcare data breaches: Insights and implications. *Healthcare, 8*. https://doi.org/10.3390/healthcare8020133

Smart, W. (2018). *Lessons learned review of the WannaCry ransomware cyber-attack* (pp. 10–1038). Department of Health and Social Care.

Suguna, S., & Suhasini, A. (2014). Overview of data backup and disaster recovery in the cloud. In *International Conference on Information Communication and Embedded Systems (ICICES2014)* (pp. 1–7). IEEE. https://doi.org/10.1109/ICICES.2014.7033804

Tao, H. A. (2019). Secured data collection with hardware-based ciphers for IoT-based healthcare. *IEEE Internet of Things Journal, 6*, 410–420. https://doi.org/10.1109/JIOT.2018.2854714

Vankamamidi, S., & Naresh, S. S. (2020). Internet of things in healthcare: Architecture applications challenges and solution. *CSSE-Computer Systems Science and Engineering, 6*, 411–421.

Wikina, S. B. (2014). What caused the breach? An examination of the use of information technology and health data breaches. *Perspectives in Health Information Management, 11*.

Woodward, P. A. (2015). Cybersecurity vulnerabilities in medical devices: A complex environment and multifaceted problem. *Medical Devices: Evidence and Research*, 305–316. https://doi.org/10.2147/MDER.S50048

Yaqoob, T. (2019). Security vulnerabilities, attacks, countermeasures, and regulations of networked medical devices—a review. *IEEE Communications Surveys & Tutorials, 21*(4), 3723–3768. https://doi.org/10.1109/COMST.2019.2914094

Zare, H. M. (2018). Cybersecurity vulnerabilities assessment (a systematic review approach). In *Information Technology-New Generations: 15th International Conference on Information Technology*. Springer International Publishing.

Chapter 9
Cybersecurity Governance and Ethics

9.1 Introduction

Data governance is the specification of decision rights and an accountability framework to ensure the appropriate behavior in the valuation, creation, consumption, and control of data and analytics (Gartner, 2024). It refers to the exercise of authority and control over the management of data. Data governance aims to increase data value and minimize data-related costs and risks. In the healthcare context, it is a collection of procedures and plans that ensure the availability, integrity, security, and usability of the structured and unstructured data available to the healthcare organization. The best data governance practice outlines the healthcare data governance framework, guiding principles, organization-wide applications, and best practices. It is not a new topic, but it is still challenging for many healthcare organizations to implement and achieve (Oachs, 2020). Healthcare data governance includes the people, processes, and systems used to manage data throughout the lifecycle. Figure 9.1 shows the data governance lifecycle of a healthcare organization (AHIMA, 2022). The data lifecycle includes creation, process, use, storage/archival, or disposal. It also involves defining policies and procedures for data retention, archival, and disposal following regulatory requirements.

- *Capture*: Recording data in health information systems.
- *Process*: A series of actions are taken to create a product and service.
- *Use:* Access, sharing, and analysis.
- *Store:* Maintaining and archiving of data.
- *Dispose:* Destruction of data.

One of the biggest challenges when using health data is interoperability, as these data are available in various formats and collected from different sources such as electronic health records (EHRs), medical devices, health surveys, and clinical trials. Data governance can also help establish data exchange standards, formats, and

D. P. Sharma et al., *Understanding Cybersecurity Management in Healthcare*,
Progress in IS, https://doi.org/10.1007/978-3-031-68034-2_9

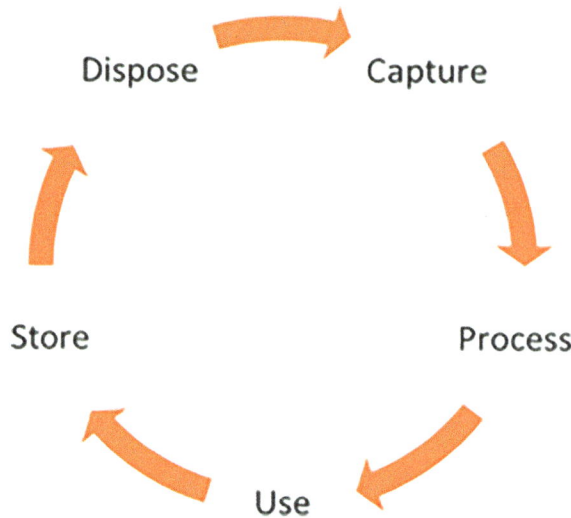

Fig. 9.1 Data lifecycle in healthcare

sharing policies, enabling seamless integration across different systems and providers. Standardized data governance approaches enable communication, transparent sharing, and the potential of operational data insights for data-intensive medical research to improve patient care. Data governance mainly focuses on safe access to patient data and the value of research to data owners, patients, and members of the public (Fatemeh Torabi, 2024).

Data governance improves patient care, enables data-driven decision-making, minimizes compliance risks, and maintains trust in the integrity and confidentiality of healthcare data.

9.2   Data Governance Framework in Healthcare

A healthcare data governance framework is a comprehensive system designed to handle the availability, integrity, usability, and security of data within an organization (Zou 2014). A healthcare organization should establish a basic data framework for the collection, retention, use, accessibility, and sharing of healthcare data, consisting of policies, procedures, standards, ownership, decision rights, roles and responsibilities, and accountability related to the data (Oachs, 2020). The framework identifies the essential data governance capabilities in these three areas, which are people, process, and technology (KPMG, 2018). Healthcare organizations need to establish an operational framework to determine major components and their relationship to each other. For example, the Canadian Institute for Health Information

(CIHI) developed a framework for Health Data and Information Governance and Capability Framework that consists of four subject areas, each area covering a subset of the 28 health data information (HDI) capabilities (CIHI, 2020). Figure 9.2 shows CIHI's HDI Governance and Capability Framework, including its four areas and requirements.

- *Strategy and governance*: This provides an effective HDI program's overall direction, accountability, and oversight. Capabilities in this area include an articulated strategy for the intended outcomes of the strategic use of HDI, governance and accountability models, and processes to monitor and report compliance.
- *Policies and processes:* It defines activities for appropriate collection, processing, analysis, and sharing of trusted HDI. Capabilities in this area include data management, quality, conformance, privacy, security, access, and partnerships that collectively define how the organization operates internally and externally to ensure efficiency, effectiveness, integrity, and protection.
- *Assets and standards*: This establishes the HDI assets, the policies, and processes required to enable strategic and operational outcomes. Capabilities include enterprise data assets, standards, models, and analytics insights that form the organization or network's collective data foundation.
- *People and knowledge*: It empowers stakeholders and the workforce to facilitate and evolve effective and sustained policies, processes, designs, and governance. Capabilities include engagement, education, and communication within and outside the organization.

Fig. 9.2 Health data and information governance and capability framework (CIHI, 2020)

9.2.1 The Role of Healthcare Data Governance in Big Data Analytics

Large amounts of heterogeneous medical data have become available in various healthcare organizations (Juzwishin 2019). Big data technology enables us to work with data from different formats and sources using advanced tools different from traditional relational databases. The main characteristics of big data are volume, variety, and velocity (O'Driscoll, 2013). Big data needs to have effective data governance, which includes measures to manage and control the use of data and to enhance data quality, availability, and integrity (Juddoo, 2018). Cloud computing and big data technologies can be used to deal with complex medical and biological big datasets such as genomic sequences (Quail, 2012) (Pollack, 2011). A data technology like Apache Hadoop provides distributed and parallel data processing and analysis of large-scale (petabyte (PB)) datasets (O'Driscoll, 2013).

The extensive data processing capabilities of cloud computing facilitate the analysis of complex healthcare data from diverse. Biomedical and healthcare tools such as genomics, mobile biometric sensors, and smartphone apps generate a large amount of data. The collective extensive data analysis of healthcare data is continuously helping build a better predictive framework (Sabyasachi Dash, 2019). Healthcare data governance establishes a process for ensuring the quality, accuracy, and consistency of data used in big data analytics. It enables predictive modeling, survival analysis, patient similarity, genetic data analysis, disease progression, treatment responses, and healthcare resource utilization (Guo, 2023).

Figure 9.3 shows an extensive data governance framework for healthcare data based on the governance activities associated with processing regional health information networks in China (QLi, 2019). It consists of 3 domains and 12 elements. Three domains with their elements are as follows:

- *Drive domain:* This domain determines whether it can run. Its elements include considerable data strategy planning, laws and regulations, open transactions, and industry support.
- *Capability domain*: This domain determines how far it can run. The elements of this domain include healthcare big data organization, collection, storage, process and analysis, and usage).
- *Support domain*: This domain determines how fast it can run. Its elements include healthcare, considerable data resource planning, standards systems, and privacy and security protection.

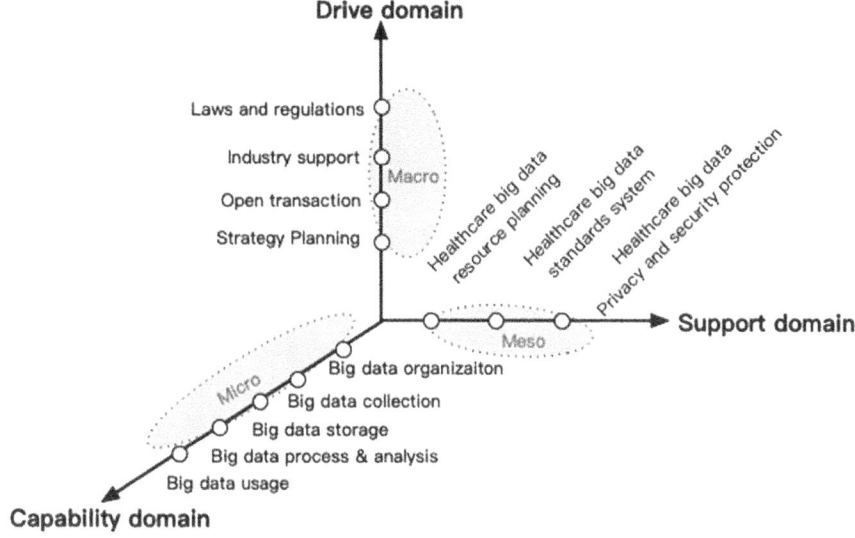

Fig. 9.3 A framework for big data governance (QLi, 2019)

9.3   Steps to Healthcare Data Governance

A healthcare organization can effectively steward data growth and maintain trust with five manageable steps toward data governance (Hess, 2021; Turner 2022).

1. *Identify the organizational priorities:* Data analytics services help the organization's strategic goals, so the first step in developing a new data governance program is to identify the organizational priorities. This requires understanding the top five targets the executive team wants everyone in the organization to help deliver over the next year.
2. *Identify the data governance priorities:* This step identifies the data governance opportunities that overlap with the organizational priorities identified in step 1.
3. *Identify and recruit the early adopters:* List the intersecting priorities identified in step 2 and the desired characteristics of a data governance leader, and determine which leaders are likely early adopters of data governance. Early adopters should understand data governance on a more than casual level and be aware of the challenges and benefits.
4. *Identify the scope of the opportunity appropriately:* Sets the scope and opportunity by focusing on specific data governance opportunities within a particular area of interest, such as clinical domain, patient population, and geographic region.
5. *Enable early adopters to become enterprise data governance leaders and mentors:* This shift in perspective from local to organizational naturally coincides with each early adopter's transition from team leader to enterprise data governance leader.

Table 9.1 Key process of IT-strategy-driven alignment

Key processes	Activities involved
1. Identifying technological innovation	Identifying new technology
2. Clarifying IT strategy	Choosing technology
	Planning for detailed solutions
	Selecting vendors
3. Shaping business strategy	Articulating strategy
4. Transforming organizational infrastructure and process	Reorganizing organizational infrastructure
	Reorganizing organizational processes

Table 9.2 Key process of business-strategy-driven alignment

Key processes	Activities involved
1. Clarifying business strategy	Identifying misalignment
2. Modifying IT strategy	Choosing technology
	Defining functions
	Collaborating with vendors
3. Transforming organizational infrastructure and process	Arranging IT and business infrastructure

9.4   Strategic Alignment

A strategy is a long-term plan for achieving an organization's objectives. Strategy alignment in healthcare can help providers choose new information systems that support objectives and strategies. It also lists actions and characteristics that managers might use as checklists in current and future alignment efforts and in cultivating broad support for alignment (Rao, 2009). Strategic planning in healthcare helps you set business goals and decide how to allocate resources to achieve these goals. It helps to reduce efforts to create strategic plans (Winter, 2001).

A strategic alignment can be divided into IT and business strategic-driven alignments based on the activities and processes involved (Sha et al., 2020). The key processes and involving activities of IT-strategy-driven and business-strategy-driven alignment are summarized in Tables 9.1 and 9.2, respectively.

9.5   Privacy and Security in Healthcare

Ensuring the security, privacy, and protection of patient's healthcare data is critical for all healthcare personnel and organizations. In healthcare, privacy refers to the patient's right to control access to their personal and sensitive health information. Security refers to the protection measures and tools used to safeguard patient information from unauthorized access and abuse, manipulation, deletion, and denial of access. The health-related information of a patient should be secure and private within the healthcare providers and individuals. Patients hesitate to disclose health information if they don't trust the healthcare information systems. Therefore, the security and privacy of healthcare data play a crucial role PIPEDA (n.d.).

A healthcare information system generates or collects medical data from different data sources such as patient's warbles, smartphones, caregivers, and in-patient monitoring. Once data is generated, it is stored in the local databases and the remote system using a network connection. Various security and privacy methods must be applied to protect patients' sensitive data and systems from cyberattacks. Some common security and privacy mechanisms are access control, pseudonymity, data encryption, authentication, authorization, blockchain, etc. The exploitation of healthcare data and systems by the attackers could also bring about disastrous consequences, leading to financial, social, ethical, and legal implications and even loss of life in some cases (Pandey, 2019).

9.5.1 Security Concerns in Healthcare

Security concerns in healthcare data refer to risks and vulnerabilities that compromise the confidentiality, integrity, and availability of sensitive patient health information. Implementing comprehensive, proactive, multi-faced, robust security mechanisms can help protect healthcare data and/or systems and reduce the risk of cyberattacks. A healthcare organization can apply security measures at different levels (Pandey, 2019).

- *Physical security:* Physical security of the hardware (server, storage, security devices, etc.) holding healthcare information is very important. A data center may be infringed upon by individual/individuals for sabotaging it or tampering/ stealing the data. An internal member of the organization may also try to modify, steal, or delete data if the authentication-based access system is not in place.
- *Application security:* EHR records are generally accessed using EHR software that implements various functionalities ranging from access to addition, modification, sharing, and customization using the application software (e.g., web applications). Anti-virus software, antispam, and Web Application Firewall (WAF) can secure the application (i.e., the patient web portal). Application developers also should have proper plans for maintenance, management, monitoring, upgrading, patching operations, and recovery from an outage of an application or OS crash.
- *Server security:* All data and the main application reside in a physical or virtual server. Enabling a firewall, using an access control list, and using proper authentication and authorization mechanisms help ensure server security.
- *Periphery security:* Hardware-based periphery security can secure all computing resources used by the healthcare system. Security methods such as IDS, IPS, and firewalls can be used for periphery security.

- *Storage and communication security:* Healthcare data are often stored on servers or in network-attached storage (NAS) or storage area networks (SAN). An attacker can always access the storage, thereby exploiting the data. Security methods such as full disk encryption, encrypted communication channels/end-to-end encryption, and VPN use can be used for storage and communication security.
- *Ubiquitous device security:* Physicians can message their peer physicians about their work and share or exchange healthcare information via their handheld (e.g., mobile devices). The security of these message exchanges can be another concern in medical data protection. It is difficult for the organization's IT security team to monitor individual handheld devices. In addition, there is a risk of mobile devices being lost or stolen and chances of data breaches. Encryption of mobile device data and end-to-end communication channel encryption can be used for ubiquitous device security.
- *Preserving confidentiality*: Data encryption ensures confidentiality. Encryption algorithms such as DES, AES, and RSA are generally used to ensure confidentiality and privacy. In addition, it can be ensured by providing access to authorized persons with information. Authentication mechanisms such as passwords, biometrics (finger/eye scan, facial recognition), and OTP (one-time password) can also be used to preserve confidentiality.
- *Data integrity:* Data integrity is a property that ensures that data are unaltered. Data may be changed intentionally or unintentionally in some circumstances, like during data entry system upgrades or transfers. Cryptographic algorithms and message authentication protocols, such as secure hash function/algorithm (SHA) and message digest (MD5), can be used to ensure data integrity.
- *Data availability:* Healthcare systems may be targeted using request overloading or a denial-of-service attack. Some unwanted outages, like system (server, storage, etc.) crashes, may also happen. Attackers may also bring down systems and data availability. Keeping multiple backups and fault-tolerant systems with high availability ensures data availability.

9.5.2 Privacy Concerns in Healthcare

Multiple stakeholders in the patient data include patients, healthcare providers, and software professionals who maintain the data. Who is the actual owner, or who controls the patient data? It is a complex and often debatable question. Traditionally, healthcare data belongs to the provider that collects and maintains it. However, patients have increasingly recognized the right to control and access their health information. A healthcare provider can modify the data, but they shouldn't have the right to delete it. Patients may decide to delete their health records but can't modify the healthcare provider's entries. Laws and regulations such as HIPAA (HIPPA, 2023) and GDPR (GDRP, 2024) grant patients certain rights over their healthcare data, such as the right to access, correct, and control the sharing of their information.

Excessive use of mobile phones and other handheld devices increases the risk of information dissemination through social media platforms. Sharing medical and other sensitive data on social media with their friends may violate privacy regulations (Ayres, 2013).

Blockchain technology is an immutable, time-stamped, distributed ledger storing data among multiple parties. Blockchains and special protocols can be used for varying degrees of privacy and anonymity and could be used to protect healthcare data. The blockchain-based framework ensures secure access to medical records and protects the patients' private information (Vora et al., 2018).

9.6   Legal, Regulatory, and Compliances

Various recognized authoritative bodies introduce cybersecurity regulatory frameworks and standards to evaluate how organizations protect themselves and their customer data (Alder 2024). Cybersecurity compliance frameworks ensure that an organization implements appropriate security controls, policies, and best security practices to adhere to regulatory requirements outlined by various governing bodies and industry standards. In a healthcare organization, adhering to cybersecurity compliance standards has helped strengthen its security posture, protect patient data privacy, and prevent cyberattacks. Some of the common cybersecurity laws, regulatory, and compliance frameworks are as follows:

- *ISO/IEC 27001* is a standard for an organization's information security management systems (ISMS). It defines the requirements an ISMS must meet. This standard provides companies of any size and from all sectors of activity with guidance for establishing, implementing, maintaining, and continually improving an information security management system (ISO/IEC27001, 2022).
- *System and Organization Controls 2 (SOC 2):* SOC 2 is a security standard compliance framework for service organizations created by the American Institute of Certified Public Accountants (AICPA) that specifies how organizations should protect customer data from unauthorized access, security incidents, and other vulnerabilities. It has five trust services criteria such as security, availability, processing integrity, confidentiality, and privacy (COC2, 2021).
- *General Data Protection Regulation (GDPR):* GDPR is a legal framework that sets guidelines for collecting and processing personal information, including healthcare information, from individuals. It is a comprehensive data protection regulation for organizations that handle individuals' data within the European Union (EU) countries. It also provides individuals with several rights regarding their data. Healthcare organizations that process data of EU patients must comply with GDPR's requirements, which include obtaining explicit consent for data processing, ensuring data subject rights, implementing appropriate technical and organizational measures, and reporting data breaches within strict timelines (GDRP, 2024).

- *California Consumer Privacy Act (CCPA):* CCPA is a Consumer Privacy Act implemented by the State of California Department of Justice, Office of The Attorney General, USA. It gives consumers more control over the personal information businesses collect about them, and the CCPA regulations guide how to implement the law. It imposes obligations on companies that collect, use, or sell consumers' personal information, including healthcare organizations. Compliance with the CCPA involves providing transparency about data practices, honoring consumer rights to access and delete personal information, and implementing reasonable security measures (CCPA, 2018).
- *Health Insurance Portability and Accountability Act (HIPAA):* HIPAA is a US Federal law that requires the creation of national standards to protect sensitive patient health information from being disclosed without the patient's consent or knowledge. The US Department of Health and Human Services (HHS) issued the HIPAA Privacy Rule to implement the requirements of HIPAA. HIPAA's Privacy Rule regulates the use and disclosure of individually identifiable information by health plans, providers, and other covered entities. Privacy rules encompass standards for individuals' rights to understand and control how their healthcare information is used. The main goal is to ensure that individuals' healthcare information is adequately protected while allowing the flow of healthcare information needed to provide and promote high-quality healthcare services and protect the public's health and well-being. It permits important uses of information while protecting the privacy of people who seek care and healing. The HIPAA Security Rule complements the privacy rule by establishing national standards for safeguarding electronic protected health information (ePHI). It requires covered entities to implement security measures to protect against unauthorized access, use, or disclosure of ePHI. This includes implementing safeguards such as access controls, encryption, and regular security risk assessments. It ensures the confidentiality, integrity, and availability of all ePHI, detects and safeguards against anticipated cyber threats, protects against anticipated, impermissible uses or disclosures that are not allowed by the rule, and certifies compliance by the workforce (HIPPA, 2023).
- *The Health Information Technology for Economic and Clinical Health (HITECH) Act*: The HITECH Act is part of the American Recovery and Reinvestment Act 2009, developed to promote the adoption and meaningful use of healthcare information and advanced technology. It addresses the privacy and security concerns associated with the electronic transmission of healthcare information to strengthen the civil and criminal enforcement of the HIPAA rules. It significantly increases the penalty amount for each violation and sets a maximum penalty amount of $1.5 million for all violations of an identical provision (HITECH, 2009).
- *Personal Health Information Protection Act (PHIPA):* PHIPA was established by the Ontario Province of Canada in 2004. It provides a set of rules for collecting, using, and disclosing personal health information by healthcare providers and practitioners (PHIP, 2004).
- *Payment Card Industry Data Security Standard (PCI-DSS):* PCI-DSS is a global data security standard that provides a baseline of technical and operational

requirements designed to protect payment card information. Per PCI-DSS requirements, all organizations, including healthcare providers, must maintain a secure environment for protecting payment card information, including storage, processing, and card data transmission. Every organization adhering to PCI-DSS must be validated and maintain its cybersecurity regulatory compliances. It incurs fines or charges if any organization fails to comply with PCI-DSS requirements (PCI-DSS, 2024).

9.7   IT Governance

IT governance deals with the strategic direction of IT at the board level, with the necessary oversight to align IT goals with business objectives, realize IT business value, and minimize IT risks (Moustafa Elazhary, 2023). IT governance structure defines clear roles, responsibilities, and accountability for IT decisions. It is a management control exercised by the board and senior management to achieve the business objectives under normal or turbulent environmental conditions. IT governance mechanisms provide IT strategic direction to ensure realizing organizational goals with appropriate management by maintaining a balance between IT value and IT risks.

IT governance in healthcare is a framework that implements a well-defined IT strategy to ensure a more successful use of IT in hospitals (Rosenmöller, 2013). It is essential in healthcare organizations to identify the role and insight of IT stakeholders and hospital senior managers in major IT decisions. The roles and responsibilities of the key actors can be clearly defined through decision-making structures (Shahi & Sadoughi, 2014).

In the modern IT governance landscape, several frameworks have been established to provide guidelines, practices, and processes to ensure that an organization's IT operations align with its strategic objectives, risk management goals, and regulatory requirements. Three common IT governance frameworks are as follows:

- *ISO/IEC 38500:* This international standard for IT governance guides governing bodies and their advisors on the effective, efficient, and acceptable use of IT in their organizations. It applies to managing management processes and decisions relating to an organization's information and communication services (ISO/IEC, 2024).
- *Control Objectives for Information and Related Technologies (COBIT):* COBIT is a framework for effective IT governance and management. It was developed by the Information Systems Audit and Control Association (ISACA) to serve as a comprehensive guide for organizations seeking to manage and govern their IT services. The primary objective of COBIT is to ensure that IT investments align seamlessly with broader business goals and deliver tangible value to stakeholders across the spectrum. It helps organizations meet business challenges in regulatory

compliance, risk management, and aligning IT strategy with organizational goals (COBIT, 2019).

- *Global Technology Audit Guide (GTAG):* Many internationally recognized IT governance frameworks can be used to supplement this guidance. Frameworks such as ISO/IEC 38500 and COBIT® cover in more detail the processes and mechanisms needed to develop, implement, evaluate, and improve an IT governance program. GTAG is focused on the methods and mechanisms that internal audits can use to assess whether the IT governance program supports the organization's strategies and objectives (GTAG, 2021).

9.8   Awareness and Adherence

Cybersecurity awareness education training is an approach that enables the understanding of information security and motivates employees to practice the best cybersecurity strategies that help protect valuable and sensitive information (Asma & Alhashmi 2021). It is essential to increase staff awareness and compliance with the information security policies, practices, and relevant guidance related to their duties in the organization (Abawajy, 2014). Cybersecurity awareness increases staff awareness, which helps decrease cyberattacks caused by human-related vulnerabilities such as human error and phishing scam emails. Cybersecurity awareness helps healthcare staff such as IT staff working in hospitals, doctors, end-users, and other staff to identify and recognize the potential cybersecurity vulnerabilities and cyber threats such as social engineering, email phishing attacks, email use, and use of portable media devices in the context of hospitals and healthcare. It helps them to know how the information security processes and data protection procedures are implemented in the healthcare system. Different training schemes can be developed for the various categories of staff such as IT personnel, users (medical personnel such as doctors, nurses, and lab technologies), and managers such as executive directors and CEOs who work at decision-making levels (Rajamäki et al., 2018).

A cyber-safe working environment can be created by implementing strict cybersecurity measures, setting clear security policies and procedures, and developing comprehensive employee awareness cybersecurity programs. Cybersecurity awareness programs promote the education of the healthcare staff about cybersecurity measures and provide training on how to secure information access, manipulation, and transfer of data across different healthcare systems. The healthcare regulations and compliances (HIPAA, GDPR, etc.) require healthcare personnel to be regularly educated and provided with the needed training regarding patient information security measures (Dari Alhuwail, 2021). Cybersecurity awareness training programs should be conducted periodically.

The main goal of a cybersecurity awareness program is to raise employee information security awareness in an organization. The success or failure of the cybersecurity awareness program will rely heavily on how the awareness information is delivered. There are many cybersecurity awareness delivery models. The commonly used cybersecurity awareness delivery methods are as follows (Abawajy, 2014):

- *Conventional delivery methods:* These delivery methods use leaflets, posters, and newsletters.
- *Instructor-led delivery methods*: In this method, local or external information security experts conduct formal presentations, such as lectures, seminars, and workshops, to help raise the staff's information security awareness.
- *Online delivery methods:* These are virtual delivery methods that include different forms of online security awareness delivery models such as email broadcasting, online synchronous and asynchronous discussion, information uploading, blogging, animation, and multimedia.
- *Game-based delivery methods:* These methods are highly interactive and offer an effective alternative to, or supplement for, more traditional modes of awareness. Online games combine graphics, play, and training concepts to create compelling training experiences. The benefit of the game-based awareness delivery method is that it can challenge, motivate, and engage the participants.
- *Video-based delivery methods:* Educational videos are used for cybersecurity awareness. In this method, there is no need for a classroom trainer. Online video is a medium that provides visual and audio learning for participants.
- *Simulation-based delivery methods:* In a simulation-based delivery method, users are sent simulated phishing emails to test users' vulnerability to phishing attacks and then follow up with training. In this simulation, an email with an embedded link to an external website is sent to the staff and tells them to click on the link where they would input their login credentials. If a staff member acts upon the request and clicks the link in the email, remedial training is provided to the staff, typically on a webpage where training materials are hosted. Following the remedial training, another simulated phishing email can be used to check whether the ability to detect phishing threats has improved.

9.9   Chapter Summary

This chapter delves into cybersecurity governance and ethics, including the data lifecycle in healthcare, healthcare data governance frameworks, the role of data governance in big data analytics, an extensive data governance framework, and strategic alignments. It also presents security and privacy concerns in healthcare, legal, regulatory, and compliance issues, IT governance and standard frameworks, and cybersecurity awareness and adherence in healthcare.

After understanding cybersecurity governance and ethics in healthcare, the following questions are addressed in this chapter:

- What is data governance? Explain data governance life-cycle phases in healthcare.
- How can data governance framework be used in healthcare? Discuss its components.

- What is the role of healthcare data governance in big data analytics? Explain different domains of the data governance framework for big data.
- How do healthcare organizations steward data growth and maintain trust? What are the five manageable steps toward data governance?
- What is a strategic alignment? How do IT-driven strategic alignments differ from a business-driven strategy?
- What are the healthcare system's legal, regulatory, and compliance requirements?
- What are the security and privacy concerns in healthcare?
- What is IT governance? What are the typical IT governance frameworks?
- What is cybersecurity awareness? What are the different delivery methods used in cybersecurity awareness?

References

Abawajy, J. (2014). User preference of cyber security awareness delivery methods. *Behavior & Information Technology*, 237–248. https://doi.org/10.1080/0144929X.2012.708787

AHIMA. (2022). *Healthcare data governance.* The American Health Information Management Association (AHIMA). Retrieved from https://www.ahima.org/media/pmcb0fr5/healthcare-data-governance-practice-brief-final.pdf

Alder, S. (2024, Feb 20). *What is healthcare regulatory compliance?* The HIPAA Journal. Retrieved from https://www.hipaajournal.com/healthcare-regulatory-compliance/

Asma, A., & Alhashmi, A. D. (2021). Taxonomy of cybersecurity awareness delivery methods: A countermeasure for phishing threats. *International Journal of Advanced Computer Science and Applications., 12.* https://doi.org/10.14569/IJACSA.2021.0121004

Ayres, E. J. (2013). The impact of social media on business and ethical practices in dietetics. *Journal of the Academy of Nutrition and Dietetics, 113*, 1539–1543. https://doi.org/10.1016/j.jand.2013.09.020

CCPA. (2018). *California consumer privacy act (CCPA).* State of California Department of Justice. Retrieved from https://www.oag.ca.gov/privacy/ccpa

CIHI. (2020). *Canadian Institute for Health Information. CIHI's health data and information governance and capability framework.* Canadian Institute for Health Information (CIHI).

COBIT. (2019). *Control objectives for information and related technologies (COBIT) ISACA's framework.* Information Systems Audit and Control Association (ISACA). Retrieved from https://www.isaca.org/resources/cobit

COC2. (2021, Jul). *SOC 2®–SOC for service organizations: Trust Services Criteria.* American Institute of Certified Public Accountants (AICPA). Retrieved from https://www.aicpa-cima.com/topic/audit-assurance/audit-and-assurance-greater-than-soc-2

Dari Alhuwail, E. A.-J. (2021). Information security awareness and behaviors of health care professionals at public health care facilities. *Applied Clinical Informatics*, 924–932. https://doi.org/10.1055/s-0041-1735527

Fatemeh Torabi, E. S. (2024). A common framework for health data governance standards. *Nature Medicine, 30*, 26–29. https://doi.org/10.1038/s41591-023-02686-w

Gartner. (2024). *Data governance.* Data Governance. Retrieved April 2, 2024, from https://www.gartner.com/en/information-technology/glossary/data-governance

GDRP. (2024). *General data protection regulation (GDPR).* General data protection regulation (GDPR). Retrieved April 2, 2024, from https://gdpr-info.eu/

GTAG. (2021, Sep 10). *GTAG: Auditing IT governance.* Global technology audit guide (GTAG). Retrieved from https://www.theiia.org/en/content/guidance/recommended/supplemental/gtags/gtag-auditing-it-governance/

Guo, C. A. (2023). Big data analytics in healthcare. In *Knowledge technology and systems: Toward establishing knowledge systems science* (pp. 27–70). Springer.

Hess, S. (2021, June 24). *Five practical steps towards healthcare data governance.* Health catalyst. Retrieved from https://www.healthcatalyst.com/insights/healthcare-data-governance-5-step-strategy.

HIPPA. (2023). *Health information privacy.* U.S. Department of health and human services (HHS). Retrieved from https://www.hhs.gov/hipaa/index.html

HITECH. (2009). *Health information technology for economic and clinical health (HITECH) act.* Retrieved from https://www.hhs.gov/hipaa/for-professionals/special-topics/hitech-act-enforcement-interim-final-rule/index.html

ISO/IEC. (2024). *Information technology–governance of IT for the organization (ISO/IEC 38500:2024).* Retrieved from https://www.iso.org/standard/81684.html

ISO/IEC27001. (2022). *Information security, cybersecurity, and privacy protection.* ISO. Retrieved from https://www.iso.org/standard/27001

Juddoo, S. (2018). Data governance in the health industry: Investigating data quality dimensions within a big data context. *Applied System Innovation., 1.* https://doi.org/10.3390/asi1040043

Juzwishin, D. W. (2019). Big data challenges from a healthcare governance perspective. In Househ, Mowafa and Kushniruk, Andre W and Borycki, Elizabeth M (pp. 69-82). Springer International Publishing. doi:https://doi.org/10.1007/978-3-030-06109-8_6.

KPMG. (2018). *Data governance: Driving value in healthcare.* KPMG International. Retrieved from https://assets.https://kpmg.com/content/dam/kpmg/co/pdf/2018/07/data-governance-driving-value-in-health.pdf

Moustafa Elazhary, A. P. (2023). How information technology governance influences organizational agility: The role of market turbulence. *Information Systems Management, 40*, 148–168. https://doi.org/10.1080/10580530.2022.2055813

O'Driscoll, A. A. (2013). 'Big data,' Hadoop and cloud computing in genomics. *Journal of Biomedical Informatics, 46*, 774–781.

Oachs, P. A. (2020). In A. W. Pamela & K. Oachs (Eds.), *Health information management: Concepts, principles, and practice* (6th ed.). American Health Information Management Association (AHIMA) Press. Retrieved from https://books.google.ca/books?id=msNnwwEACAAJ

Pandey, A. K. (2019). Security and privacy of electronic healthcare records: Concepts, paradigms and solutions. In S. T. Sudeep Tanwar, Security and privacy of electronic healthcare records concepts, paradigms and solutions (pp. 17–39). The Institution of Engineering and Technology.

PCI-DSS. (2024). *Payment card industry data security standard (PCI DSS) v4.0.* Retrieved from https://www.pcisecuritystandards.org/

PHIP. (2004). *Personal health information protection act (PHIP).* Retrieved April 4, 2024, from https://www.ontario.ca/laws/statute/04p03

PIPEDA. (n.d.). *The personal information protection and electronic documents act (PIPEDA).* Retrieved from https://www.priv.gc.ca/en/privacy-topics/privacy-laws-in-canada/the-personal-information-protection-and-electronic-documents-act-pipeda/

Pollack, A. (2011). DNA sequencing caught in the deluge of data. *New York Times.*

QLi, Q. A. (2019). A framework for big data governance to advance RHINs: A case study of China. *IEEE Access, 7*, 50330–50338. https://doi.org/10.1109/ACCESS.2019.2910838

Quail, M. A. (2012). A tale of three next-generation sequencing platforms: Comparison of ion torrent, Pacific biosciences, and Illumina MiSeq sequencers. *BMC Genomics, 13*, 1–13.

Rajamäki, J., Nevmerzhitskaya, J., & Virág, C. (2018). Cybersecurity education and training in hospitals. In *Proactive resilience educational framework (Prosilience EF)* (pp. 2042–2046). IEEE. https://doi.org/10.1109/EDUCON.2018.8363488

Rao, M. B. (2009). The alignment of information systems with organizational objectives and strategies in health care. *International Journal of Medical Informatics, 78*, 446–456. https://doi.org/10.1016/j.ijmedinf.2009.02.004

Rosenmöller, M. (2013). IT governance in healthcare institutions. In D. W. Carlisle George (Ed.), *eHealth: Legal, ethical and governance challenges* (pp. 329–348). Springer Berlin Heidelberg. https://doi.org/10.1007/978-3-642-22474-4_14

Sabyasachi Dash, S. K. (2019). Big data in healthcare: Management. *Journal of Big Data., 6.* https://doi.org/10.1186/s40537-019-0217-0

Sha, X., Chen, J., & Teoh, S. Y. (2020). The dynamics of IT-business strategic alignment: Evidence from healthcare information systems implementation. *Information Technology & People*, 1465–1488. https://doi.org/10.1108/ITP-08-2019-0414

Shahi, M., & Sadoughi, F. (2014). Information technology governance domains in hospitals: a case study in Iran. *Global Journal of Health Science*, 200–208. https://doi.org/10.5539/gjhs.v7n3p200

Turner, M. (2022, March 29). *Five steps to creating effective data governance in healthcare.* The Journal of Mhealth. Retrieved from https://thejournalofmhealth.com/five-steps-to-creating-effective-data-governance-in-healthcare/

Vora, J., Nayyar, A., Tanwar, S., Tyagi, S., Kumar, N., Obaidat, M. S., & Rodrigues, J. J. (2018). *BHEEM: A blockchain-based framework for securing electronic health records* (pp. 1–6). IEEE. https://doi.org/10.1109/GLOCOMW.2018.8644088

Winter, A. W.-S.-U. (2001). Strategic information management plans: The basis for systematic information management in hospitals. *International Journal of Medical Informatics, 64*, 99–109.

Zou, Q. A.-B.-R.-Y.-L. (2014). Survey of MapReduce frame operation in bioinformatics. *Briefings in Bioinformatics, 15*, 637–647.

Chapter 10
Cybersecurity Challenges, Best Practices, and Future Work in Healthcare

10.1 Cybersecurity Concerns in Digital Healthcare

As healthcare professionals, IT professionals, and decision-makers in healthcare organizations, your role in exploring and addressing the potential security and privacy concerns in healthcare systems is crucial and highly valued (Jawad, 2024). Figure 10.1 shows the key potential cybersecurity concerns in digital healthcare systems. These common potential security concerns and the best practices that are used to ensure security and privacy in the healthcare industry are discussed as follows:

- *Data breaches and unauthorized access*: Data breaches can occur due to various factors, including vulnerabilities in software systems, weak authentication mechanisms, or inadequate security protocols. To address these concerns, a healthcare organization can implement robust security measures such as secure storage methods and strong access controls to protect patient data at rest and in transit.
- *Cybersecurity attacks:* Potential cyberattacks such as ransomware attacks, malware infections, phishing attempts, and DDoS attacks can disrupt healthcare services, compromise the confidentiality and integrity of patient data, and even impact patient safety. To protect from these attacks, a healthcare organization can adopt multi-layered approaches such as firewalls, intrusion detection systems (IDS), and antivirus software. Regular vulnerability assessments and penetration testing can help identify and address potential vulnerabilities before exploiting them. The most common way to protect patient data from ransomware attacks is to keep data backup up to date and change all your credentials as soon as possible. DDoS attacks can be protected by using network and application monitoring tools and identifying traffic trends and patterns. Keeping your device and software updated, using a non-administrator account, and not opening emails and other attachments from unknown or untrusted senders can help reduce malware

D. P. Sharma et al., *Understanding Cybersecurity Management in Healthcare*, Progress in IS, https://doi.org/10.1007/978-3-031-68034-2_10

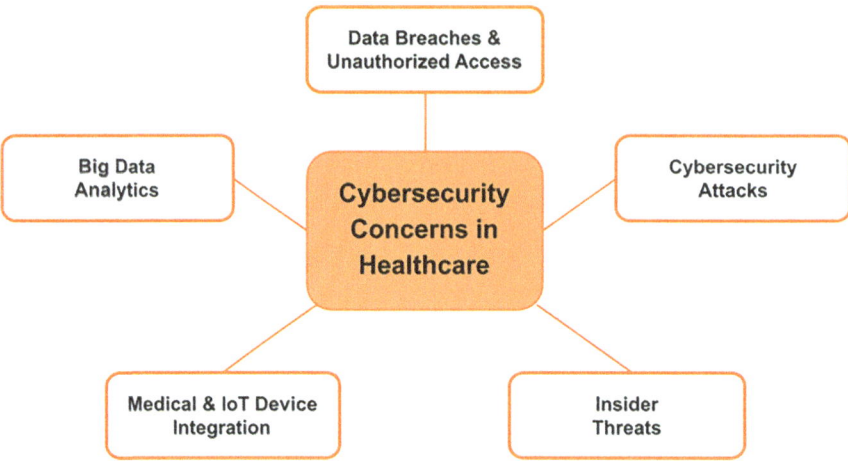

Fig. 10.1 Key cybersecurity concern in healthcare

attacks. Educating your employees and conducting training sessions with mock phishing scenarios and simulations could help prevent phishing attacks.

- *Insider threats:* An insider threat is a malicious threat to a healthcare organization from current employees, former employees, contractors, business associates, and others with access to patient data and IT systems. To address insider threats, a healthcare organization should implement role-based access controls, ensuring that employees only have access to the data necessary for their job responsibilities. Monitoring suspicious activities enables timely intervention in case of unauthorized access or data misuse.

- *Medical and IoT device integration*: Integrating medical devices and Internet of Things (IoT) devices in healthcare introduces additional cybersecurity risks. For example, pacemakers, insulin pumps, or connected IoT wearables to healthcare networks can become a potential target for attackers. Exploitation of security vulnerabilities in these devices can lead to unauthorized access, tampering, or disruption of healthcare services. To mitigate these vulnerabilities, healthcare organizations can adopt risk assessments, regular software updates and patches, and implement robust authentication mechanisms to access the devices.

- *Big data analytics*: Using big data analytics in healthcare can raise privacy issues. It reveals detailed information on an individual patient's health conditions, behaviors, and lifestyle choices, which increases the risk of potential re-identification and the misuse of personal information. To address these concerns, privacy-enhancing technologies such as differential privacy can be employed to protect patient privacy while enabling valuable data analysis. Standards and compliance with privacy regulations ensure patient privacy.

10.2   Mitigation Methods for Security and Privacy Concerns in Healthcare

Security and privacy are critical considerations in a modern digital healthcare system (CISA 2024; NIST 2018). Figure 10.2 shows the essential mitigation methods for protecting healthcare data from future cyberattacks. These methods are considered the best practices and can be used to ensure security and privacy in the healthcare industry. These methods are described as follows:

- *Two-factor authentication and biometric verification:* Robust authentication and access control mechanisms help mitigate security and privacy concerns in healthcare systems. Robust authentication methods such as two-factor or biometric verification can help ensure that only authorized individuals can access patient data. Role-based access controls should be implemented to limit access privileges based on job responsibilities and the principle of least privilege.
- *Encryption and data protection:* The encryption methods ensure that data remain confidential. Robust encryption algorithms can be used to encrypt data both at rest and during transmission. Additionally, healthcare organizations can employ secure storage methods and backups to prevent data loss or unauthorized modifications.
- *Continuous security monitoring:* Healthcare system operational and network traffic activities can be monitored by implementing advanced intrusion detection systems (IDS) and intrusion prevention systems (IPS) or security information and event management solutions. These security monitoring systems can help identify and respond to threats in real time.

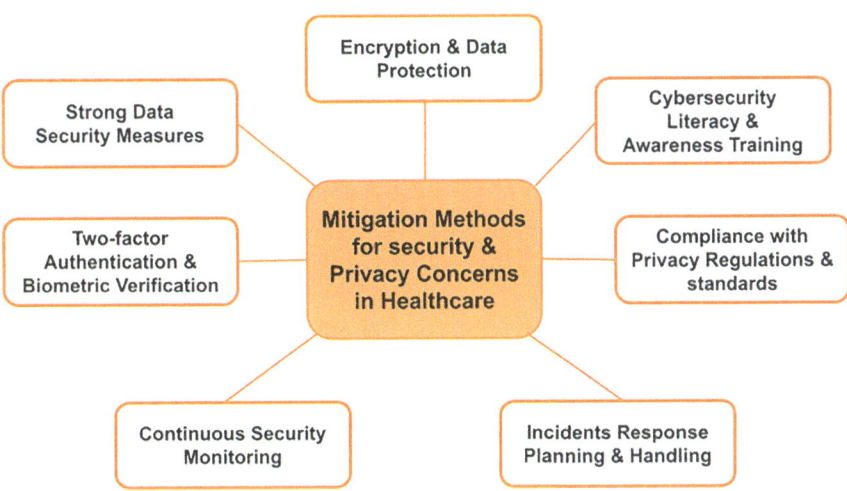

Fig. 10.2   Mitigation methods for security and privacy concerns in healthcare

- *Incident response planning and handling:* The impact of cybersecurity attacks can be minimized by preparing a well-defined incident response plan that includes containment, eradication, and recovery procedures.
- *Cybersecurity literacy and awareness training:* Continuous training and awareness programs are very important for healthcare professionals and staff to understand potential cyber threats and best practices. The training topics can include password hygiene, identifying phishing attempts, secure data handling practices, etc. Ensuring employee awareness of their roles, responsibilities, and data security and privacy obligations can improve cybersecurity.
- *Strong data security measures and risk assessment:* Employ state-of-the-art encryption algorithms, firewalls, and intrusion detection systems to protect patient data from unauthorized access or breaches. Healthcare organizations can leverage the NIST Cybersecurity Framework, which guides them in managing cybersecurity risks and helps protect patients and other sensitive information. It allows an organization to determine its cybersecurity goals, assess its current cybersecurity practices, or lack thereof, and help identify gaps for remediation (NIST, The NIST Cybersecurity Framework (CSF) 2.0, 2024). A risk-based assessment scans the healthcare system to identify, investigate, and prioritize the most critical assets and vulnerabilities. The selection of the proper cybersecurity risk assessment and management tools is crucial to the healthcare industry for identifying, prioritizing, and mitigating cyber risks. Organizations should carefully evaluate their requirements, budget, and regulatory compliance and select the security and risk assessment tools that meet their security requirements. This evaluation can be carried out in consultation with cybersecurity experts. Vulnerability scanning tools are used to find security loopholes and risks in the networks and systems. Nessus (2024) and OpenVAS (2024) are two standard vulnerability scanning tools. Regular security audits and risk assessments can help identify vulnerabilities and update systems with the latest security practices.
- *Compliance with privacy regulations and standards:* Healthcare organizations should ensure compliance with relevant data privacy regulations such as the Health Insurance Portability and Accountability Act (HIPAA) in the USA (HIPPA, 2023) or the General Data Protection Regulation (GDPR) in the European Union (GDRP, 2024). These frameworks outline guidelines for handling patient data, ensuring privacy, and maintaining data integrity. Compliance with these regulations and standards ensures that commitment to privacy and data protection of patients' personal and healthcare information is handled responsibly and lawfully.

10.3 Five Key Cyberattacks and Best Practices in Healthcare

Ransomware, DDoS, insider threats, malware, and phishing attacks are the five vital potential cyberattacks in digital healthcare systems (Salama et al., 2024). Figure 10.3 shows the five critical cyberattacks in the healthcare industry. Similarly, Table 10.1

summarizes the cybersecurity best practices for protecting from these five cyberattacks in healthcare. The descriptions of these five cyberattacks with their best practices are as follows:

- *Ransomware attacks:* A ransomware attack is a type of malware in which hackers encrypt your critical data so that you cannot access it until you pay the demanded ransom. The most common way to protect your data from ransomware attacks is to keep a backup and change all your credentials as soon as possible.
- *DDoS attack*: A DDoS attack is another potential cyberattack in healthcare systems. Cybercriminals flood a network with malicious, harmful traffic that prevents normal operation and communication. There are several ways to prevent your devices from DDoS attacks. For example, secure your router by changing the default password, use network and application monitoring tools to identify traffic trends and patterns, etc.
- *Insider threat:* An insider threat is a malicious threat to an organization from current employees, former employees, contractors, business associates, and others with access to critical data and IT systems. Policies, procedures, and technologies that help prevent privilege misuse can manage insider threats. Tools such as continuous risk assessment, security incident management, and automatic monitoring can help mitigate internal threats.
- *Malware attacks*: A malware attack is a typical cyberattack where malicious software executes unauthorized actions on your system. The malicious software performs different attacks, such as ransomware, spyware, trojans, worms, and viruses. Keeping your device and software updated, using a non-administrator account as much as possible, not opening emails and other attachments from unknown or untrusted senders, etc., can help to reduce the malware attack.

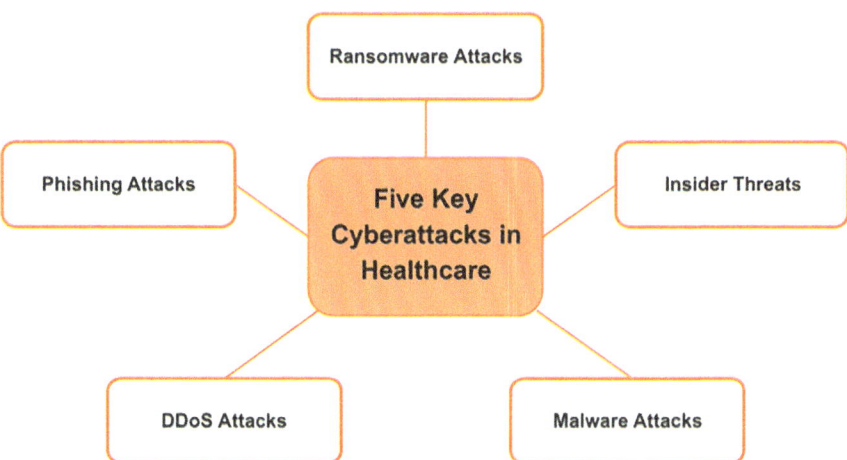

Fig. 10.3 Five key cyberattacks in healthcare

Table 10.1 Cybersecurity best practices for protecting from the potential common cyberattacks in healthcare

Potential cyberattacks	Key best practices
Ransomware attacks	Keep data backup up to date Change user credentials as soon as possible Keep your device's software updated
DDoS attacks	Use network and application monitoring tools to identify traffic trends and patterns
Insider threats	Use continuous risk assessment and automatic incident monitoring tools Define proper security policies and procedures
Malware attacks	Keep your device and software updated Use a non-administrator account as much as possible Do not open emails and other attachments from unknown or untrusted sender
Phishing attacks	Educate your employees about the phishing attacks with training sessions Conduct mock/simulated phishing scenarios.

- *Phishing attacks*: Phishing is a most common type of social engineering attack where an attacker sends a fraudulent message using email, social media, instant messaging, SMS, or phone calls to obtain sensitive personal information from the victims. Attackers can use different methods of phishing, for example, phishing via emails, vishing, and smishing. Phishing via email is the most common phishing attack method, and attackers use spam emails, malicious websites, or malware attachments. Two-factor authentication, VPN services, and regular cybersecurity awareness training can help protect your system or data from phishing attacks.

10.4   Challenges of Personal Cybersecurity in Healthcare

Healthcare systems face challenges in safeguarding personal data and privacy from cyber threats and ensuring the system's integrity. Here are some of the main challenges:

- Preventing identity theft and fraud by protecting personal data
- Ensuring the accessibility of EHRs with adequate security measures to prevent data breaches
- Assuring the security and privacy of personal data when using online healthcare platforms
- Increasing individual awareness and training on cybersecurity threats, such as phishing emails and other cybercrime tactics
- Providing secure networked medical devices to prevent cyber attackers from accessing and manipulating personal data
- Maintaining a secure environment to prevent hackers from targeting unpatched vulnerabilities in outdated legacy systems within healthcare organizations

While these are some of the most common personal cybersecurity challenges, other cybersecurity challenges are specific to patients or healthcare professionals, such as doctors and staff, as outlined below:

1. *Challenges of patient cybersecurity in healthcare*

    - Maintaining patient trust in their privacy and the competence of the health-care system
    - Protecting patients' sensitive medical records against ransomware, malware, DDoS attacks, and data breaches to prevent identity theft and fraud
    - Protecting patient data from unauthorized access by encrypting it
    - Protecting patient data security and privacy when using remote healthcare services
    - Averting adverse effects on patients, such as delayed treatments, medication errors, and inaccuracies in diagnosis and treatment caused by cyberattacks on health and well-being

2. *Challenges of doctors' cybersecurity in healthcare*

    - Balancing allocating resources for cybersecurity while prioritizing personal healthcare needs within a limited budget.
    - Keeping a balance between clinical focus and cybersecurity to mitigate doctors' vulnerabilities
    - Implementing cybersecurity measures to safeguard their privacy and professional reputation from cybersecurity breaches
    - Targeting their information prevents cybercriminals from causing significant financial losses and identity theft
    - Assuring patient privacy and protecting sensitive information
    - Integrating cybersecurity practices into healthcare delivery, preventing cyber-attacks that delay treatment and misdiagnose patients, and protecting patients from data corruption and ransomware

3. *Challenges of staff cybersecurity in healthcare*

    - Preventing data breaches, cybersecurity threats, phishing emails, and other cybercrime tactics by continuous training and awareness
    - Maintaining vigilance to recognize cyber threats and prevent security errors, especially during heavy workloads
    - Keeping up with evolving threats through continuous education

4. *Challenges of software security in healthcare*
    The security of healthcare software faces numerous challenges that threaten the confidentiality of patient data, the integrity of the system, and the safety of patients. Some of these challenges include:

    - Managing credentials effectively to avoid issues such as poor default user-names, weak passwords, and hard-coded credentials

- Addressing buffer overflow vulnerabilities, the most common software vulnerabilities, by improving software design and testing practices to prevent program crashes and protect patient health and sensitive medical data
- Enhancing authentication security and reducing the risk of unauthorized access by eliminating hard-coded credentials and implementing an "initial login" mode requiring solid and distinct passwords
- Protecting patient data from interception and unauthorized access by implementing robust encryption
- Preventing legacy systems and outdated software from becoming easy targets for cyberattacks due to limited vendor support by updating them
- Mitigating insider threats by enhancing access protocols, retraining employees, imposing sanctions, and taking corrective actions to prevent unauthorized access and disclosure of sensitive information
- Managing third-party involvement in healthcare software to reduce the risk of security breaches by implementing robust cybersecurity measures and addressing challenges posed by technologies like cloud computing
- Ensuring patient safety and system integrity by securing communication channels and network schema and following secure software practices
- Protecting healthcare software against cyberattacks by continuously monitoring security

5. *Challenges of infra-security in healthcare*

   Addressing infra-security challenges in healthcare is essential for protecting patient data, ensuring seamless healthcare delivery, preventing cyber threats, and, thus, maintaining the integrity and confidentiality of sensitive information. Some of these challenges are:

- Ensuring the confidentiality, integrity, availability, ownership, and privacy of healthcare information to protect sensitive data
- Implementing effective control and audit mechanisms to monitor and secure healthcare data
- Protecting healthcare infrastructures and networks from unauthorized access, vulnerabilities, and cyber threats
- Preventing identity theft, tax fraudulence, medical fraud, bank fraud, and insurance fraud
- Protecting the privacy and reputation of high-profile patients from defamation and data breaches
- Extending and securing health applications on tablets, laptops, and smartphones
- Preventing data breaches, data loss, and account hijacking
- Providing strong authentication, authorization, and access control
- Ensuring secure data access, safe data transmission, and deleting data when no longer needed
- Securing interfaces and APIs against vulnerabilities and misuse
- Protecting against hackers, as well as malicious insiders

6. *Challenges of apps security in healthcare*

- Managing large volumes of medical data from a variety of sources by using advanced machine learning algorithms and data processing techniques.
- Avoiding compatibility and security issues by developing standardized communication protocols among devices and systems
- Updating outdated infrastructure and integrating modern healthcare apps
- Ensuring data unification by making diverse healthcare devices compatible and enabling seamless data exchange for effective data use
- Ensuring healthcare apps comply with varying privacy and security regulations across countries and regions
- Investing in secure healthcare apps and infrastructure requires significant investment with long-term benefits, which justifies the cost factor
- Building trust with patients, healthcare providers, and the public regarding data usage through transparent communication and strategies
- Implementing robust authentication and access control measures to protect sensitive data
- Preventing cloud resource abuse and ensuring proper management and security of cloud-based healthcare apps
- Securing mobile devices that access healthcare apps against threats such as malware, loss, and unauthorized access
- Training users to recognize and avoid cyberattacks
- Implementing continuous monitoring of healthcare apps and having an effective incident response plan to address security breaches quickly

Addressing these challenges requires a comprehensive approach to healthcare software security, including implementing robust authentication mechanisms, encrypting sensitive data, regularly updating software and systems, conducting security audits and assessments, and fostering a culture of security awareness and compliance throughout the organization. By proactively addressing these challenges, healthcare organizations can mitigate the risk of healthcare software security vulnerabilities.

10.5   Cybersecurity Best Practices for Healthcare Professionals and IT System Administrators

Healthcare professionals and IT system administrators play crucial roles in safeguarding modern digital healthcare systems. As these two users have different roles and responsibilities, they can implement different cybersecurity best practices so that the deployed best practices can significantly enhance the security posture of their healthcare organizations, protect sensitive patient data, and maintain the trust of their patients. Based on their roles, ten common best practice activities with their outcomes are discussed.

10.5.1   Healthcare Professionals

Healthcare professionals such as doctors, nurses, and other clinical staff play a significant role in maintaining the security and privacy of patient data. Applying cybersecurity best practices significantly enhances the security posture of healthcare systems. The common 10 security best practices for healthcare professionals are summarized in Table 10.2.

10.5.2   IT and System Administrators

Information technology (IT) and system administrators are specialized professionals responsible for managing and maintaining the information technology and network infrastructure that supports healthcare services. IT and system administrators can significantly enhance the security posture of healthcare organizations, protect sensitive patient data, and ensure compliance with regulatory requirements by

Table 10.2 Cybersecurity best practices for healthcare professionals

Activities	Outcomes
Use strong password and multi-factor authentication (MFA)	Reduce the risk of unauthorized access Protect sensitive data
Ensure patient data encryption both at rest and in transit	Protect patients from unauthorized access to healthcare data at rest and in transit
Use VPN, firewall, and IDS	Ensure end-to-end secure connection Monitor network traffic and protect the internal network from unauthorized access and malicious activity
Keep regular software updates	Enhance features, functionalities, and performance Fix bugs and security holes Protect from malware (e.g., ransomware) and sophisticated attacks
Secure physical access to devices with strong passwords	Enhance data protection Reduce the risk of data breaches
Install and maintain advanced antivirus and antimalware software	Detect a wide variety of malware, including viruses, trojans, ransomware, and spyware, and help mitigate the risk of malware infections Protect patient data
Report incident	Minimize the impact of the incident Prevent future attacks
Ensure regulatory compliances	Ensure security measures comply with regulatory compliances (e.g., HIPAA and GDPR) requirements and other relevant regulations
Participate in cybersecurity awareness training.	Stay informed about the latest cyber threats and state-of-the-art best practices
Educate patients	Educate patients on how to protect their healthcare information when accessing online healthcare services and data

Table 10.3 Cybersecurity best Practices for IT and system administrators

Activities	Outcomes
Risk and vulnerability analysis	Identify, prioritize, and mitigate cybersecurity risks and vulnerabilities
Access control and identity management	Prevent unauthorized access to systems and data
Vulnerability and patch management	Prioritize patching based on the severity of vulnerabilities and their impact on healthcare systems and services Ensure installed applications software, operating systems, and underlying firmware are regularly updated with the latest security patches
Implements firewalls, IDS, and IPS	Monitor network traffic and protect the internal network from unauthorized access and malicious activity
Deploy endpoint detection and response (EDR) tools	Detect and prevent malware infections Provide remediation suggestions to restore affected systems Manage and secure all endpoint devices, including desktop computers, laptops, mobile devices, servers, and other medical devices
Prepare incident response plan	Outlines procedures (plan) for detecting, responding, and recovering from potential future cyberattacks
Implement advanced data encryption and data loss prevention solutions	Protect from unauthorized access to patients and other sensitive healthcare data at use, rest, and transit Secure data being used by health information system applications or endpoint systems Protect data stored at network locations/sites (on-premises or cloud) Ensure the safe transmission of patient-sensitive data while it moves across the network
Use continuous monitoring tools	Detect and respond to cyberattacks in real time. Protect the healthcare systems from emerging cyber threats and vulnerabilities
Regulatory compliance	Ensure security measures comply with regulatory compliances (e.g., HIPAA and GDPR) requirements and other relevant regulations
Training and awareness	Educate all healthcare professionals and staff on cybersecurity threats, best practices, policies, and procedures.

applying these security best practices. The common 10 security best practices for IT and system administrators in healthcare systems are summarized in Table 10.3.

10.6   Cybersecurity Future Work in Healthcare

Cybersecurity concerns in the healthcare sector are growing as sensitive healthcare and digitalized personal health records become more widely available (Salama et al., 2024). The future of cybersecurity in healthcare necessitates a forward-looking approach to address emerging cyber threats and ensure the protection of sensitive patient data and healthcare systems (Islam et al. 2022; Nicola Rieke 2020). Here are some areas for cybersecurity future work in healthcare:

- *Privacy-enhancing technologies:* The development of privacy-enhancing techniques, including differential privacy, secure multi-party computation, and homomorphic encryption, is imperative for enabling privacy protection while collecting and analyzing data collaboratively (Liu et al., 2024).
- *Federated learning (FL) and differential privacy (DP):* FL and DP are two innovative technologies that offer a powerful approach to enhancing the privacy and security of healthcare data. These methods allow for patient-sensitive data in research and analytics without compromising individual privacy. Federated learning is a decentralized approach to machine learning where the patient's data remain on local devices and only model updates. This method enhances privacy and security by keeping sensitive data within the local environment. It significantly helps preserve patients' private data from being exposed to attackers. DP is a mathematical framework that provides a quantifiable privacy protection measure when medical data analysis is done. It introduces noise into the data or the query results, ensuring that the inclusion or exclusion of a single data point does not significantly affect the outcome, thus protecting individual data points. In recent years, there has been a surge in the development of novel algorithms for differential privacy for healthcare data analysis (Brisimi et al., 2018; Wei et al., 2020).
- *Securing Internet of Medical Things (IoMT) devices*: IoMT is a significant application of the IoT that benefits human welfare; it also presents security and privacy risks in collecting and processing healthcare data. Quantum blockchain can provide a higher level of security for handling medical data involving the Internet of Medical Things (IoMT) (Qu et al., 2024). Quantum blockchain is to combine quantum technology and blockchain. Blockchains are publicly distributed ledgers that record information and enable tamper-proof data storage by continuously adding new blocks.
- *Post-quantum cryptography:* Cryptographic algorithms (e.g., lattice-based, hash-based, code-based, and multivariate polynomial cryptosystems) are resistant to quantum attacks. Integrating post-quantum cryptography, searchable encryption, and blockchain technology can be used for security and privacy preservation in healthcare (Xu et al., 2022). Combining post-quantum public-key searchable encryption and blockchain methods protects against current and future cyber threats and facilitates efficient and compliant data sharing and collaboration among healthcare stakeholders.

10.7 Chapter Summary

This chapter delves into cybersecurity challenges, state-of-the-art best practices, and future healthcare data privacy and security work. It presents security and privacy concerns in healthcare with best practices and cybersecurity mitigation methods for security and privacy concerns in healthcare, identifying the potential five common cyberattacks and best practices used to protect healthcare data. It also presents cybersecurity challenges for patients, doctors, infrastructure, software, apps, etc. It lists the cybersecurity best practices for healthcare professionals and IT system administrators. Finally, we discuss some potential future research directions in healthcare data privacy.

After understanding cybersecurity challenges, best practices, and future work in the healthcare industry, the following questions are addressed in this chapter:

- What are key cybersecurity concerns and mitigation methods in digital healthcare systems?
- What are the most common cyberattacks in the healthcare industry, and what are the best practices for preventing them?
- What are the cybersecurity challenges for personnel, patients, doctors, and staff in healthcare?
- What are the cybersecurity challenges with healthcare software, apps, and infrastructure?
- What are the cybersecurity best practices for healthcare professionals?
- What are the cybersecurity best practices for IT system administrators?
- What are the potential future work directions for cybersecurity in the healthcare industry?
- How can federated learning and differential privacy methods enhance the privacy and security of healthcare data?

References

Brisimi, T. S., Chen, R., Mela, T., Olshevsky, A., Paschalidis, I. C., & Shi, W. (2018). Federated learning of predictive models from federated electronic health records. *International Journal of Medical Informatics, 112*, 1386–5056. https://doi.org/10.1016/j.ijmedinf.2018.01.007

CISA. (2024, February 23). *Cyber threats to medical technology and communication technology protocols*. American cyber defense agency. Retrieved from https://www.cisa.gov/resources-tools/resources/cyber-threats-medical-technology-and-communication-technology-protocols

GDRP. (2024). *General data protection regulation (GDPR)*. Retrieved April 2, 2024, from https://gdpr-info.eu/

HIPPA. (2023). *Health information privacy*. U.S. Department of Health and Human Services (HHS). Retrieved from https://www.hhs.gov/hipaa/index.html

Islam, T. U., Ghasemi, R., & Mohammed, A. N. (2022). Privacy-preserving federated learning model for healthcare data. In *2022 IEEE 12th Annual Computing and Communication Workshop and Conference (CCWC)* (pp. 0281–0287). IEEE. https://doi.org/10.1109/CCWC54503.2022.9720752

Jawad, L. A. (2024). Security and privacy in digital healthcare systems: Challenges and mitigation strategies. *Abhigyan, 42*(1), 23–31. https://doi.org/10.1177/09702385241233073

Liu, W., Zhang, Y., Yang, H., & Meng, Q. (2024). A survey on differential privacy for medical data analysis. *Annals of Data Science, 733–747*, 1. https://doi.org/10.1007/s40745-023-00475-3

Nessus. (2024, May 6). *Tenable nessus*. Retrieved from https://www.tenable.com/products/nessus.

Nicola Rieke, J. H.-H. (2020). The future of digital health with federated learning. *NPJ Digital Medicine, 3*, 119. https://doi.org/10.1038/s41746-020-00323-1

NIST. (2018). *Cybersecurity framework V1.1.* NIST. Retrieved from https://www.nist.gov/cyberframework/framework

NIST. (2024). *The NIST cybersecurity framework (CSF) 2.0.* National Institute of Standards and Technology. Retrieved from https://www.nist.gov/cyberframework/csf-11-archive

OpenVAS. (2024, May 5). *Greenbone OpenVAS.* Retrieved from https://openvas.org/

Qu, Z., Meng, Y., Liu, B., Muhammad, G., & Tiwari, P. (2024). QB-IMD: A secure medical data processing system with privacy protection based on quantum Blockchain for IoMT. *IEEE Internet of Things Journal, 11*, 40–49. https://doi.org/10.1109/JIOT.2023.3285388

Salama, R., Altrjman, C., & Al-Turjman, F. (2024). 8–Healthcare cybersecurity challenges: A look at current and future trends. In F. Al-Turjman (Ed.), *Computational intelligence and Blockchain in complex systems* (pp. 97–111). Morgan Kaufmann. https://doi.org/10.1016/B978-0-443-13268-1.00003-0

Wei, K., Li, J., Ding, M., Ma, C., Yang, H. H., Farokhi, F., et al. (2020). Federated learning with differential privacy: Algorithms and performance analysis. *IEEE Transactions on Information Forensics and Security, 15*, 3454–3469. https://doi.org/10.1109/TIFS.2020.2988575

Xu, G., Xu, S., Cao, Y., Yun, F., Cui, Y., Yu, Y., & Xiao, K. (2022). PPSEB: A postquantum public-key searchable encryption scheme on Blockchain for E-healthcare scenarios. *Security and Communication Networks., 2022*, 1. https://doi.org/10.1155/2022/3368819

Chapter 11
Conclusion

In the intricate world of healthcare, characterized by its diversity and constant evolution, the commitment to providing affordable, quality care stands as a cornerstone principle. As we navigated through the various layers of the healthcare system in Chap. 1, we emphasized the importance of adopting a patient-centered approach, recognizing the myriad stakeholders involved, from medical professionals to policymakers. Amidst these complexities, one of the most pressing challenges facing healthcare today is cybersecurity. In an era of increasing digital interconnectedness, the risks of data breaches and unauthorized access loom large, necessitating robust cybersecurity measures to uphold patient trust and safety. This sets the stage for a deeper exploration of cybersecurity in subsequent chapters.

Chapter 2 delves into the basic concepts of cybersecurity relevant to the healthcare system, shedding light on threats, attacks, vulnerabilities, and countermeasures aimed at preventing cyberattacks and safeguarding data. We explore contemporary cyber threats such as malware, phishing, ransomware, and insider threats, alongside best practices for mitigating these risks. The CIA model—ensuring confidentiality, integrity, and availability of data—forms the foundation, augmented by principles of accountability and authenticity in the CIAAA model. Moreover, we delve into cybersecurity regulations and laws applicable to healthcare jurisdictions, highlighting the importance of compliance and steps to meet regulatory requirements. The chapter concludes with an examination of cybersecurity training and development methods for healthcare professionals, emphasizing the importance of education in bolstering cybersecurity resilience.

Chapter 3 builds upon the foundational understanding of cybersecurity, emphasizing its pivotal role in safeguarding sensitive patient data, preserving medical system integrity, and ensuring patient safety and quality. Against the backdrop of an increasingly digitalized healthcare landscape, we underscore the rising significance of cybersecurity and its applications in data protection, medical equipment security, and regulatory compliance. This chapter sets the stage for deeper dives into different

© The Author(s), under exclusive license to Springer Nature
Switzerland AG 2024
D. P. Sharma et al., *Understanding Cybersecurity Management in Healthcare*,
Progress in IS, https://doi.org/10.1007/978-3-031-68034-2_11

categories of security in subsequent chapters, including data and information security, personal security, and healthcare system and infrastructure security.

Moving forward, Chap. 4 delves into the realm of data and information security within healthcare, shedding light on methods for protecting healthcare information and securing electronic health records, administrative data, and clinical trial data. We explore authentication and authorization techniques, encryption strategies, and data masking methods, alongside common data threats and vulnerabilities. Regulatory frameworks and industry best practices for data protection and privacy are also examined, underlining the importance of compliance in safeguarding patient information.

In Chap. 5, the focus shifts to personal security in healthcare, emphasizing the critical importance of cybersecurity for patients, doctors, and staff. With the prevalence of cyber threats on the rise, robust measures are essential to safeguard patient data, privacy, and organizational integrity. Through collaboration, vigilance, and comprehensive training, healthcare professionals can bolster their defenses against evolving cyber threats, ensuring the security of patient care within a digitalized healthcare ecosystem.

Chapter 6 delves into the vital task of protecting healthcare infrastructure from cyberattacks, highlighting the role of infra-security strategies in maintaining patient data confidentiality, integrity, and availability. By exploring different infra-security approaches, stakeholders can enhance trust, operational efficiency, and resilience against evolving cybersecurity challenges.

In the following chapters, we delve into the detection and prevention of cyberattacks in healthcare, exploring strategies and technologies to identify and mitigate cyber threats. Through this comprehensive exploration, we aim to provide readers with a holistic understanding of cybersecurity in healthcare, empowering stakeholders to navigate the complexities of an increasingly digitalized healthcare landscape while safeguarding patient trust, safety, and quality of care.

This book serves as a comprehensive resource for a diverse audience across the healthcare sector, including patients, medical professionals, healthcare administrators, policymakers, cybersecurity specialists, and IT professionals. Medical professionals, including doctors, nurses, and allied healthcare professionals, can benefit from gaining insights into cybersecurity measures to protect patient data and ensure the integrity of medical systems. Healthcare administrators and policymakers can utilize the knowledge presented in this book to implement robust cybersecurity protocols within their organizations and develop policies to address emerging cyber threats. Cybersecurity specialists and IT professionals will find valuable information on the specific cybersecurity challenges faced by the healthcare industry and effective strategies for mitigating these risks. Overall, anyone involved in healthcare delivery, administration, or technology management can leverage the insights provided in this book to enhance cybersecurity practices and safeguard patient privacy and safety in an increasingly digitized healthcare landscape.

Correction to: Understanding Cybersecurity Management in Healthcare

Correction to:
D. P. Sharma et al., *Understanding Cybersecurity Management in Healthcare*, Progress in IS
https://doi.org/10.1007/978-3-031-68034-2

The abstracts in all chapters have been revised on Springerlink.

The updated version of this book can be found at
https://doi.org/10.1007/978-3-031-68034-2

GPSR Compliance

The European Union's (EU) General Product Safety Regulation (GPSR) is a set of rules that requires consumer products to be safe and our obligations to ensure this.

If you have any concerns about our products, you can contact us on ProductSafety@springernature.com

In case Publisher is established outside the EU, the EU authorized representative is:

Springer Nature Customer Service Center GmbH
Europaplatz 3
69115 Heidelberg, Germany

The manufacturer's authorised representative in the EU is Springer
Nature Customer Service Centre GmbH, Europaplatz 3, 69115 Heidelberg,
Germany. If you have any concerns regarding our products, please
contact ProductSafety@springernature.com

Printed and bound by CPI Group (UK) Ltd, Croydon, CR0 4YY
27/04/2026
02097566-0001